Witnessing

Witnessing

Beyond Recognition

KELLY OLIVER

 University of Minnesota Press
Minneapolis
London

A version of part of chapter 1 was published as "Beyond Recognition: Witnessing Ethics," *Philosophy Today* 44, no. 1 (spring 2000); copyright 2000 DePaul University, reprinted here with permission from DePaul University. A version of part of chapter 3 was published as "What Is Transformative about the Performative? From Repetition to Working Through," *Studies in Practical Philosophy* 1, no. 2 (fall 1999); copyright Humanities Press, Inc., reprinted with permission from Humanities Press, Inc.

Published by the University of Minnesota Press
111 Third Avenue South, Suite 290
Minneapolis, MN 55401-2520
http://www.upress.umn.edu

Library of Congress Cataloging-in-Publication Data

Oliver, Kelly, 1958–
    Witnessing : beyond recognition / Kelly Oliver.
        p.   cm.
    Includes bibliographical references and index.
    ISBN 0-8166-3627-3 (alk. paper) — ISBN 0-8166-3628-1 (pbk. : alk. paper)
    1. Recognition (Philosophy)   2. Perception (Philosophy)   3. Social perception.
  I. Title.
    B828.45 .O55 2001
    128—dc21

                                                              00-009646

Printed in the United States of America on acid-free paper

The University of Minnesota is an equal-opportunity educator and employer.

11 10 09 08 07 06 05 04 03 02 01   10 9 8 7 6 5 4 3 2 1

For Ruthy

who has survived unimaginable torture,
and who, in the last year,
has taught me
more about the anxieties,
response-abilities,
joys,
courage,
vigilance,
and necessity
of loving
than books ever could.

Contents

Acknowledgments

I would like to thank audience members at various presentations of this project (at Notre Dame University, Purdue University, University of Washington, Seattle University, State University of New York at Stony Brook, Villanova University, Modern Language Association) for their helpful questions, comments, and suggestions. Thanks to Rita Alphonso for research assistance. I would also like to thank my colleagues Beverly Haviland, Eva Kittay, and Edward Casey for pointing me in some exciting and fruitful directions. Thanks to Courtney Martin and Steve Edwin for the index.

Thanks to the graduate students in my seminars during 1998–99 for stimulating discussions of some of the issues that concern me here. Thanks to Shaun Gallagher, Robert Bernasconi, Ewa Ziarek, and Cynthia Willett for exceptionally helpful suggestions and advice on an earlier draft of the manuscript. Special thanks to Benigno Trigo for continuing conversations about these issues and provocative insights that contribute to some of my favorite parts of the book. As always, thanks to my friends and family (with and without fur), whose sustenance enables me to write.

Introduction: Beyond Recognition

Dori Laub, a psychoanalyst interviewing survivors as part of the Video Archive for Holocaust Testimonies at Yale University, remarks on a tension between historians and psychoanalysts involved in the project. He describes a lively debate that began after the group watched the taped testimony of a woman who was an eyewitness to the Auschwitz uprising in which prisoners set fire to the camp. The woman reported four chimneys going up in flames and exploding, but historians insisted that since there was only one chimney blown up, her testimony was incorrect and should be discredited in its entirety because she proved herself an unreliable witness. One historian suggested that her testimony should be discounted because she "ascribes importance to an attempt that, historically, made no difference" (Felman and Laub 1992, 61). The psychoanalysts responded that the woman was not testifying to the number of chimneys blown up but to something more "radical" and more "crucial"—namely, the seemingly unimaginable occurrence of Jewish resistance at Auschwitz, that is to say, the *historical truth* of Jewish resistance at Auschwitz. Laub concludes that what the historians, listening for empirical facts, could not hear, was the "very secret of survival and of resistance to extermination" (62). The Auschwitz survivor saw something unfamiliar, Jewish resistance, which gave her the courage to resist. She saw something that in one sense did not happen—four chimneys blowing up—but that in another made all the difference to what happened. Seeing the impossible—what did not happen—gave her the strength to make what seemed impossible possible: surviving the Holocaust.

While the historians were listening to hear confirmation of what they already knew, the psychoanalysts were listening to hear something new, something beyond comprehension. While the historians were trying to recognize empirical facts in the survivors' testimonies, the psychoanalysts were trying to acknowledge that the import of these testimonies was unrecognizable.

1

Although undeniably powerful in their impact, the empirical facts of the Holocaust are dead to the process of witnessing, that which cannot be reported by the eyewitness, the unseen in vision and the unspoken in speech, that which is beyond recognition in history, the process of witnessing itself. The process of witnessing, which relies on address and response—always in tension with eyewitness testimony—complicates the notion of historical truth and moves us beyond any easy dichotomy between history and psychoanalysis.

The tension between recognizing the familiar in order to confirm what we already know and listening for the unfamiliar that disrupts what we already know is at the heart of contemporary theories of recognition. How is it possible to recognize the unfamiliar and disruptive? If it is unfamiliar, how can we perceive it or know it or recognize it? These questions are related to the question of how we experience anything new or different. Conceptually, these questions seem to lead to paradoxes or aporias that can leave us with the belief that we experience newness only through what we already know and therefore that we cannot experience newness at all. Of course, we do experience newness and difference. How could we possibly become functioning adults if we didn't? If we always experienced the world only in terms of what we already knew, then we couldn't learn anything at all. We would remain infants unable to make distinctions and therefore unable to function.

Many of the paradoxes of difference or newness are the result of how we conceive of ourselves. First, we end up with paradoxes if we believe that we encounter difference and newness only or primarily intellectually, especially if we believe that the intellect is distinct from perception, sensation, passion, or embodiment in general. After all, how can we both know and not know something at the same time? The intellect and reason notoriously lead us into contradictions. This hermeneutical problem has troubled philosophers from Plato's *Meno* (1987a) to Jacques Derrida's "Psyche: Inventions of the Other" (1992). Second, we end up with paradoxes if we believe that we are self-same and our identities are unified, especially if we conceive of identity in opposition to difference. How can a unified, self-contained being ever come in contact with something or someone wholly other to itself? If the self is bounded and experiences only that which is within its boundaries, then how can it encounter anything outside of its own boundaries?

Certainly, how we conceive of ourselves determines how we conceive of others, and vice versa. If we conceive of ourselves as self-identical, and we conceive of identity as opposed to difference, and we conceive of anything or anyone outside of the boundaries of ourselves as different, then we will conceive of anything different or outside of ourselves as a threat to our own identity. Identity will be pitted against difference. Relations will be hostile. Hostile relations will lead to hostile actions, and the result will be war, domination, and torture. All of this is to say that our conceptions of ourselves determine our conceptions of others and our conceptions of our relationships with others. Moreover, our conceptions of our relationships determine how we behave toward others and ourselves. There is an intimate and necessary correspondence between how we conceive of others and how we treat them.

As a philosopher who is interested in social and political problems, then, I believe that it is important to examine and diagnose our self-conceptions as they affect our conceptions of others and relationships, and our actions toward and in them. Julia Kristeva says that any philosophy of language presupposes a particular notion of the subject. So, too, any social or political theory presupposes a particular notion of the subject. In fact, our actions, policies, stereotypes, fantasies, and desires also presuppose notions of what it is to be a subject and to "have" subjectivity. How we conceive of ourselves as subjects and how we conceive of our subjectivity are at the foundation of what we believe about ourselves, the world, and other people, and we act accordingly. This is why in order to begin to understand domination and oppression it is imperative to investigate who we think we are and how we imagine others.

Relations of domination and oppression presuppose particular notions of subjects and others, subjectivity and objectification. One of my arguments throughout *Witnessing* is that the dichotomy between subject and other or subject and object is itself a result of the pathology of oppression. To see oneself as a subject and to see other people as *the other* or objects not only alienates one from those around him or her but also enables the dehumanization inherent in oppression and domination. It is easier to justify domination, oppression, and torture if one's victims are imagined as inferior, less human, or merely objects who exist to serve subjects. Within this familiar scenario, to see oneself as a subject is to imagine oneself as self-sovereign. This sense of myself as a subject gives the impression that I am an individual who possesses a sovereign will, while this sense of my own subjectivity gives the impression that I have agency and that I can act in the world. To see other people as objects or the other denies them the sovereignty and agency of subjectivity. To see other people as objects or the other is to imagine them as unable to govern themselves as subjects.

Since the Enlightenment a lot of attention has been paid to the subject and his or her agency. Since World War II, however, attention has been turning to the one who has been marginalized, oppressed, enslaved, and tortured as an object or as the other. Attention is turning to the effects of this marginalization and objectification on the subjectivity and agency of its victims. What happens to someone's sense of herself as a subject and her sense of her subjectivity or agency when she is objectified through discrimination, domination, oppression, enslavement, or torture? Some contemporary theorists argue that subjectivity and the process of becoming a subject constitute a process of subordination and enslavement.[1] This neo-Hegelian position makes it difficult to distinguish between domination and enslavement that are inherent in the process of becoming a subject and oppression that is not necessary. This is especially problematic for theorists, like Jacques Derrida and Judith Butler, who maintain that social oppression and domination are manifestations, or repetitions, of the oppression and domination at the heart of subjectivity itself.

Contemporary theory is still dominated by conceptions of identity and subjectivity that inherit a Hegelian notion of recognition. In various ways, these theories describe how we recognize ourselves in our likeness as the same or in opposition to what is (or those who are) different from ourselves. Relations with others are described as struggles for recognition. But if we start from the assumption that relations are essentially antagonistic struggles for recognition, then it is no wonder that contemporary theorists spend so much energy trying to imagine how these struggles can lead to compassionate personal relations, ethical social relations, or democratic political relations. From the presumption that human relations are essentially warlike, how can we imagine them as peaceful?

Theories of identity and subjectivity based on recognition are implicit if not explicit in almost all types of contemporary theory. It is difficult to find a contemporary social theory that doesn't in some way employ a notion of recognition. In spite of its prominence, most of the time that *recognition* is used, its meaning is assumed but not defined or analyzed. In general, in work that relies on a notion of recognition there is the sense that individual identity is constituted intersubjectively; that we come to recognize ourselves as subjects or active agents through recognition from others; that a positive sense of self is dependent on positive recognition from others, while a negative sense of self is the result of negative recognition or lack of recognition from others. Some poststructuralists employ theories of recognition against Enlightenment notions of autonomy: if our subjectivity or our sense of self or agency is dependent on relations with others, then autonomy is an illusion. For example, Judith Butler concludes that "[the subject] can never produce itself autonomously," and moreover that only by forfeiting the notion of autonomy can survival become possible (Butler 1997b, 196). On the other hand, some critical theorists employ theories of recognition to explain how we develop a sense of our own autonomy necessary for survival. For example, Axel Honneth (1996) believes that we see ourselves as autonomous only by virtue of relations of positive recognition with others: when others trust us, only then can we trust ourselves; when others respect us as capable of judgment and action, only then can we respect ourselves as autonomous agents.

Regardless of their stand on autonomy, most of the time both these groups of theorists insist that subjectivity is dialogic because the subject is a response to an address from the other. For example, Charles Taylor insists that "the crucial feature of human life is its fundamentally dialogical character. . . . We define our identity always in dialogue with, sometimes in struggle against, the things our significant others want to see in us" (1994, 32–33). Axel Honneth says that "the reproduction of social life is governed by the imperative of mutual recognition, because one can develop a practical relation-to-self only when one has learned to view oneself, from the normative perspective of one's partners in interaction, as their social addressee" (1996, 92). And Judith Butler maintains that "the discursive condition of social recognition precedes and conditions the formation of the subject. . . . I can only say 'I' to the extent that I have first been addressed" (1993, 225).

Not surprisingly, while theorists of recognition like Taylor, Honneth, and Butler discuss subjectivity or identity in terms of recognition that comes through dialogue or discourse, they don't realize the full import of thinking of subjectivity as response-ability, or response to address. As different as the discourses of critical theory and poststructuralist theory seem to be, they are both populated with subjects warring with others, often referred to as *objects*, subjects struggling to deny their dependence on others. Subjects still dominate in spite of their dependence on dialogue with their "others" and "objects." By insisting that subjectivity is based on antagonism, these theorists undermine the deep sense of response-ability implied in claiming that subjectivity is dialogic. While subjectivity is necessarily intersubjective and dialogic, it is not necessarily antagonistic. The tension at the heart of subjectivity need not produce antagonism between people. More than this, we cannot conceive of subjectivity as both fundamentally antagonistic and fundamentally dialogic in the rich sense of dialogue as response-ability that I propose, using the notion of witnessing.

As much as my own thinking is indebted to poststructuralist theories, with poststructuralists it seems that the other is sometimes mute, impoverished, unavailable, still to come, almost worshipped (à la Derrida and Emmanuel Lévinas), or the other is the invisible, unspoken, nonexistent, the underside of the subject (à la Foucault and Butler). With critical theorists the other is usually either the one who confers recognition on us (à la Honneth and Jürgen Habermas) or the one on whom we confer recognition (à la Taylor and Nancy Fraser), but in all cases an object for the subject. All of these articulations of the other raise this question for me: what of the subjectivity of this so-called other? What of the subject position of those othered by these discourses of subjectivity? What of their speech, their present, their existence? Surely, they don't just think of themselves as mute, still to come, invisible, or nonexistent. Whether these theories celebrate the presence of an autonomous subject produced through intersubjective relations or mourn the loss of that presence produced through the absence inherent in intersubjective relations, the subject—as presence or absence—still dominates its others.

In *Witnessing: Beyond Recognition,* on the one hand, I challenge the Hegelian notion that subjectivity is the result of hostile conflict—Axel Honneth's struggle for recognition or Judith Butler's subordination that makes the subject's turn inward possible. On the other hand, I challenge notions of subjectivity based on a logic of exclusion—Butler's foreclosed object of desire or Julia Kristeva's abject. In various ways contemporary theories that propose a hostile conflict between subject and other and theories that propose that identity is formed by excluding the other continue to define the other in terms of the subject. The rhetoric of the other in itself denies subjectivity to those othered within dominant culture. Throughout *Witnessing,* I am concerned with these questions: what of the subjectivity of those othered? Can we develop a theory of subjectivity by starting from the position of those othered within dominant culture? What of the subject position of the othered? And what is the relationship of subject position as it is prescribed by social context to subjectivity itself?

The metacritical question is, then, in what ways do these theories of subjectivity centered on *the other* work against the other whom they privilege? And how might we think of subjectivity outside of these exclusionary frameworks within which subjects exist only at the expense of their others? Can we think of dialogic subjectivity as noncontestatory conversation? Can we conceive of the intersubjectivity of the subject without relying on the Hegelian warring struggle for recognition that dominates contemporary theory? To answer this question affirmatively, I engage some of the work of various contemporary theorists of recognition, subjectivity, and abjection, moving toward an ethics of witnessing.

My project here is to begin developing a theory of subjectivity by starting from the position of those othered. What can we learn about subjectivity in general by starting from the perspective of othered subjectivity? How do domination and subordination affect subjectivity? I suggest that by starting from othered subjectivity, we learn that subordination, oppression, and subjectification are not necessary elements of subjectivity itself. Rather, subordination, oppression, and subjectification undermine the very possibility of subjectivity. At the extreme, torture and enslavement can destroy essential parts of subjectivity that must be revived or reconstructed in order for the survivor to be able to act as an agent. Being othered, oppressed, subordinated, or tortured affects a person at the level of her subjectivity, her sense of herself as a subject and agent. Oppression and subordination render individuals or groups of people as other by objectifying them. Objectification undermines subjectivity: to put it simply, objects are not subjects. Through the process of bearing witness to oppression and subordination, those othered can begin to repair damaged subjectivity by taking up a position as speaking subjects. What we learn from beginning with the subject position of those othered is that the speaking subject is a subject by virtue of address-ability and response-ability. Address-ability and response-ability are the roots of subjectivity, which are damaged by the objectifying operations of oppression and subordination.

Address-ability and response-ability are what I identify with the process of witnessing. Subjectivity is the result of the process of witnessing. Witnessing is not only the basis for othered subjectivity; witnessing is also the basis for all subjectivity; and oppression and subordination work to destroy the possibility of witnessing and thereby undermine subjectivity. Against theorists who maintain that subordination or trauma is necessary in order to become a subject, I argue that subordination or trauma undermines the possibility of becoming or maintaining subjectivity by destroying or damaging the possibility of witnessing.

While the experience of marginalization or othering is traumatic for its victims—and that experience needs witnesses—relational or dialogic subjectivity is not founded on trauma. Since those who have been othered have been victimized, trauma is part of what makes subjectivity othered, but it is not part of what makes subjectivity subjectivity. Witnessing works to ameliorate the trauma particular to othered subjectivity. This is because witnessing is the essential dynamic of all subjectivity, its constitutive event and process. While trauma undermines subjectivity and witnessing restores it, the process of witnessing is not reduced to the testimony to trauma. So, too, subjectivity is not reduced to the effects of trauma. One important implication of this thesis is that those who have been othered suffer from traumas directed at their subjectivity, traumas directed at their identities and sense of themselves as agents. In other words, oppression and subordination affect their victims at the level of their sense of themselves as subjects, at the level of subjectivity.

In order to understand the effects of oppression on someone's sense of herself as a subject and her sense of her subjectivity, we need to understand more about how subjectivity is formed and functions. What does oppression do to compromise a subject's sense of agency and thereby the ability to act? What elements of subjectivity are the targets of oppression and enslavement? How are victims rendered docile or speechless? On the other hand, how are agency and subjectivity restored to survivors? For example, in the testimony of a woman to a Jewish uprising at a concentration camp, what are the effective and affective differences between hearing inaccuracies, unreliability, and hallucinations and hearing the possibility of agency and resistance? What are the effective and affective differences between listening for what we already know and recognize in her testimony and listening for what we don't know, for what is beyond recognition? What kind of recognition, if any, do survivors want and need?

Contemporary debates in social theory around issues of multiculturalism have focused on the demand or struggle for recognition by marginalized or oppressed people, groups, and cultures. The work of Charles Taylor and Axel Honneth, in particular, has crystallized issues of multiculturalism and justice around the notion of recognition. I want to challenge what has become a fundamental tenet of this trend in debates over multiculturalism—namely, that the social struggles manifested in critical race theory, queer theory, feminist theory, and various social movements are struggles for recognition.[2] For instance, I would argue that testimonies from the aftermath of the Holocaust and slavery do not merely articulate a demand to be recognized or to be seen. Further, they bear witness to a pathos beyond recognition and to something other than the horror of their objectification. They are also testifying to the process of witnessing that both reconstructs damaged subjectivity and constitutes the heart of all subjectivity. The victims of oppression, slavery, and torture are not merely seeking visibility and recognition, but they are also seeking witnesses to horrors beyond recognition. The demand for recognition manifest in testimonies from those othered by dominant culture is transformed by the accompanying demands for retribution and compassion.

If, as I suggest, those othered by dominant culture are seeking not only, or even primarily, recognition but also bearing witness to something beyond recognition, then our notions of recognition must be reevaluated. Certainly, notions of recognition that throw us back into a Hegelian master-slave relationship do not help us overcome domination. If recognition is conceived as being conferred on others by the dominant group, then it merely repeats the dynamic of hierarchies, privilege, and domination. Even if oppressed people are making demands for recognition, insofar as those who are dominant are empowered to confer it, we are thrown back into the hierarchy of domination. This is to say that if the operations of recognition require a recognizer and a recognizee, then we have done no more than replicate the master-slave, subject-other/object hierarchy in this new form.

Additionally, the need to demand recognition from the dominant culture or group is a symptom of the pathology of oppression. Oppression creates the need and demand for recognition. It is not just that the injustices of oppression create the need for justice. More than this, the pathology of oppression creates the need in the oppressed to be recognized by their oppressors, the very people most likely not to recognize them. The internalization of stereotypes of inferiority and superiority leave the oppressed with the sense that they are lacking something that only their *superior* dominators have or can give them. The very notion of recognition as it is deployed in various contemporary theoretical contexts is, then, a symptom of the pathology of oppression itself. Implied in this diagnosis is the conclusion that struggles for recognition and theories that embrace those struggles may indeed presuppose and thereby perpetuate the very hierarchies, domination, and injustice that they attempt to overcome.

The notion of recognition becomes more problematic in models where what is recognized is always only something familiar to the subject.[3] In this case, the subject and what is known to him and his experience are once again privileged. Any real contact with difference or otherness becomes impossible because recognition requires the assimilation of difference into something familiar. When recognition repeats the master-slave or subject-object hierarchy, then it is also bound to assimilate difference back into sameness. The subject recognizes the other only when he can see something familiar in that other, for example, when he can see that the other is a person too. Only when we begin to think of the recognition of what is beyond recognition can we begin to think of the recognition of difference.

Some contemporary theorists seem to think that we can begin to move beyond recognition by focusing on *misrecognition.* But insofar as misrecognition presupposes an ideal recognition we are still operating within an economy of recognition.[4] The move to misrecognition can be read as the displacement of a nostalgia for an ideal of successful recognition and recuperation of the self against otherness or nostalgia for an autonomous subject who creates his own world. While theories of misrecognition have the advantage of challenging us to be vigilant in exposing the illusion of familiarity or sameness, most of them also propose an antagonistic subject-object/other relationship. Influenced by Lacan's account of misrecognition in the mirror stage, theorists like Julia Kristeva and Judith Butler propose that identity and one's sense of oneself as a subject come from abjecting or excluding otherness; otherness and difference are abjected in order to secure the subject's always precarious boundaries against the threat of fragmentation. In this type of scenario, we fortify ourselves on the level of individual subjective identity as well as group and national identity by drawing artificial but strict boundaries between ourselves and others. Whatever characteristics we prefer not to associate with ourselves—those characteristics we deem unacceptable, dirty, or improper—we project onto the others. Others and otherness become threats to our very sense of ourselves as subjects.

While this neo-Hegelian model is very effective in *explaining* the existence of war and oppression, if *normalized* it makes it impossible to imagine peaceful compassionate relations with others across or through differences. Kristeva tries to get around the absolute alienation and impossibility of relationship suggested by Lacan's notion of misrecognition by insisting that otherness is always internal to subjectivity and encounters with others and that otherness can become an embrace of the return of the repressed. Because of the otherness within, the boundaries of subjectivity are always shifting and precarious. Kristeva maintains that only by elaborating and interpreting our relation to repressed otherness can we come to terms with difference, even love it. Suspicious of any discourse on love, Butler, on the other hand, focuses less on how we can imagine peaceful and compassionate relations and more on how to diagnose warring oppressive relations. She argues that the boundaries of subjective identity shift because of performative repetitions that open up the possibility of transformation in the spaces where the operations of abjection and exclusion fail. While Kristeva's theory as she presents it in *Powers of Horror* seems to oscillate between the merely descriptive and normative, Butler's theory seems dangerously normative on the questions of abjection and subjugation.

What is lacking in Butler's account of performative repetition and suggested in Kristeva's insistence on elaboration and interpretation is the Freudian notion of "working-through." In order to imagine peaceful and compassionate relations, we must be able to imagine working-through whatever we might find threatening in relations to otherness and difference. A social theory of transformation needs a notion of working-through. More than this, it is necessary to reconceive of subjective identity in a way that does not require abjecting or excluding others or otherness in order to have a sense of oneself as a subject. Subjectivity is not the result of exclusion. If it is, it is certainly not only the result of exclusion but also of relationship through difference. None of us develops a sense of ourselves as subjects with any sort of identity apart from relations with others. Neither the notion of recognition nor the notion of misrecognition can provide a model of subjective identity that opens beyond the deadly antagonistic Hegelian model.

We need a new model of subjectivity, a model that does not ground identity in hostility toward others but, rather, one that opens onto the possibility of working-through hostilities. With regard to subjectivity, theories that describe the nature of subjectivity as violent and antagonistic work as normative theories, insofar as within their framework there is no escaping violence and antagonism. We need to describe subjectivity in ways that support the normative force of ethical obligations to be responsible to others rather than exclude or kill them. With the notion of witnessing, I propose an alternative description of how subjectivity is formed and sustained, which implies within it the normative force of ethical obligations.

One of the main reasons that recognition always either returns us to the recognition of sameness or becomes misrecognition that leads to hostility is that recognition seems to depend on a particular notion of vision. Whether or not they employ a notion of recognition explicitly, many contemporary theorists of society and culture talk about power in terms of visibility.[5] To be empowered is to be visible; to be disempowered is to be rendered invisible. To be recognized is to be visible; to be misrecognized or not recognized is to be rendered invisible. Dominance and marginality are discussed in terms of visibility and invisibility.[6] Contemporary theorists of recognition conceive of recognition and misrecognition in terms of visual metaphors. Philosophers such as Emmanuel Lévinas and Luce Irigaray have challenged this emphasis on vision in the history of philosophy, specifically with regard to recognition. The problem, however, is not with vision per se but with the particular notion of vision presupposed in theories of recognition or misrecognition.

From Jean-Paul Sartre's accusing *look,* to Jacques Lacan's insistence that the *gaze* necessarily alienates through misrecognition, through Charles Taylor's embrace of an *examination* of the worth of other cultures in order to confer recognition, vision is reduced to an objectifying gaze. Recognition or misrecognition supposedly results from vision attempting to bridge the abyss of empty space between the subject and its object. Vision supposedly fixes the object in a gaze either in order to examine it or as the result of misrecognizing itself. Either way, the seeing subject is imagined as cut off from its object by the abyss of empty space that vision must span in order to reconcile subject and object. In this way, vision is on the one hand presumed to be a distancing sense that requires a gap between subject and object, and on the other hand vision is presumed to link subject and object through the vector of the subject's (in terms of recognition) or object's (in terms of misrecognition) gaze.

It is this notion of vision as both alienating and bridging, and the notion of space as empty abyss, that gives rise to many problems with theories of recognition/misrecognition. Only if we imagine ourselves forever cut off from others and the world around us do we need to create elaborate schemes for bridging that gap. We create an impossible problem for ourselves by presuming to be separated in the first place. By presuming that we are fundamentally separated from the world and other people by the void of empty space, we at once eliminate the possibility of connection and relationships even while we make desperate attempts to bridge that abyss. Moving from vision back to subjectivity, by presupposing that relationships are fundamentally hostile, we doom any attempts to formulate the possibility of cooperative relationships. The impossibility of solving the problem is, then, already built into any solution that we attempt.

Space, however, is not an empty void. It is full of air, light, and the circulation of various forms of electrical, thermal, mechanical, and chemical energies that sustain us and connect us to each other and the world. If space is not empty, and if vision connects us rather than separates us, if vision is indeed a proximal sense like touch, then visual recognition is neither the assimilation of all difference into sameness nor the alienation, exclusion, or abjection of all difference. Rather, since vision connects us to the world and other people, then we can imagine an alternative form of recognition, which gives rise to an alternative conception of subjectivity and identity. We need not give up on vision or turn from vision to some other sense; rather, we can reformulate vision and what it means to see.

Most psychologists and neuroscientists agree that we don't have just five senses (Gibson 1966, 48). In addition, many psychologists have concluded that the senses are intermodal and that the motor system is central to perception (Hurley 1998; Meltzoff and Moore 1977, 1983; Gallagher and Meltzoff 1996).[7] If we don't have five separate senses but, rather, systems of sensation and perception that operate through the entire body, then vision operates in conjunction with more seemingly proximal senses. More than this, the visual system is coordinated with the vestibular and motor systems.[8]

The work of psychologists Andrew Meltzoff and Keith Moore has shown that newborn infants can imitate the facial and manual gestures of adults (1977, 1983). Their studies show that this imitation is not the result of either conditioning or innate releasing mechanisms; rather, it is the result of an inherent coordination between the visual systems and motor systems that pre-exists any conditioning or demand for recognition. They hypothesize that

> this imitation is mediated by a representational system that allows infants to unite within one common framework their own body transformations and those of others. According to this view, both visual and motor transformations of the body can be represented in common form and directly compared. Infants could thereby relate proprioceptive motor information about their own unseen body movements to their representation of the visually perceived model and create the match required. . . . the proclivity to represent actions intermodally is the starting point of infant psychological development, not an end point reached after many months of postnatal development. (1983, 708)

The implications of this research for my project are significant. Meltzoff and Moore show that sensory, perceptional, and motor systems are linked from birth. Specifically, visual systems work in conjunction with motor and proprioceptive systems such that imitation is the result not of some sort of recognition but, rather, of coordinated sensory systems. This conclusion suggests that infants are responsive to their environment from birth and that sociosomatic interpersonal interaction is innate rather than acquired through any Lacanian mirror-stage recognition. Primitive social interactions such as imitation are the result of complex sensory-perceptual systems that are inherently responsive. Similarly, Shaun Gallagher and Andrew Meltzoff conclude that "recent studies of newborn imitation suggest that an experiential connection between self and others exists right from birth" that "is already an experience of pre-verbal communication in the language of gesture and action" (1996, 212, 227).

Psychologist J. J. Gibson maintains that we have perceptual systems that rely on coordinated information reception by different regions and organs in the body. For example, vision is dependent on a basic orientation and responsiveness to the force of gravity, which is possible through the coordination of the responsiveness of hairs in the inner ear along with tactile sensations in the feet and other parts of the body. In order to see, we first have to orient ourselves and keep ourselves steady in relation to the force of gravity. Vision, touch, and basic orientation to the earth work together to produce sight.

In addition, all perception and sensation result from our receptivity to energy in our environment—electrical energy, chemical energy, thermal energy, mechanical energy, photic energy or light, magnetic energy, and so forth. Vision, like other types of perception, is a response to energy, specifically differences in photic energy. Air, light, and various forms of energy are the mediums through which we experience the world. We are connected to the world through the circulation of energy that enables our perception, thought, language, and life itself. Indeed, we are conduits for energy of various sorts. Our relations to other people, like our relations to the environment, are constituted by the circulation and exchange of energy. With living beings, especially human beings, we exchange social energy in addition to chemical energy, thermal energy, electric energy, and so on.

Vision, like all other types of perception and sensation, is just as much affected by social energy as it is by any other form of energy. This is why theorists can talk about the politics of vision or the visibility or invisibility of the oppressed. To see and to be seen are not just the results of mechanical and photic energies, but also of social energies.[9] What we see is influenced by what we believe about the world. So, too, what we see is influenced by how we feel about the world and other people. What people around us believe and feel about the world and others also influences what we see. This is why, for example, Patricia Williams can talk about the invisibility of the homeless or the hypervisibility of black males in crime statistics and Judith Butler can talk about the invisibility of homosexuals and the hypervisibility of gay men in media coverage of AIDS. Vision is the result of the circulation of various forms of energy, including social energy. Social and political theorists cannot afford to ignore the importance of social energy to sight.

All human relationships are the result of the flow and circulation of energy—thermal energy, chemical energy, electrical energy, and social energy. Social energy includes affective energy, which can move between people. In our relationships, we constantly negotiate affective energy transfers. Just as we can train ourselves to be more attuned to photic, mechanical, or chemical energy in our environment, so too can we train ourselves to be more attuned to affective energy in our relationships. The art critic trains her eye to distinguish between subtle changes in photic energy or light. The musician trains her ear to distinguish between subtle changes in sound waves or tone. The food or wine connoisseur trains her palate to distinguish between subtle changes in chemical energy or taste. Similarly, some people, usually women, are "trained" to be more attuned to changes in affective energy or mood.

If vision is the result of the circulation of various forms of energy through the mediums of air, light, and other elements, including language, then it is not an alienating but a connecting sense. Approaching otherness and difference through vision as one part of a dynamic system of perception opens up the possibility of address beyond the humiliation, subordination, and objectification of the gaze. Conceived as circulation, vision, along with other perceptual and sensorial systems, allows for an openness and connection to otherness and difference not possible in neo-Hegelian struggles for recognition. With this alternative conception of vision, we can begin to transform the notion of recognition beyond its limited visual-based metaphors. Vision as the result of circulation of energies opens up the possibility of addressing the subjectivity of those othered within dominant culture as more than another version of the familiar or something wholly alien and alienating. Indeed, this conception of our relationship and responsiveness to the environment and other people suggests a fundamental ethical obligation.

Thus we are fundamentally connected to our environment and other people through the circulation of energies that sustain us. The possibility of any perception or sensation associated with subjectivity is the result of our *responsiveness* to the energy in our environment. Because our dependence on the energy in our environment brings with it ethical obligations, insofar as we *are* by virtue of our environment and by virtue of relationships with other people, we have ethical requirements rooted in the very possibility of subjectivity itself. We are obligated to respond to our environment and other people in ways that open up rather than close off the possibility of response. This obligation is an obligation to life itself.

Analyzing the nature of relations of dependency, Eva Kittay argues that a subject who "refuses to support this bond absolves itself from its most fundamental obligation—its obligation to its founding possibility" (1998, 131). The responsibility inherent in subjectivity itself is this same type of fundamental obligation. Subjectivity is founded on the ability to respond to, and address, others—what I am calling witnessing. Insofar as subjectivity is made possible by the ability to respond, response-ability is its founding possibility. The responsibility inherent in subjectivity has the double sense of the condition of possibility of response, response-ability, on the one hand, and the ethical obligation to respond and to enable response-ability from others born out of that founding possibility, on the other.

This ethical obligation at the heart of subjectivity is inherent in the process of witnessing. Moving from recognition to witnessing provides alternative notions of ethical, social, and political responsibility entailed by this conception of subjectivity. Our conceptions of ourselves as subjects, our subjective identities, along with our conceptions of others, hang in the balance.

Witnessing as address and response is the necessary ground for subjectivity. Yet this witnessing is always in tension with another dimension of witnessing, "seeing" for oneself.

Witnessing is defined in the *Oxford English Dictionary* as the action of bearing witness or giving testimony, the fact of being present and observing something; *witnessing* is from *witness*, defined as to bear witness, to testify, to give evidence, to be a spectator or auditor of something, to be present as an observer, to see with one's own eyes. It is important to note that witnessing has both the juridical connotations of seeing with one's own eyes and the religious connotations of testifying to that which cannot be seen, in other words, bearing witness. It is this double meaning that makes witnessing such a powerful alternative to recognition in reconceiving subjectivity and therefore ethical relations.

The double meaning of witnessing—*eyewitness* testimony based on first-hand knowledge, on the one hand, and *bearing witness* to something beyond recognition that can't be seen, on the other—is the heart of subjectivity. The tension between eyewitness testimony and bearing witness both positions the subject in finite history and necessitates the infinite response-ability of subjectivity. The tension between eyewitness testimony and bearing witness, between historical facts and psychoanalytic truth, between subject position and subjectivity, between the performative and the constative, is the dynamic operator that moves us beyond the melancholic choice between either dead historical facts or traumatic repetition of violence.

The double meaning of *witness* takes us back to the example with which I began: the Holocaust survivor testifying as an eyewitness to the Jewish uprising at Auschwitz. As an eyewitness, she testifies (incorrectly) to the events of that particular day when prisoners blew up a chimney. However, she bears witness to something that in itself cannot be seen, the conditions of possibility of Jewish resistance and survival. As an eyewitness she occupies a particular historical position in a concrete context that constitutes her actuality as well as her possibilities. She was a Jew in the midst of deadly anti-Semitism. She was a prisoner in a concentration camp. She was a woman in the mid–twentieth century. Her position as a subject is related to the particularities of her historical and social circumstances. In order to evaluate her testimony as an eyewitness, it is crucial to consider her sociohistorical subject position and not just the "accuracy" of her testimony. Indeed, the accuracy of her testimony has everything to do with her subject position. It is, in fact, her subject position that makes historians particularly interested in her testimony as a Holocaust survivor. Her testimony is unique because she was an eyewitness; she was there. But it is not just because she was there, but why and how she was there that make her testimony unique. The testimony of another eyewitness to the same event—a Nazi guard at the camp, or someone outside the camp who noticed flames in the air—would have a very different meaning, even if he also claimed to see four chimneys blowing up. Perhaps within the context of the Holocaust Testimonies at Yale, surrounded by mostly male professors, the fact that this witness was a woman makes a difference to how she speaks and how she is heard. Only by considering her subject position can we learn something about the "truth" of history, even from the "inaccuracies" of her testimony.

Moreover, insofar as she is also bearing witness to what cannot be seen, she testifies to the process of witnessing itself. From his work with Holocaust survivors, and being a survivor himself, Dori Laub concludes that psychic survival depends on an addressable other, what he calls an "inner witness." It is the possibility of address that sustains psychic life and the subject's sense of its subjective agency. If the possibility of address is annihilated, then subjectivity is also annihilated. To conceive of oneself as a subject is to have the ability to address oneself to another, real or imaginary, actual or potential. Subjectivity is the result of, and depends on, the process of witnessing— address-ability and response-ability. Oppression, domination, enslavement, and torture work to undermine and destroy the ability to respond and thereby undermine and destroy subjectivity. Part of the psychoanalyst's task in treating survivors is reconstructing the address-ability that makes witnessing subjectivity possible.

Our experience of ourselves as subjects is maintained in the tension between our subject positions and our subjectivity. Subject positions, although mobile, are constituted in our social interactions and our positions within our culture and context. They are determined by history and circumstance. Subject positions are our relations to the finite world of human history and relations—what we might call politics. Subjectivity, on the other hand, is experienced as the sense of agency and response-ability that are constituted in the infinite encounter with otherness, which is fundamentally ethical. And although subjectivity is logically prior to any possible subject position, in our experience both are always profoundly interconnected. This is why our experience of our own subjectivity is the result of the productive tension between finite subject position and infinite response-ability of witnessing.

The productive tension at the foundation of the notion of witnessing is the paradox of the eyewitness. The possibility of getting beyond a mere repetition of either history or trauma is the result of the tension between history and testifying to what one already knows from firsthand experience, on the one hand, and psychoanalysis and bearing witness to what is beyond knowledge or recognition, on the other. Both historical truths and the structure of subjectivity are supported by the tension created by the necessary connection between history and psychoanalysis, testimony and witnessing. By strapping two opposite poles together, this support structure works on the principle of tension. Witnessing has the double sense of testifying to something that you have seen with your own eyes and bearing witness to something that you cannot see; there is the juridical sense of bearing witness to what you know from firsthand knowledge as an eyewitness and the religious sense of bearing witness to what you believe through faith. Subject positions and subjectivity are constituted through the tension between these two senses of witnessing. The poles of support for subjectivity are subject positions that are historically determined, at one pole, and the condition of possibility for subjectivity itself that is an infinite response-ability, at the other. The tension between these two supports both subject positions and subjectivity. Oppression and domination work on both levels to destroy the structure of subjectivity, both of which are necessary for the subject's sense of agency.

The question is how can we witness and bear witness to oppression, domination, subordination, enslavement, and torture in ways that open up the possibility of a more humane and ethical future beyond violence? How can acknowledging both subject positions and the response-ability inherent in the process of witnessing mobilize a different, nonthreatening, compassionate, yet critical relationship to difference? How can we move beyond an us-versus-them or every-man-for-himself image of relationships? Vigilance in elaborating and interpreting the process of witnessing—both in the sense of historical facts and historically located subject positions on the one hand, and in the sense of the response-ability opened or closed in the performance of bearing witness on the other—enables working-through rather than merely the repetition of trauma and violence.

In order to conceive of peaceful social relations, democratic political relations, and compassionate personal relations, we must reconceive of ourselves. That is to say, we must reconceive of what it means to be a self, a subject, to have subjectivity, to consider oneself an active agent. If we are selves, subjects, and have subjectivity and agency by virtue of our dialogic relationships with others, then we are not opposed to others. We are by virtue of others. If subjectivity is the process of witnessing sustained through response-ability, then we have a responsibility to response-ability, to the ability to respond. We have an obligation not only to respond but also to respond in a way that opens up rather than closes off the possibility of response by others.

This is what I take Lévinas to mean when he says that we are responsible for the other's responsibility, that we always have one more responsibility. We are responsible for the other's ability to respond. To serve subjectivity, and therefore humanity, we must be vigilant in our attempts to continually open and reopen the possibility of response. We have a responsibility to open ourselves to the responses that constitute us as subjects.

There are, of course, responses that work to close off rather than open up the possibility of response. There are false witnesses and false witnessing that attempt to close off response from others, otherness, or difference. And there are various ways to engage in false witnessing, many of them encouraged within cultures of dominance and subordination. Identifying, elaborating, interpreting, and working-through our own blind spots that lead to false witnessing require constant vigilance in self-reflection—including reflection on what it means to be a self and what it means to reflect. I would argue, for example, that claims of "reverse discrimination" by white students when they are not admitted to universities is a form of false witnessing. To claim that affirmative action is a type of reverse discrimination ignores both the differential sociohistorical subject positions of whites and racial minorities and our ethical responsibility to open up rather than close off responses from others. The double axis of subjectivity is denied in the current discourse of reverse discrimination. Indeed, the discourse of reverse discrimination presupposes a problematic conception of subjectivity that leads to ethical and political problems.

There is a direct connection between the response-ability of subjectivity and ethical and political responsibility. The way in which we conceive of subjectivity affects the way that we conceive of our relationships and responsibilities to others, especially others whom we perceive as different from ourselves. This is why in order to get to the root of social, political, or cultural analysis, it is necessary to examine and diagnose the conceptions of subjectivity presupposed in various discourses, institutions, and practices. How we conceive of ourselves determines how we act and how we conceive of, and treat, other people. If we conceive of subjectivity as a process of witnessing that requires response-ability and address-ability in relation to other people, especially through difference, then we will also realize an ethical and social responsibility to those others who sustain us.

Rather than seeing others with the objectifying gaze of a self-sufficient subject examining, subordinating, or struggling with the other, we can see others with loving eyes that invite loving response. Reconstructing subjectivity entails reconstructing notions of self, self-reflection, relationships, and love. What is love beyond domination? What is love beyond recognition? It is love as working-through that demands constant vigilance toward response-ability in relationships. The loving eye is a critical eye, always on the lookout for the blind spots that close off the possibility of response-ability and openness to otherness and difference. Love is an ethics of differences that thrives on the adventure of otherness. This means that love is an ethical and social responsibility to open personal and public space in which otherness and difference can be articulated. Love requires a commitment to the advent and nurturing of difference.

Love is the responsibility to become attuned to our responses to the world and other people, and to the energies that sustain us. Loving eyes are responsive to the circulation of various forms of energy, especially psychic and affective energy, that enable subjectivity and life itself. Just as the various parts of the body cannot function without the circulation of blood and oxygen, the psyche cannot function without the circulation of affective energy. When response is cut off, the circulation of affective and psychic energies that sustain the process of witnessing, subjectivity, and life itself, is cut off. We have an ethical and social responsibility to be vigilant in our attempts to open up the circulation and flow of affective energy in all of our relationships. Subjectivity itself is the circulation of energy sustained through the process of witnessing. Witnessing is the heart of the circulation of energy that connects us, and obligates us, to each other. The spark of subjectivity is maintained by bearing witness to what is beyond recognition, the process of witnessing itself.

I. Recognition

1. Domination, Multiculturalism, and the Pathology of Recognition

Psychic Recognition

Frantz Fanon is considered an important advocate of recognition for colonized and oppressed people. *Black Skin, White Masks* (1967) has been read as Fanon's attempt to apply the Hegelian master-slave dialectic to colonization.[1] A close reading of this work, however, reveals that rather than merely endorse recognition for colonized people, Fanon problematizes the connection between recognition and identity. In fact, by extending Fanon's analysis, it is possible to interpret the recognition model of identity as the particular pathology of colonial or oppressive cultures. While it seems obvious that oppressed people may engage in struggles for recognition in response to their lack of recognition from the dominant culture, it is less obvious that recognition itself is part of the pathology of oppression and domination. Just as money has been the hard currency for which women and slaves have been exchanged (directly and indirectly), recognition is the soft currency with which oppressed people are exchanged within the global economy. In this way, recognition, like capital, is essential to the economy of domination, which is not to say that oppressed people should not fight for both capital and recognition.

A close reading of Fanon's analysis of the struggle for recognition within a colonial situation unsettles contemporary discussions of recognition by theorists like Charles Taylor, Axel Honneth, and Nancy Fraser. In various ways, these three argue that recognition from the dominant culture is necessary to develop a strong sense of one's own personal and group identity. Taylor explicitly describes the intellectual criteria appropriate for the dominant culture or person to confer recognition on another less powerful culture or person. Honneth, with Fraser following, describes identity as a struggle for personal, social, and political recognition. What Fanon's analysis shows is that these theories presuppose rather than challenge the pathology of recognition inherent in colonial and oppressive cultures.

Within the pathology of recognition, subjectivity is conferred by those in power and on those they deem powerless and disempowered. The desire to be seen, to be recognized, is the paradoxical desire created by oppression. It is the desire to become objectified in order to be recognized by the sovereign subject to whom the oppressed is beholden for his or her own self-worth. Oppression turns people into faceless objects or lesser subjects. The lack of visage in objects renders them invisible in any ethical or political sense. Political and ethical agency, linked to sovereign subjects, also becomes the property of those empowered within dominant culture to dispense according to their mercies. In turn, subjectivity becomes the domain of domination, the property of those empowered to confer on their "inferiors." Subjectivity itself becomes the sign of superiority within the logic of oppression that divides the world into superior subjects and inferior objects.

Fanon argues that the so-called inferiority complex of the oppressed is the result of both economic "inferiority" and the internalization of stereotypes of inferiority. The values of dominant culture are not so much internalized psychologically but forced onto the bodies of the oppressed. The oppressed are chained to the body, represented as unable to think, to reason, to reflect, to speak properly. They are reduced to an egoless, passive body that is at the same time in need of control and discipline. Oppression operates by denying the oppressed access to any internal life. Paradoxically, then, the internalization process of oppression and colonization results in the collapse of internal space—the psyche, mind, or soul. In order to render the oppressed inhuman, the oppressors represent them as animals at the mercy of their bodily instincts with no access to an interior mental life. This is why Fanon argues that in the case of racism the internalization of the dominant values is really what he calls an "epidermalization": stereotypes of inferiority are absorbed in the skin, which signals that inferiority within racist culture.

Fanon describes the process through which racism works over the body: "In the white world the man of color encounters difficulties in the development of his bodily schema. Consciousness of the body is solely a negating activity.... A slow composition of my *self* as a body in the middle of a spatial and temporal world—such seems to be the schema" (1967, 110–11). Fanon next describes his attempts to sketch a "historico-racial schema" below the corporeal schema using the "details, anecdotes, stories" woven by white society in order to "construct a physiological self" (111). Yet in this attempt, he discovers that the corporeal schema gives way to "a racial epidermal schema" (112). It is not the body, after all, but the skin to which he is chained and by which he is determined. Fanon describes this objectification by white society as "an amputation, an excision, a hemorrhage that spattered my whole body with black blood" (112). Racism objectifies by turning skin and blood into objects and then reducing one's very being to that black object. By so doing, as Fanon says, "my body was given back to me sprawled out, distorted, re-colored, clad in mourning in that white winter day" (113). With racism the body becomes nothing more than skin, abjected by dominant culture, alien to the one whose bodily integrity it paradoxically both protects and destroys.

In her work on Fanon, Ann Pellegrini suggests that Fanon's fragmented body "complicates Freud's claim that the 'ego is first and foremost a bodily ego; it is not merely a surface entity, but is itself the projection of a surface'" (1997, 103). She argues that Fanon's "body in pieces" displays multiple projections and surfaces, not the unified surface of Freud's bodily ego. She claims that whereas for the "later Freud" identification is necessary and transformative, for Fanon it is pathogenic and self-destructive (103). Extending Pellegrini's analysis, Fanon's notion of epidermalization further complicates and problematizes Freud's notion of a bodily ego. If, as Freud suggests in *The Ego and the Id*, the ego is "a mental projection of the surface of the body," and the surface of the body turns out to be the site of political struggle and oppression, then the mental projection of that surface is going to be inflected by oppression (Freud 1923, 26). The mental projection, or ego, of the oppressed, mirroring the experience of the body, will be fragmented and in pieces. Rather than enable the projection necessary to maintain the psychic space of the ego, the epidermalization of racially oppressed people reduces projection to the surface in a way that collapses the psychic space necessary for an active ego and the operations of projection itself. Racist epidermalization gives new meaning to Freud's suggestions that the ego is a mental projection of the surface of the body when that surface signifies inferiority and lack of agency; ultimately, the surface of the body signifies lack of ego. While epidermalization is the particular pathology of those racially oppressed, Fanon's analysis suggests that we could develop different symptomologies and characteristics of other forms of oppression.[2]

Throughout *Black Skin, White Masks* he describes the process through which colonized people take on the ideals of their colonizers so that the identity of colonized people is defined solely in relation to the "superior" colonizer. Fanon maintains that "it is the racist who creates his inferior" (1967, 93), and both the inferiority of the oppressed and the superiority of the dominant are pathological (60). He argues that there is no "black man" and there is no "white man" (231). Rather, black and white exist by virtue of their relationship. More specifically, black exists always in relation to a standard or norm that is white (110). We could say that in a racist culture, the superego is white. The colonized or oppressed "internalizes" the attitudes of the colonizers and oppressors to the point where he idealizes the colonizer and denies or hates himself.[3] Fanon diagnoses the way in which white domination creates a paradox of identity whereby blacks recognize themselves either as evil and inferior or as white. Within the pathology of colonialism and oppression, in order for identity to exist these are the two choices (197).

Fanon insists, however, that we can go beyond either alternative by appealing to humanity beyond the pathology of colonial identification. Fanon's humanism is an antidote to what he describes as the dehumanization of oppression. As he says in *The Wretched of the Earth,* the colonized operate as the natural background for the human presence of the colonizer (Fanon 1968, 250). It is this dehumanization that motivates the struggle for recognition by oppressed people. Dehumanization creates the desire and need for recognition from the dominant culture. By so doing, however, the desire for recognition reinforces the dominance of the oppressor and the subordination of the oppressed. For it is the dominant culture and its representatives who have the power to confer or withhold recognition. While the oppressed are constantly seeking acknowledgment from those who continue to subordinate them, they put themselves and their very identities at the mercy of their oppressors. As Fanon describes the situation:

> I begin to suffer from not being white to the degree that the white man imposes discrimination on me, makes me a colonized native, robs me of all worth, all individuality, tells me that I am a parasite on the world, that I must bring myself as quickly as possible into step with the white world, "that I am a brute beast, that my people and I are like a walking dung-heap that disgustingly fertilizes sweet sugar cane and silky cotton, that I have no use in the world." Then I will quite simply try to make myself white: that is I will compel the white man to *acknowledge* that I am human. (1967, 98; my emphasis)

It is only after oppressed people are dehumanized that they seek acknowledgment or recognition of their humanity. More perverse is that they seek recognition of their humanity from the very group that has denied them of it in the first place. In the words of Ann Pellegrini, "The double bind of the colonized is that s/he must seek recognition from those most resistant to recognizing her as a subject in the first place" (1997, 99). An effective aspect of the pathology of oppression is that those who are dominant have the power to create, confer, or withhold recognition, which operates as cultural currency. Struggles for recognition, then, are caught up in the logic of colonialism and oppression that made them necessary in the first place. Fanon repeatedly describes the powerful jaws of the trap of recognition that sprawls out the body and psyche of the oppressed. He describes the black Antillean's desire to be white, the need to find appeasement and permission in the white man's eyes, the burning desire to show the white man that he is wrong about the black man (1967, 63, 76, 118). Fanon's colonized black man is preoccupied with the attention of the white man (1967, 54); everything he does is done for the white man (1967, 212); his moral and human worth is dependent on recognition from the white man (1967, 154). Colonization has soldered his self-identity to the recognition of his oppressor.

With anger and sarcasm, Fanon describes the push and pull of recognition given by one group, demanded by another. For example, he says that

> I was told by a friend who was a teacher in the United States, "The presence of the Negroes beside the whites is in a way an insurance policy on humanness. When the whites feel that they have become too mechanized, they turn to men of color and ask them for a little human sustenance." At last I had been *recognized*, I was no longer a zero. I had to soon change my tune. Only momentarily at a loss, the white man explained to me that, genetically, I represented a stage of development. (1967, 129; my emphasis)

One page earlier, Fanon reacts with sarcasm to a poem about "the Negro's emotion" and "sensitivity," saying, "so here we have the Negro rehabilitated, 'standing before the bar,' ruling the world with his intuition, the Negro *recognized*, set on his feet again, sought after, taken up, and he is a Negro—no, he is not a Negro but the Negro, exciting the fecund antennae of the world" (127; my emphasis). It becomes obvious that Fanon does not embrace a recognition that enslaves the oppressed to their oppressors for their own sense of self-worth.

The only time that Fanon appears to embrace a notion of recognition is in his discussion of Hegel's master-slave dialectic (in the section of *Black Skin, White Masks* titled "The Negro and Hegel"). Even there, he is quick to point out that the situation of slaves and former slaves is not at all captured in Hegel's master-slave scenario. In fact, in a footnote Fanon makes it clear that his point in discussing Hegel has been to show that "the master differs basically from the master described by Hegel" (220).

In Hegel's master-slave model, self-recognition is the result of a life-and-death struggle with another self-consciousness. The self can only recognize itself when it is recognized by another self-consciousness. The recognition of the other, however, turns the self into an object of its own consciousness.

Unable to take the position of an object and a subject for itself at the same time, the self must recuperate its subjectivity by first recognizing itself *in the other*, thereby identifying with the other's recognition of itself, and then *supersede the other*. This last moment is crucial. To return to itself from the place of the other, the self must supersede the otherness of its self-recognition. It must overcome its self-alienation in its relation to the other. This dialectic struggle between self and other is a violent battle in which the self must either kill the other or commit suicide to avoid the inevitable murder of the other. For Hegel, of course, this is merely one stage in the development of consciousness, a stage superseded by Reason.

In Hegel's model the goal is reciprocity between master and slave, whereas in real slavery, as Fanon suggests, the master laughs at the consciousness of the slave:

> What he wants from the slave is not recognition but work. In the same way, the slave here is in no way identifiable with the slave who loses himself in the object and finds in his work the source of his liberation. The Negro wants to be like the master. Therefore, he is less independent than the Hegelian slave is. In Hegel the slave turns away from the master and turns toward the object. Here the slave turns toward the master and abandons the object. (1967, 220–21)

The slave is not the Hegelian slave, because he seeks recognition from the master. Even if Fanon takes the Hegelian model of mutual reciprocal recognition as an ideal (and it is not clear that he does), he insists that the real situation in no way resembles this ideal. The very fact that Fanon points out Hegel's dialectic of master and slave in his phenomenology of self-consciousness as so far from describing the self-consciousness of real masters and slaves presents a challenge to the Hegelian scenario.

Fanon's description of Hegel's master-slave dialectic, which should not be read as an endorsement, emphasizes not only the reciprocity that is missing from real master-slave relations but also insists that the "former slave wants to make himself recognized" (1967, 217). The slave does not want recognition conferred on him by the master but wants to be the agent of his own recognition. Describing the Hegelian struggle for recognition, Fanon seems to suggest that when there are masters and slaves, recognition is impossible: "In a savage struggle I am willing to accept convulsions of death, invincible dissolution, but also the possibility of the impossible" (218).

What Fanon realizes is that the logic of recognition that is part and parcel of colonialism and oppression makes those in power the active agents of recognition and those without power the passive recipients. This is why rather than embrace a recognition model of identity and self-worth, or unproblematically endorse the struggle for recognition of oppressed people, Fanon suggests that active meaning making and self-creation are necessary to fight oppression and overcome the psychic damage of colonization. Fanon ends his section on Hegel by questioning Johann Gottlieb Fichte's idea that "the self takes its place by opposing itself" (1967, 222). Contra Fichte (and presumably Hegel, too) Fanon believes that "man is a yes" to life, love, and generosity but also a no to scorn, degradation, exploitation, and the butchery of freedom. He concludes that to be a yes, humans must be educated to be "actional" and not just "reactional" (222). In a sense, humans must learn not to oppose themselves. Fanon argues that one of the main reasons that Hegel's dialectic cannot apply to real master-slave situations is that "the Black man was acted upon. Values that had not been created by his actions, values that had not been born of the systolic tide of his blood, danced in a hued whirl round him" (1967, 220). The oppressed must learn to be actional and create their own meaning.

Colonization makes the dominant group the creator of values and meaning for the oppressed. Even if the enslaved are freed and given the rights of citizenship, insofar as they are not allowed to create their own values, they remain oppressed. It is not recognition per se that is at stake in overcoming oppression; rather, for Fanon it is the power to create meaning and value for oneself. That is to say, it is precisely the ability to overcome the logic of recognition instilled by the colonial situation—a logic that demands that values are conferred from the dominant culture without any active agency on the part of the oppressed themselves—that enables freedom and respect.

Following Fanon, bell hooks insists that overcoming oppression does not require seeking recognition from the oppressors but being the source of one's own meaning making. She argues that rather than seek recognition from their oppressors, blacks must recognize themselves:

> Fundamental to the process of decentering the oppressive other and claiming our right to subjectivity is the insistence that we must determine how we will be and not rely on colonizing responses to determine our legitimacy. *We are not looking to that Other for recognition.* We are recognizing ourselves and willingly making contact with all who would engage us in a constructive manner. (1990, 22; my emphasis)

Like Fanon, hooks diagnoses the struggle for recognition by the dominant culture as a symptom of the pathology of oppression. Rather than seek recognition from the dominant culture, which means accepting dominant values, those oppressed within and by that culture, hooks argues, need to create their own values.

Fanon sees his own task as one of creating values and finding meaning through analysis, description, and disclosing the mechanics of psychological oppression (168). He hopes that his book "will be a mirror with a progressive infrastructure, in which it will be possible to discern the Negro on the road to disalienation" (184). Fanon imagines reforming the mirroring logic of colonialism into a progressive disalienating device for reflection and self-reflection of nonreactionary values—that is, the creative reflection of values that are not conferred by one's oppressors. Yet Fanon is well aware of the paradox of this hope since *Black Skin, White Masks* is a testimony to the effects of a world in which *my* meaning, or more accurately *my* meaninglessness, is already made for *me* (134). It becomes clear through Fanon's analysis, however, that the alienation of oppressed people is not merely the result of their coming into a world in which their meaning has already been made; in that, the oppressed are not unique. Rather, Fanon suggests that the alienation of oppressed people is the result of a double alienation from the world of meaning and specifically from the meaning of their own bodies.

At this point an analysis of Fanon's explicit and implicit engagement with Lacan's mirror stage will help explain why maintaining that the alienation of oppression "is the case with every individual" only "conceals a basic problem" in extending the psychology of the oppressor to the psychology of the oppressed (1967, 110). Of particular importance in applying Fanon's analysis to Lacan's mirror stage essay is the relation between what Lacan calls the "specular I" and the "social I." Lacan postulates that the specular I—the I of the mirror stage—sets up the social I. He suggests that the alienation inherent in the specular image becomes a central component of all relationships with others, which makes all relationships aggressive and hostile at some level. It is in the development of the relation between the psyche and the social that Fanon's theories provide their most powerful challenge to, and productive revision of, psychoanalytic theory. Whereas Lacan and other Freudian psychoanalysts attribute alienation to a split in the ego caused by discrepancies between the ideal-ego and reality, in the case of the colonized Fanon identifies an alienation that is not inherent in individuality but is social in nature: "It will be seen that the black man's alienation is not an individual question" (Fanon 1967, 11). While neither Freud's nor Lacan's account of the ego or its development takes us outside of the social, I will argue that Fanon's shift in focus from the individual to the social in diagnosing psychic formation presents us with a *reversed mirror stage.*

In *Black Skin, White Masks* Fanon explicitly engages with Lacan's mirror stage in a long footnote when Fanon diagnoses what he calls the "Negrophobia" that results from whites projecting their own unacceptable desires onto blacks. The footnote begins with Fanon asking what would happen if the mirror image the young whites saw were black. He goes on to claim that blacks are the other for whites, presumably in the sense of that which whites exclude as other from their own identities. In tandem, he argues that the mirror image for young blacks is neutral or ultimately white. In this way, taking Lacan's emphasis on the imaginary and fictional direction in the mirror stage, Fanon claims that the mirror image is not primarily a visual perception, for "perception always occurs on the level of the imaginary"; this is how Antilleans perceive themselves and their fellows "in white terms" (163).

Perhaps the question of why blacks do not see themselves in "their own kind" is instigated by Lacan's strange interest in biological experiments with pigeons and locusts that demonstrate that their sexual development depends on the visual perception of a similar image. Lacan gives these examples as further evidence of the importance of imitation in the psychological development of humans. Since Fanon's footnote on Lacan appears at the sentence "What is important to us here is to show that with the Negro the cycle of the *biological* begins," Lacan's appeal to biology seems to raise the question for Fanon that if in the white world blacks represent the biological, then why are blacks an exception to this biology of homeomorphic identification? Lacan maintains that "the facts of mimicry are no less instructive when conceived as cases of heteromorphic identification," and as we know it is ultimately misrecognition that defines the mirror stage (Lacan 1977, 3). Yet Fanon's challenge to Lacan's notion of the mirror stage lies beyond his explicit engagement with it.

Lacan maintains that the function of the mirror stage is to "establish a relation between the organism and its reality—or, as they say, between the *Innenwelt* [inner-world] and the *Umwelt* [outer-world]" (Lacan 1977, 4). Because of the "specific prematurity of birth in man," the imaginary or fictional direction of the mirror with its images compensates for the motor coordination and skills lacking in the "premature" infant. Through the mirror stage, the infant breaks "out of the circle of the *Innenwelt* into the *Umwelt*" by virtue of what Lacan calls the orthopedic image of itself as a totality with agency in the world (4; cf. 2). In the beginning, the

> jubilant assumption of his specular image by the child at the *infans* stage, still sunk in his motor incapacity and nursling dependence, would seem to exhibit in an exemplary situation the symbolic matrix in which the *I* is precipitated in

a primordial form, before it is objectified in the dialectic identification with the other, and before language restores to it, in the universal, its function as a subject. (1977, 2)

In this way, the mirror stage sets up and prefigures the subject's dependence on the dialectic identification with the other. The specular gives birth to the social by presenting a mirror image through which the child can construct itself as a whole and as the seat of agency. Lacan emphasizes that the specular image in the mirror stage creates the fiction of agency prior to the social:

> The important point is that this form situates the agency of the ego, before its social determination, in a fictional direction, which will always remain irreducible for the individual alone, or rather which will only rejoin the coming-into-being of the subject asymptotically, whatever the success of the dialectical syntheses by which he must resolve as *I* his discordance with his own reality. (2)

This process is what Lacan calls the "deflection of the specular *I* into the social *I*" (5).

The mirror stage, then, has several constituent stages. Through it, the child goes from experiencing itself as a fragmented body-out-of-control to gaining a sense of itself as a totality with agency to act on the world. What Lacan calls this "temporal dialectic" soon gives way, however, to "the assumption of the armour of an alienating identity, which will mark with its rigid structure the subject's entire mental development" (4). This alienation is caused by the fact that the individual's sense of itself as an active agent or ego is produced through fiction, practically a hallucination or mirage, or what Lacan also calls a misrecognition of itself in the mirror (2, 6). There is always a split between the inner world and the outer world, between the subject and its Ideal-I, or perfectly delightful mirror image. Experiencing the alienation from its ideal will become the essence of the social: "This moment in which the mirror-stage comes to an end [the moment of the deflection of the specular *I* into the social *I*] inaugurates, by the identification with the imago of the counterpart and the drama of primordial jealousy . . . , the dialectic that will henceforth link the *I* to socially elaborated situations" (1977, 5). The alienation inherent in subjectivity brings with it aggression and hostility in relation to others, with whom the drama of the mirror stage is necessarily repeated.

The pathological mirror of racism has the opposite effect of the Lacanian mirror. Rather than produce the ego with its agency as a fictional defense against alienation, the alienation in the racist mirror destroys the ego. While the Lacanian mirror stage creates a fictional identification that compensates for fragmentation and powerlessness, the racist mirror binds the black subject to an egoless body that is fragmented and powerless. Whereas Lacan describes the orthopedic function of the Ideal-I encountered in the mirror image, which gives the child the empowering fiction of its own agency and unity, Fanon describes the pathological function of the white Ideal-I encountered by blacks in the white mirror of identity. Rather than give blacks the empowering fiction of agency and unity, the white ideal reflects back powerlessness and fragmentation. Fanon maintains that until the black child becomes aware of its blackness in relation to whiteness as defined by white culture, its psychological development is "normal." But when the black child sees itself for the first time reflected in the mirror of white culture, it undergoes a reversed mirror stage.

As if describing the experience of the reversed mirror stage of the oppressed, Fanon says that "my body was given back to me sprawled out, distorted, recolored, clad in mourning in that white winter day" (1967, 113). In the mirror of white domination the black body is not reflected as whole or an active agent but as "animal," "bad," "mean," "ugly," and not human (113). In the reversed mirror stage, racism, through epidermalization, reduces the ego to skin, not even a fragmented body. Rather than create or maintain the illusion of agency and wholeness that supports the ego, the subject is deflated to a flattened sense of self as nothing but skin.

In this reversed mirror stage Fanon describes a *double alienation* and a *double misrecognition* within a racist society that force blacks to choose between identifying as whites, as evil blacks, or not existing at all. This double sense of alienation or socially split subjectivity inherent in racism is described in its contemporary context by Patricia Williams:

> For black people, the systematic, often nonsensical denial of racial experiences engenders a sense of split identity attending that which is obviously inexpressible; an assimilative tyranny of neutrality as self-erasure. It creates an environment in which one cannot escape the clanging of symbolism of oneself. This is heightened by contrast to all the silent, shifty discomfort of suffering condescension. There's that clunky social box, larger than your body, taking up all that space. You need two chairs at the table, one for you, one for your blackness. (1998, 27)

Instead of setting up the fiction of the ego and its agency, this double misrecognition collapses the ego and undermines the sense of agency (Fanon

1967, 154). As he concludes his study in *The Wretched of the Earth* of the psychic disorders caused by colonialism, Fanon says that these disorders make a "mass attack against the ego" (1968, 252). The double alienation and misrecognition inherent in racism appear, it seems, at a stage akin to Freud's, and later Lacan's, secondary narcissism. But rather than work to form the ego through an identification with another person as in secondary narcissism, racism makes an identification with the white oppressor both necessary and impossible for people of color. Furthermore, Fanon suggests that racist identifications undermine—not solidify—the ego. So unlike the identifications with the other formative to the ego in secondary narcissism, the identification with the oppressive other in the reversed mirror stage works to destroy the ego.

For Fanon, the psychic and social are so intimately connected that it seems impossible to identify, as Lacan does in his early essay "The Mirror Stage," a primordial specular I before its social determination. As Fanon argues in his discussion of Lacan, the specular is always the result of the collective unconscious that constructs perception. There is no specular prior to the social. By this Fanon does not simply mean that individual psychic development is always necessarily social or that subjectivity is always necessarily intersubjectivity. While Lacan's later formulation of the gaze in relation to subject formation may be more akin to Fanon's thoroughly social I, still he does not distinguish between the alienation inherent in all subject formation and racist or sexist alienation in particular (cf. Lacan 1981, especially 67–78).

Fanon insists that racist social structures create racist psychic structures—structures that reproduce the inferiority/superiority pathology of oppression. It becomes impossible to describe psychic structures and operations without also describing social structures and operations. In her study of Fanon, Ann Pellegrini concludes that although

> white and black subjects alike form their body-selves intersubjectively, in a dialectic of inside/outside . . . , what starkly distinguishes "white" and "black" experiences of bodily self-consciousness, however, is their differential situation within the historico-psychical network of "race." . . . the push-pull between "what is real and what is psychical" is all the more jarring for subjects who must embody and signify the borderlands of dominant frames of reference. (1997, 103)

When Fanon discusses the effect of social forces on the psyche, he is not merely referring to the fact that language or the symbolic order precedes any individual's ascension to it. He does not simply mean that because meaning is created prior to the individual, alienation is inevitable. Rather, particular kinds of degrading or dehumanizing meanings and the social forces of domination and oppression prevent the individual from participating in meaning making and tie subjectivity to some/one body part and thereby produce a double alienation and a double misrecognition, which are not inherent in all subject formation but are peculiar to the pathology of oppression. While the alienation that psychoanalysts like Lacan describe as inherent in the psyche is the result of a gap between the inner world of the individual and the outer world of reality or society, what I am calling the double alienation described by Fanon is the result of the dominant culture's denial of individuality to members of the oppressed group. While Freudian psychoanalysts place the individual or ego at the center of the psyche, Fanon places the social at the center of the oppressed psyche.

Adapting and historicizing Carl Jung's notion of a collective unconscious, Fanon diagnoses what happens when an individual is confronted with the collective unconscious of the dominant culture that oppresses him. The double alienation unique to oppression is crystallized in that moment when an individual realizes that she is denied individuality and access to meaning making by a culture that chains her to a group identity. Fanon's analysis suggests that whereas white culture values individuality and the merits associated with this individualism, oppression works through denying individuality to the oppressed by stereotyping them. The racialized other is seen as always and only a representative of a group, while the "race-neutral" or "normal" dominant white is seen as an individual whose merit is self-determined. What I am calling the reversed mirror stage, then, is inaugurated in the moment when the individual first experiences him- or herself as chained to a group in a dehumanizing or denigrating way. The reversed mirror stage begins with the recognition of oneself through the eyes of the dominant culture and continues with the double alienation that results from identifying with the very collective unconscious through which one has been othered. While Lacan's mirror stage begins with the solidification of the ego and ends with a defensive alienation that the ego uses against others to protect itself, Fanon's reversed mirror stage begins with a challenge to the ego and ends with the debilitating double alienation that leaves the ego defenseless against being othered within the dominant culture.

Whereas within the Lacanian scenario the gap between the inner and outer worlds that results in alienation makes a virtue of necessity when it gives rise to the fiction of the active agency of the ego, for Fanon the gap between the ego as active agency and the cultural fiction of the inferiority and powerlessness of colonized people makes vice necessary. In *The Wretched of the Earth*, Fanon attributes what he sees as the competitiveness and crime spawned in colonial environments to the poverty of the oppressed, for whom both economic and psychological resources for survival are scarce (1968, 308). If the psychology of oppressed people is one of comparison and the will to dominate their peers, Fanon maintains that the cause is the colonial environment. We could say that a colonial or oppressive environment creates the psychology of comparison and the will to dominate by means of the connection between recognition and identity (1967, 213). Because the oppressed are forced to compare themselves to their oppressors who put themselves up as the norm or standard against which the oppressed are found inferior, the oppressed are thrown into a vicious circle of finding their own self-worth by virtue of this impossible comparison. Comparison and domination are thus inherent in the recognition model of identity, a model that helps to maintain oppression and colonialism on a psychological level.

If the racist reversal of the mirror stage that Fanon's analysis suggests is a type of secondary narcissism, then its operation is more akin to Freud's description of the narcissistic identification in melancholia. In "Mourning and Melancholia" Freud depicts melancholia as an identification with a lost object. In mourning, "it is the world which has become poor and empty; in melancholia it is the ego itself." Melancholia, unlike mourning, displays "an extraordinary diminution in self-regard, an impoverishment of ego on a grand scale" (1989, 584). This diminution of self-regard is caused by the subject's identification with the lost object who had been the source of disappointment. More than this, Freud attributes self-reproaches to the mourner's delusion that he is to blame for the loss of the loved object (587–88). As Freud describes it, the subject holds onto his love for the lost object through his identification with it. In this way, although he berates the lost object as himself, he refuses to lose it. Freud maintains that

> in this way an object-loss was transformed into an ego-loss and the conflict between the ego and the loved person into a cleavage between the critical activity of the ego and the ego as altered by identification. . . . The narcissistic identification with the object then becomes a substitute for the erotic cathexis, the result of which is that in spite of the conflict with the loved person the love-relation need not be given up. (586–87)

Revising Freud's theory in light of Fanon's notion of the redoubled alienation experienced by colonized peoples when they come to see themselves in the eyes of their oppressors, we could say that the forced internalization of the oppressor's superiority and their own inferiority results in a type of melancholic identification with the cultural loss of their own lovable and loved ego. The dominant culture forces the oppressed to "internalize" an objectified ideal of himself; this is to say, the oppressed are forced to identify with the position of Other for the dominant culture. In this position of Other, the oppressed can only identify with an abject object prohibited and shunned by the harsh ego-ideal or superego of the dominant culture.

When the child or young adult begins to experience the racism of her culture, she is put in the position of the Other, longing for a sense of self as belonging and loved that is missing within dominant culture. In this version of melancholy, rather than incorporate the other into the self and berate it, the self is put in the position of the other, projected out of itself as abject and disappointing, while the lost love is a loss of any positive sense of self as an agent or a beloved. The lost love is not an object but the subject itself, and the subject becomes object by way of the introjection of the racist ideals of the dominant culture. The beratement and feelings of inferiority introjected from racist culture are directed at the subject's own ego, which produces the melancholy subject of racism. Freud's description of the mourner's self-blame for the loss of the object is apt in a situation where dominant culture blames the victim for his own victimization. Along with abjecting itself as the other of dominant culture, the oppressed subject internalizes the sense of blame thrust upon it. The only sense of agency or responsibility afforded the racialized other or those othered by racism is the responsibility for what Fanon calls his or her own inferiority complex.

Fanon's *Black Skin, White Masks* can be read as a melancholy text, in which he longs for his lost sense of himself as white. He laments the day that he was forced to see himself as black. As Fanon reminds us, within the colonial situation *black* and *white* are relative terms and have no meaning in themselves. This means that what he longs for when he longs for his past image of himself as white is really his past image of himself as a social agent, which results from finding a loving, supportive space within the social with which to identify himself. When he laments being forced to face his blackness, he is bemoaning the lack of that loving space for black identity. In this way, Fanon's text displays his own melancholic relationship to his lost ideal image—an ideal that he begins to regain through social and political activism aimed at creating a supportive social space for black identity.

The absence of a positive sense of self and agency is the result of the absence of a loving ego-ideal. If the ego-ideal or superego is only punishing, then we are left with paranoia or masochism (paranoia in that we are constantly under the harsh surveillance of the Law, or masochism in that we are constantly deserving punishment from the Law). The narcissistic structure, which supports all subjective identity, requires what Julia Kristeva calls a loving imaginary father. The imaginary father is the flip side of the law, the love that supports a positive sense of self (1987). For Kristeva, without this loving aspect of the social, the ego is left identified with an abject (maternal) body excluded from the world of meaning. Ultimately, the loving paternal support for the narcissistic structure gives meaning to signification by connecting affect and words. Without loving support from the social, we are homeless, without a sense of belonging. More than this, for Kristeva, without this loving support, psychic space collapses, leaving the subject with a sense of emptiness and meaninglessness (1987, 1995, 1996, 1997b, 2000).

Kristeva's diagnosis of this collapse or flattening of psychic space that results from a lack of loving idealization in the social consensus (1997a, 162) resonates with Fanon's diagnosis of the "internalization" or introjection of a lack of internal or psychic space that comes from the specific lack of a loving idealization of oppressed peoples within the social consensus that oppresses them. Oppression collapses the psyche by othering the subject through dehumanizing operations and representations that construct the other as animal and chain him to his body rather than acknowledging his subjectivity and psyche/soul.

From Fanon's analysis of the effects of oppression on the ego, we can extrapolate at least three axes of critical engagement with psychoanalytic theory. First, the mirror stage model does not account for the double alienation and double misrecognition experienced by victims of racism. In fact, this model conflates all types of alienation and reduces them to the primary alienation at the heart of subjectivity—a move that effectively denies the uniqueness of racial alienation. Second, the notions of both primary and secondary narcissism that explain the formation of the ego are inadequate to explain the disintegration of the ego that results from narcissistic identifications of victims with their oppressors. Third, psychoanalytic postulations of rejection, exclusion, projection, and abjection inherent in ego or subject formation effectively perpetuate colonization and oppression insofar as they do not identify rejection, exclusion, projection, and abjection with the logic of colonization and oppression themselves. Rather than describe the rejection, exclusion, projection, or abjection of certain undesirable characteristics onto the other as part of the operations of oppression and colonization, Freudian psychoanalysis explains this operation as inherent in ego, subject, or identity formation.

From Hegel's notion of self-consciousness as a struggle for recognition to Lacan's notion of psychic compensation for misrecognition in the mirror stage, models of identity and subjectivity based on recognition are symptoms of the pathology of oppression and domination. In the Hegelian scenario the hope for reciprocal recognition and equality is won through enslavement and domination. Within Hegelian mutual recognition both self-consciousnesses must be the same; difference is the threatening otherness that alienates and motivates the murderous urges inherent in the struggle for recognition. While Lacan exposes the ideal of mutual recognition as a delusion, the centrality and inescapability of misrecognition make communication or love (across difference) just as impossible. While psychoanalysis better enables us to diagnose murderous urges or paranoid alienation in relationships between people, alone it is not able to diagnose the social context that creates those urges or paranoia. Fanon brings psychoanalysis and social analysis together to show the ways in which the social and psychic work together to form our sense of ourselves as subjects and our sense of our own and others' identities.

It is Fanon's hope that by reflecting back the white mirror of double alienation with his own "progressive" mirror, he can begin the process of disalienation.[4] He attempts to mirror the mirror of racism in order to expose the mechanics of oppression (1967, 168). By doubling the mirror, Fanon hopes to counteract the double alienation caused by oppression. Whereas Lacan's orthopedic mirror reflects a specular image seen by the eyes, Fanon imagines another "correcting mirror" not of the physical eyes but of the mind's eye. Lacan calls the mirror stage the threshold of the visible world. Insofar as the Lacanian mirror stage describes a movement from the eyes to the eye—from vision to Vision, Fanon describes a movement back from the eye to the eyes—from Vision to vision.[5] Reflection is one of the antidotes to the tyranny of the visible world in which people are divided by colors. Throughout his work, Fanon stresses the importance of reflection and self-reflection in overcoming the logic of oppression. One must be vigilant in self-reflection to see the ways in which one's own identity and attempts toward liberation are complicit with one's oppression.

Fanon concludes *Black Skin, White Masks* with his "final prayer": "O my body, make of me always a man who questions!" (232). This final remark suggests a dialectical relationship or symbiosis between the mind's eye and the eyes, between questioning and the body. Fanon calls on his body and not his mind to make him self-reflective and interpretative. This final prayer also connects the body with man or humanity, a connection denied within the colonial environment, which denies humanity on the basis of body types or skin colors. For it is the ability to question, to interpret, to reflect that is called into question when humanity is called into question through racism. Within a racist or sexist culture certain bodies are not able to legitimately question, interpret, or reflect. Those human abilities are reserved for bodies posing as disembodied neutral forces of nature or truth. Yet in his final prayer, Fanon calls on his body to remind him of his humanity, a humanity lost through the perversions of colonial domination and regained through love.

Just before this prayer, Fanon says that "at the conclusion of this study, I want the world to recognize, with me, the open door of every consciousness" (1967, 232). Some commentators have read this passage as Fanon's endorsement of a recognition model of identity as the means to liberation.[6] I read this passage as Fanon's call to see in every consciousness the welcoming of the other, the open door, which cannot be accomplished through a recognition model of identity insofar as that model operates according to the logic of oppression. Rather, throughout *Black Skin, White Masks,* Fanon keeps returning to a discussion of the necessity and possibility of love. Fanon begins by diagnosing the aberrations of affect that result from colonization and oppression (1967, 8). Colonization creates perverse self-destructive desires and unhealthy affect and makes love impossible.

Moreover, love, it seems, is what is lacking from some analyses of oppression. For example, in the end Fanon criticizes Octave Mannoni's theories of the pathology of oppression because Mannoni "has not tried to *feel* himself into the despair of the man of color confronting the white man" (1967, 86; my emphasis). Mannoni fails to appreciate the situation of oppression because his theories are without affective connection to his subjects. Conversely, for Fanon love is only possible when we are freed from the unconscious conflicts and inferiority complex inherent in psychological oppression (1967, 41–42). Overcoming oppression involves affective connection and love, but true love is possible only when we have overcome oppression.

Love is possible only beyond struggles, particularly struggles for recognition. Against Sartre, Fanon insists on the possibility of love:

> And, if Sartre has appeared to formulate a description of love as frustration, his *Being and Nothingness* amounting only to an analysis of dishonesty and inauthenticity, the fact remains that true, authentic love—wishing for another what one postulates for oneself, when that postulation unites the permanent values of human reality—entails the mobilization of psychic drives basically freed of unconscious conflicts. Left far, far behind, the last *sequelae* of a titanic struggle carried on against *the other* have been dissipated. Today I believe in the possibility of love; that is why I endeavor to trace its imperfections, its perversions. (1967, 41–42)

In his analysis of concrete relationships with others, Sartre devotes most of his discussion to feelings of conflict; even love is ultimately the experience of conflict (1956, 477). Love is another form of struggle for recognition and freedom, full of conflict and shame. For Sartre, the primary experience that brings me to myself is the experience of shame that results from being caught in the act by another person. Although he insists that both pride and shame are the result of the look of the other, he does not analyze pride. Instead, he spends much of his discussion describing shame in front of the other. In fact, as it turns out, pride is only the antithesis of shame; even pride is derived from the primary feeling of shame: "Pride does not exclude original shame. In fact it is on the ground of fundamental shame or shame of being an object that pride is built" (1956, 386).

Like Hegel's theory of the onset of self-consciousness through the master-slave relationship, Sartre's theory is premised on the claim that even in concrete relations each person is attempting to enslave the other:

> While I seek to enslave the Other, the Other seeks to enslave me. We are by no means dealing with unilateral relations with an object-in-itself, but with reciprocal and moving relations. The following descriptions of concrete behavior must therefore be envisaged within the perspective of conflict. Conflict is the original meaning of being-for-others. (1956, 475)

As Sartre describes the conflict, it is a conflict over freedom. The other takes my freedom, possesses it, and is the catalyst for my recognition of my freedom (1956, 473). I am imprisoned by the look of the other, yet through the look of the other I am aware of myself as a subject. As an object for another, I become aware of myself as a subject for myself; I become aware of myself as a subject who escapes objectification, even my own attempts at objectifying myself. Yet in spite of what Sartre describes as the totalizing presence of the other, the look of the other always refers back to me: "The look which the *eyes* manifest, no matter what kind of eyes they are, is a pure reference to myself" (1956, 347). The other's look is always directed *at me*. Even while my own self-consciousness is dependent on the other, for Sartre I remain the center of the universe.

Although in his discussion of freedom in *Being and Nothingness* Sartre stresses an individual's freedom and responsibility, we know from earlier sections of his book that the other plays a crucial role in my freedom. It is the look of the other that gives rise to my own recognition of my freedom. The look of the other turns me back on myself so that I can see the way in which I always escape myself; I see my possibilities. The look of the other confronts me with the nothingness at the core of my being when I see myself as an object for the other and realize that who I am is constituted in that look at the same time that I refuse to be reduced to that look. I both am and am not the object seen by the other. So begins the Sartrean struggle with the other, which supports Garcin's conclusion in *No Exit* that "there's no need for red-hot pokers. Hell is other people" (Sartre 1976, 47).

In contrast to Sartre, Fanon insists on the possibility of love beyond conflict and shame. If love provides a form of recognition, it is not the Sartrean recognition won in a struggle against the other for one's freedom. Fanon's vision of love opens the way for a love that is not self-centered but other-centered. Love for and between those othered by dominant culture opens up new possibilities for recognition. Yet against Hegel, Fanon claims—perhaps tongue in cheek—that sexual love between sexes and races can bestow a form of recognition on the oppressed that takes us outside of the Hegelian dialectic of recognition (1967, 63). Love from an individual who is part of the group dominant in the culture can elevate the individual who is part of the group subordinated in the culture; this form of recognition, however, like others I have discussed, is symptomatic of oppression.

Unlike Hegel, Fanon opts for love over reason. Following Fanon, Cornel West insists that racism cannot be cured through reason or "overcome by arguments or analyses"; rather, West claims that as a "disease of the soul," "the disease of racism is tamed by love and care." He says that this love ethic "has nothing to do with sentimental feelings or tribal connections. Rather it is a last attempt at generating a sense of agency among a downtrodden people" (1994, 29). For West, like Fanon, love is part of a critical process of re-creating a sense of agency in the fight against racism's attack on the ego.

Fanon's emphasis on love and feeling suggests an affect-based alternative to the Hegelian-Lacanian economy of desire. While desire is a lack in relation to the other that is born out of a primordial alienation, affect is a movement toward the other that is born out of love. Kristeva describes the difference between desire and affect: desire "emphasizes *lack,* whereas affect, while acknowledging the latter, gives greater importance to the movement toward the other and to mutual *attraction*" (1982, 155). Affect is an alternative to a sacrificial economy that puts either the self or other in the place of lack or alienation.

It becomes clear that for Fanon love is a matter of ethics and ethics is a matter of love—the values of human reality and wishing for the others what you wish for yourself. And this ethical commitment to love is necessarily part of a politics of liberation. Love restores the agency of the oppressed subject, an agency that is destroyed insofar as she or he is made into an object within the dominant culture. Love restores the oppressed subject to the world of subjectivity and humanity. Affective connection and loving attention can be a liberation from objectification, if only temporarily and incompletely, until everyone is free of oppression and all see and begin to walk through the welcoming, open door of every consciousness (cf. Fanon 1967, 109). Rather than limit ourselves to the oppressive logic of superior/inferior, the logic of recognition, Fanon asks, "why not the quite simple attempt to touch the other, to feel the other, to explain the other to myself?" (1967, 231). For Fanon, however, there can be no explanation of the other without some affective connection between self and other. If this is true, understanding is affective and welcoming. And touching and feeling are the true welcoming gestures toward others. Fanon's notion of the connection between politics and love is suggestive, although, as others have argued, it tends to be homophobic and patriarchal.[7] Applying Fanon's own suggestions about the competitive need for recognition spawned through the pathology of colonialism and oppression, one could say that like racism, homophobia and patriarchy are symptoms, with varying characteristics, of this pathology.

For Fanon, it seems that love operates between the social and the psyche. Love can enable a sense of psychic wholeness necessary for social agency. Although Fanon idealizes what he calls "true love," he imagines the political and social power of loving attention. Given Fanon's analysis of the social constitution of the ego, it is difficult to imagine that he suggests that true love is ahistorical, asocial, or apolitical. By imagining interracial love in the context of racism, Fanon politicizes love even as he describes its effects on the psyche of the oppressed. Love becomes the working joint between psychic self-affirmation and social and political transformation. The transformative power of love is a social and political power.

Teresa Brennan has persuasively described the power of love in the development of the psyche. In *The Interpretation of the Flesh*, Brennan argues that the ego is set up and fortified by directed attention from others, usually women who care for us (1992). This directed attention, or love, gives the ego a sense of agency and power in the world. Without this attention, especially positive attention or love, the ego is inadequately prepared to act in the world. Loving attention is what enables agency.

Loving attention on the personal level has its analogue on the social level. As Fanon suggests, oppressed people lack the ability to create meaning for themselves as a result of both the denial of a sense of social agency and the lack of the social space within which to create meaning. Social agency is tied to personal agency, and the lack of social space is tied to the lack of psychic space. Just as an individual cannot develop a sense of agency without loving attention from another and cannot develop a sense of meaning without the loving support of the social, an individual or group cannot develop a sense of social agency or social purpose without a loving social space in which to articulate that agency and meaning. In *The Sense and Nonsense of Revolt* (2000) Kristeva insists that revolution—both individual and social—from the largest to the smallest revolt, requires psychic space; that is to say, revolt requires the personal and social space within which to create our own meaning. And for Kristeva, opening this psychic space requires an identification with a loving social space. Kristeva suggests that social revolution requires love.

Although Fanon's use of love in *Black Skin, White Masks* is problematic, especially when he romanticizes "true love," and, as many commentators have argued, when his analysis is tainted by homophobia and sexism, still his insistence on love's place in ethical and political struggle suggests an alternative to Hegelian Reason as the reconciliation of the struggle for recognition. Opening a public space of love and generosity is crucial to opening a space beyond domination.

In her recent work, bell hooks insists that an ethic of love must be part of any political movement. For hooks, there is an essential relation between love and freedom: "The moment we choose to love we begin to move against domination, against oppression. The moment we choose to love we begin to move towards freedom, to act in ways that liberate ourselves and others. That action is the testimony of love as the practice of freedom" (1994a, 250). Loving is itself a sign of freedom (cf. Willet 2001). As Toni Morrison's narrator tells us in *Beloved*, "To get to a place where you could love anything you choose—not to need permission for desire—well now, *that* was freedom" (1987, 162). Fanon's imperative to "attempt to touch the other, to feel the other, to explain the other to myself," along with his belief that love can restore a sense of subjectivity, agency, and ego to those wounded by oppression so that they might create the world for themselves, beyond the pathology of recognition, conjures up the vision of this place where love shall set us free.

Intellectual Recognition

Charles Taylor attempts to theorize what it means to explain the other to ourselves. Unlike Fanon, Taylor's theory embraces a Hegelian notion of recognition and an understanding based in intellect rather than affect. For Taylor, recognition is a type of respect that is conferred or withheld depending on the worth of the individual or group in question. According to Taylor, once worth is determined, then respect or recognition is either extended or withheld. The judgment about worth is not an ethical but an intellectual judgment that can be made only after careful "study of the other," which Taylor insists begins with the ethical presumption of worth because only a "real engagement" with the other can lead to a new horizon from which to judge it (Taylor 1994, 69–70). So the standards for judging worth can or should change through studying the other from the ethical presumption of worth.

It is obvious that Taylor's is a theory presented from the position of dominance, the position of the judge of others who confers or withholds recognition. While our own worth is never questioned, other cultures and other people are objects of study, which in the best scenario enrich or contribute something of value to our own: if they don't have worth for us, then they don't have worth. As Taylor says, either they do or they don't; and "we" can act as objective judges if we study hard enough. Taylor assigns us the dubious position of judge and juror because he seems to believe that the West is morally and intellectually superior to the rest of the world (1989, especially 396–97).[8] Recognition, for Taylor, is a type of market exchange: we give recognition in exchange for something of value to us.

Not only is Taylor's theory presented from the position of dominance, but also it presupposes the subject and its object or other. In spite of his attention to the history of subjectivity, and in spite of his insistence that identity is dialogic, Taylor does not consider how the subject and its values or its others are produced within that dialogue. Taylor's dialogue presumes interlocutors seemingly already formed who seek only membership into the new world order or recognition of their worth from the superpowers of subjectivity. He scoffs at the "neo-Nietzscheans" who turn subjectivity and identity into an issue of power, yet he does not attempt an explanation of how subjects and their others are formed such that certain values are embraced and others are rejected (1994, 70). Rather, at the same time that he insists that identity is produced through intersubjective relations, he appeals to intellectual standards of objectivity without questioning their means of production or the conditions of possibility for intellectual judgment. For Taylor, ethics seem to demand nothing more than the sovereign's good will toward his subordinates as he studies them for his own enrichment. Like the historian's method of looking for objective facts that were recognizable to him in survivors' testimonies, Taylor's method of engagement with others risks overlooking value that cannot be listed in an encyclopedia of worth.

An anecdote recounted by Patricia Williams resonates with Taylor's approach to others. Williams tells the story about a group walking tour of Harlem on Easter Sunday sponsored by the New York Arts Society, attended by young white professionals, with the exception of Williams. She recounts how the tour guide asked the group if they would like to stop in some churches to see the Easter services in progress. Williams reports that in response to her protests that it would be disrespectful and could disrupt the services, the group maintained that "no one will mind," that they "just want to look," and that "no harm is intended" (1991, 71; 1998, 21–25). Williams's critical reflection on this situation could just as well be directed at Taylor's method of engagement with others:

> As well-intentioned as they were, I was left with the impression that no one existed for them who could not be governed by their intentions. While acknowledging the lack of apparent malice in this behavior, I can't help thinking that it is a liability as much as a luxury to live without interaction. To live so completely impervious to one's own impact on others is a fragile privilege, which over time relies not simply on the willingness but on the inability of others—in this case blacks—to make their displeasure heard. (1991, 72)

Taylor's theory of multiculturalism and engagement with others risks the dangers identified by Williams. His theory does not take into account the effects of Western culture on those whom we choose to study, nor does it allow that the one-way gaze of the judging subject is reversible. Indeed, his notion of intellectual judgment from the ethical presumption of worth resonates with the most insensitive operations of liberal multiculturalism, which begins from the benevolence of those in power without regard for the desires of those without power. Taylor's presumption of ethical worth—a presumption easily dismissed if a culture proves unworthy—even combined with his Gadamerian notion of shifting horizons, is little protection against cultural imperialism, whatever its motivations.

Moral Recognition

Unlike Taylor, who turns our engagement with others into a matter of intellectual judgment, Axel Honneth argues that all human struggles, especially struggles over worth, are moral struggles (1996, 5). For Honneth, ethical life is based on recognition, and recognition has the obligation to reciprocity built into it (37). Honneth follows Hegel in maintaining that we can get recognition only from an equal; therefore, in order to get recognition from the other we also have to give recognition to the other. We have crossed from Taylor's one-way street of recognition to Honneth's two-way street of mutual recognition. Still, even with Honneth we may not be able to get where we want to go.

Honneth describes three forms of recognition necessary for proper independent individuality and democratic society. Love is the first and most basic form of recognition. Primary caring relationships are necessary for an individual's sense of self-confidence and trust in their own agency. The child learns to trust itself by learning to trust its mother not to abandon it (1996, 104). This assurance of care allows one to become an independent subject (105). Recognition is the affirmation of independence supported by care (107). The failure of recognition in love destroys self-confidence. Furthermore, disrespect of physical existence or bodily integrity guaranteed through loving intimate relationships can injure a person to the point of collapse (132). Rape and torture can cause one to mistrust oneself and ultimately to question one's own sense of reality (132). For Honneth, all types of recognition and self-respect are conditioned by the experience of love, which, unlike its subsequent and more properly social forms, does not emerge as a historical development (106, 108).

The second form of recognition is legal recognition, and its corresponding form of disrespect is denying legal rights. Whereas recognition in love is affective, Honneth claims that legal recognition is cognitive. Still, he describes legal recognition as analogous to love in that just as loving care supports autonomy by transferring trust from the mother to the child, social respect leads to self-respect because social subjects endowed with rights are trusted by law to make judgments and thereby come to trust themselves (118, 134). Denying legal rights can destroy self-respect and the trust in one's own ability to make judgments.

The third form of recognition Honneth calls social solidarity. Whereas legal recognition assures that every person is extended equal rights, social solidarity respects the particular worth and contribution of different groups of people (121). People gain a sense of self-esteem only when they are esteemed for accomplishments that they do not share with everyone else (125). Group identity becomes a source of self-esteem when groups are valued for certain particular characteristics that can carry over to individuals (127–28). Honneth associates the form of corresponding disrespect with shame and rage that result when the unique contributions of one's group are not valued (135–37). The lack of both types of social recognition, one conferred by law and the other by group identity, can lead to a sense of social or psychic death (135).

For Honneth, both types of social recognition are historical developments still dependent on recognition in love, which for him is not a historical development. In his preface to *The Struggle for Recognition*, Honneth says that he must postpone an encounter with feminism in spite of feminists' concerns with recognition. Had he not postponed that encounter, he might have reconsidered this claim that love is not a historical development. Even while he criticizes Hegel for not moving beyond a bourgeois notion of the family, Honneth accepts D. W. Winnicott's problematic notion of symbiotic oneness between mother and infant motivated by the infant's helplessness and the mother's "inner urge" (99). By presupposing this symbiotic relation between mother and child, Honneth must also assume some violent break, through which the child becomes independent. He follows Jessica Benjamin (1988) in maintaining that this break is like the Hegelian master-slave life-and-death struggle for recognition.

But as I argued in *Family Values* (1997), this violent break is necessary only if we imagine the mother-infant relationship as antisocial. If, however, we see that relationship as a prototype for all social relations, then it is not a symbiotic natural relation that needs to be overcome in order for the child to enter society. Honneth's claim that love is not historical leads him to accept as natural and necessary a view of motherhood and mother-child relations that reduces the mother and her relation to her child to some antisocial natural realm. And this patriarchal view of love supports the rest of his social theory, which rests on what he sees as this cornerstone of ahistorical love. So it is not surprising when Honneth quotes Joel Feinberg: "Having rights enables us to stand up like men" (1996, 120)!

Still, there are even more serious problems with Honneth's theory of recognition. First, like Taylor, he assumes preformed subjects-objects and others, whose attitudes towards themselves and others change according to their intersubjective relations. His concern is not so much with how the subject is produced or comes into being, but how the subject becomes independent, autonomous, and able to act. He doesn't ask the question "What, or who, is this subject that has these attributes?" He assumes that recognition is something that others confer on the subject in order to give that subject a sense of self-respect. Yet by assuming preformed subjects and others, Honneth addresses only the *symptoms* of lack of respect and not the *causes*. He merely says that without recognition through love, legal recognition, and the recognition of solidarity, an individual does not have self-respect, but he doesn't investigate why these types of recognition are given or withheld in the first place.

Moreover, insofar as he continually reasserts that it is only through injustice and disrespect, both of which lead to conflict, that individuals form their identities as individuals and members of groups, his theory presupposes injustice. If the condition of possibility of self-respect is that one is disrespected, then Honneth's analysis undermines his own vision. Honneth maintains that self-confidence, self-respect, and self-esteem all come through conflict and struggles for recognition. These struggles are struggles against disrespect on each of these levels, disrespect that becomes social injustice. Yet in Honneth's analysis it is only through the conflicts that result from disrespect and injustice that self-respect can emerge (128). This takes me back to my original questions: how can we think that war is necessary for peace? How can disrespect be necessary for respect? How can we start from the presumption of injustice as a *necessary* condition of possibility for justice? Is it, then, only through continued abuse and injustice that respect and justice can grow? Certainly, injustice exists. But can we assume that it is necessary and still hope for justice?

2. Identity Politics, Deconstruction, and Recognition

Recognition Remedies

Nancy Fraser addresses this problem in other terms. She makes a distinction between affirmative and transformative remedies for disrespect or lack of recognition. Affirmative remedies for unjust distribution aim at correcting inequitable outcomes without addressing the underlying structure—formal equality. Transformative remedies aim at correcting inequitable outcomes by addressing the underlying generative framework that produces the inequities in the first place—socialist politics (Fraser 1997, 23). Affirmative remedies for lack of recognition or disrespect would revalue unjustly devalued groups and individuals while leaving intact the content of the group or individual identity and differential that underlies them—identity politics (24). Transformative remedies, on the other hand, would redress disrespect by transforming the underlying structure of cultural valuation by destabilizing existing group and individual identities and thereby changing every one's sense of self—deconstruction (24).

A problem with Fraser's analysis of the distinction between affirmative and transformative remedies is that the distinction itself is symptomatic of the affirmative approach to recognition/distribution problems. As she argues, the transformative approach undermines these types of binary or oppositional approaches. To draw the distinction, as Fraser does, between affirmative and transformative measures as a distinction between something like base and superstructure prevents the type of transformative analysis she endorses. Deconstructive transformative analysis requires that we challenge the distinction between cause and effect, base and superstructure, in order to see how effects may also act as causes. In a sense, Fraser criticizes affirmative approaches because they are too simplistic, and yet her own analysis itself simplifies complex problems to what can be seen as counterproductive ends of perpetuating oppositions. Even so, the distinction between affirmative and transformative remedies and the contradictions within Fraser's analysis of them can be instructive in bringing to the fore some of the ways in which contemporary theories concerned with difference and the other still privilege the subject in its relation to both difference and the other, especially insofar as they rely on recognition.

Fraser doesn't elaborate particular theories of equality/redistribution or identity politics/recognition that she has in mind when she sets out her redistribution-recognition dilemma and its resolution, which makes it difficult to assess the viability of her account. Since I am primarily interested in issues of recognition, for my purposes here it will be useful to analyze particular examples of theories of recognition to substantiate Fraser's analysis. The theories of Maria Lugones and Iris Young provide nice complements in the debate over identity politics. Although Lugones and Young may be positioned at either pole of the identity politics issue, I want to suggest that both only provide what Fraser calls affirmative remedies for problems of recognition.

Fraser's distinction between affirmative and transformative remedies really turns on whether or not the "remedy" engages the problem at the level of subjectivity and the subject/object dualism itself. What Fraser calls affirmative remedies leave intact the subject/object opposition and merely try to bridge the gap between them. What she calls transformative remedies would attempt to deconstruct the opposition between subject and object or otherwise change the way that we conceive of the relations between subject and object by changing our conception of ourselves as subjects. Rather than set up dualisms in order to finesse them, as Fraser does, transformative remedies would need to provide an alternative conceptual framework in which identity is not formed and solidified through an oppositional logic that uses dualisms to justify either opposition and strife or awkward or artificial bridging mechanisms.

Privileging Identification

Maria Lugones embraces a strong sense of identity politics in which identities are worn almost like badges and those badges determine one's membership in a particular community. In her most well-known essay, "Playfulness, 'World' Travelling, and Loving Perception," Lugones talks about traveling from one community to another as "world travelling," which she argues should be done with an attitude of playfulness and loving perception. Lugones maintains that

> the outsider has necessarily acquired flexibility in shifting from the main-
> stream construction of life where she is constructed as an outsider to other

constructions of life where she is more or less "at home." This flexibility is necessary for the outsider but it can also be *willfully exercised* by the outsider or by those who are at ease in the mainstream. I recommend this *willful exercise,* which I call "world" travelling, and I also recommend that the willful exercise be animated by an attitude that I describe as playful. (1987, 3, my emphasis)

She also recommends "to women of color in the U.S. that we learn to love each other by learning to travel to each other's 'worlds'" (4).

Lugones defines *world* as a culture or subculture that one does or does not know she inhabits. She says that we can be different people in different worlds. She defines *loving perception* as a loving attitude that allows us to identify with others, to see ourselves in others. She argues that "there is a complex failure of love in the failure to identify with another woman, the failure to see oneself in other women who are quite different from oneself" (7). She uses the example of her relationship with her mother to illustrate what she means by identification:

To love my mother was not possible for me while I retained a sense that it was fine for me and others to see her arrogantly. Loving my mother also required that I see with her eyes, that I go into my mother's world, that I see both of us as we are constructed in her world, that I witness her own sense of herself from within her world. Only through this traveling to her "world" could I identify with her because only then could I cease to ignore her and to be excluded and separate from her. . . . So traveling to each other's "worlds" would enable us to *be* through *loving* each other. (8)

In order to travel in a way that produces this loving perception, Lugones recommends playfulness. She defines *playfulness* as an openness to surprise and creativity (16). Playfulness (like loving perception) is an attitude toward one's activities.

There are some telling problems with Lugones's notion of identity. First, her notion of identification with another by "seeing with her eyes" in itself seems like a product of arrogant perception (8). Second, Lugones's discussion of playfulness implies an unacknowledged power hierarchy that undermines the political usefulness of her notion of playful world traveling.

Lugones says that she was motivated by her own experience of seeing herself and being seen by others as playful in some worlds but not in others. In the white/Anglo world, she says that she is constructed as unplayful. Because she is marginalized within that world, it is difficult for her to play. She emphasizes that marginal groups don't have a choice about world traveling:

they do it to survive in the dominant culture. But she argues that world traveling also can and should be a willful choice, made with a playful attitude. Given that within a world in which she is marginal she cannot play because she is constructed as unplayful, however, her analysis suggests that playfulness is not a choice willfully made, but a privilege. In fact, only in a world in which she is constructed with freedom of choice can she willfully choose to world travel. Willful world traveling, especially with a playful attitude, is the privilege of those who are constructed as dominant in any given world. Those who are marginal do not have a choice about traveling and cannot do so playfully. The notion of playful world traveling, then, presupposes a power hierarchy within which the subject who chooses can travel playfully while the object who has no choice must travel but cannot do so playfully.

This unacknowledged power hierarchy deflects the need to change social institutions (which create the power structure) onto personal and individual attitudes and relationships. Rather than concentrate on the social and political institutions, policies, and structures that construct the center and the margin, that construct one group as unplayful, Lugones turns that problem into one of personal attitudes, as if changing one's attitude could be enough. Her analysis of her own experience of playfulness and seriousness makes it painfully clear that individual choice and will are at best compromised and at worst an illusion in this situation. Rather than question the boundaries of various worlds or critically examine how they are constructed, Lugones accepts them as fixed and argues that we need to develop ways of traveling across boundaries to other worlds.

For Lugones, while we may be different people in different worlds, our identity is also fixed rather than fluid. The experience Lugones describes of being another person in a different world is like flipping a switch: you are one and then the other. Her notion of being different people, like her notion of different worlds, accepts boundaries as fixed borders to be crossed rather than crossed out. Insofar as she accepts fixed boundaries and identities and recommends negotiating them, she is proposing what Fraser calls an affirmative rather than transformative remedy. Rather than address the underlying cause of marginalization or arrogant perception, she proposes an individual remedy to treat some of the symptoms of social hierarchies. But without challenging the hierarchies themselves, and the structures, institutions, and policies that create and perpetuate them, she is reinforcing the very kind of power hierarchy she attempts to work around.

A productive counterpoint to Lugones's notion of world traveling is Patricia Williams's discussion of travel in *The Alchemy of Race and Rights.*

Williams says that the question of "Who am I?" has become the question "Where am I?" (1991, 16). But for Williams neither the who nor the where is a fixed location. Rather, both the who and the where are constantly negotiations between boundaries that are never fixed but always fluid and multivalent. Identity categories are rhetorical gestures that contextualize to be sure but cannot fix insofar as boundaries are constantly trespassed and challenged by theorists and activists. The first step is "acknowledging, challenging, playing with these as rhetorical gestures," which Williams argues is necessary "for any conception of justice" because "such acknowledgment complicates the supposed purity of gender, race, voice, boundary; it allows us to acknowledge the utility of such categorization for certain purposes and the necessity of their breakdown on other occasions" (1991, 10–11). For Williams, changing circumstance or context, not one's preexisting identity or the preexisting world into which one walks, determines which identity categories are useful.

Williams's utilitarian conception of identity moves us away from the notion of identity as property. Throughout her work, Williams argues that identity is not a property. Race and gender are not properties that we do or do not possess; they are words with shifting meaning depending on changing contexts and purposes. Williams suggests that in order to survive in this changing world of signification, we need "to invert, to stretch, meaning rather than oneself" (1991, 123). Rather than trying to shape or mold oneself to be "definitionally acceptable, we need to change definitions and stretch meanings." For Williams, stretching meaning is accomplished through traveling as boundary crossing:

> I think that the hard work of a nonracist sensibility is the boundary crossing, from safe circle into wilderness: the testing of boundary, the consecration of sacrilege. It is the willingness to spoil a good party and break an encompassing circle, to travel from the safe to the unsafe. . . . It has to do with a fluid positioning that sees back and forth across boundary, which acknowledges that I can be black and good and black and bad, and that I can also be black and white, male and female, yin and yang, love and hate. (1991, 129–30)

For Williams, like Lugones, acknowledging difference requires seeing across boundaries. But for Williams, this seeing is the result of breaking down the boundaries between worlds and acknowledging the fluidity of identity rather than maintaining different selves in different worlds. Recognizing the fluidity of the self outside of the logic of noncontradiction, which would insist that one cannot be both black and white or male and female insofar as those terms as opposites, is crucial for recognizing difference.

Recognizing difference does not mean identifying with someone else by seeing through his or her eyes. Nor does it mean occupying different contradictory worlds. Rather, for Williams, it means breaking down the borders between worlds, borders that work to turn difference into opposition, and identities into property.

Privileging Difference

Throughout her work, Iris Young has tried to reformulate notions of identity and difference that avoid the fixity and seeming immutability of the notion of identity that operates in strong theories of identity politics like Lugones's. In a sense, unlike Lugones, Young privileges difference and differentiation rather than identity and identification. Yet like Lugones's notion of identity, Young's notion of difference ultimately leaves social hierarchies intact in her attempt to address the symptoms of exclusionary practices rather than the causes. In effect, Young, like Lugones, proposes what Fraser calls affirmative rather than transformative remedies for lack of recognition.

At the other end of the spectrum from Lugones, Young insists that we cannot see with another's eyes or from another's perspective. She claims that "it is neither possible nor morally desirable for persons engaged in moral interaction to adopt one another's standpoint" (1997, 39). More specifically, she explains that "when privileged people put themselves in the position of those who are less privileged, the assumptions derived from their privilege often allow them unknowingly to misrepresent the other's situation" (48). Young suggests, however, that what she calls "asymmetrical reciprocity" is possible if we change the way in which we understand what it is to understand someone else. She argues that understanding need not mean putting ourselves into another's place or relating their experience to our own. Rather, understanding someone else involves listening with an openness that allows us to get "out of ourselves" (53). With this kind of openness we can learn about another's perspective even if we cannot adopt it or even imagine it as our own. For Young recognition and understanding are mutually constitutive in that the openness of understanding she describes requires recognizing that "I cannot put myself in her position," and understanding as learning builds recognition (53).

Young's analysis to this point is persuasive. Her next step is to propose gift giving as the essential example and model of asymmetrical reciprocity. With this move, her theory begins to lose its descriptive and prescriptive power. She begins her argument with the claim that gift giving "is basic to the generation of normative structures in most societies, precisely because it establishes relations of reciprocity: I give a gift to you, and you give a gift to me, or the opening is made for the relation of gift-giving, but of a different order from the equality of contracts and exchange" (54). Quoting Jacques Derrida out of context, Young uses his analysis of the gift to make a point antithetical to his thesis. Unlike Derrida, Young concludes that gift giving can escape the logic of contracts and exchange, that gifts don't operate to obligate and put us into an economy of exchange. Of course, we don't need Derrida's analysis to know that receiving a gift does make us feel obligated to reciprocate, that indeed most of the time gifts put us into an economy of exchange. For example, if someone gives a Christmas present or birthday card, and the recipient doesn't have one to give in return, then most likely either the recipient will feel guilty or she will make the effort to get something for the giver.

Young argues that gift giving sets up an economy of asymmetrical reciprocity because the gifts are not equivalent and because they are separated by time. Yet neither the nonequivalence of gifts nor the time difference makes gift giving asymmetrical or immune to an economy of exchange similar to contract. Young's own examples make this clear. Her only example of gift giving is the exchange of quince marmalade and cranberry bread (55). While it is true that marmalade and bread are not equivalent, they surely are two of a kind, in fact, best eaten together. The problem is not that Young chooses edible gifts; the problem is that with this example she reduces gifts to things that are exchanged in an economy that bears a striking resemblance to that of commercial exchange. The temporal (and spatial) gap between the marmalade and the bread—which perhaps prevents them from being enjoyed together—does very little to transform gift giving into something other than an exchange like any other. Commercial exchange also displays this kind of temporal gap; in fact, contracts are signed because of the temporal gap between the payment for and the receipt of goods.

Young uses the gift-giving scenario as her model for communicative action. She maintains that conversation operates like an exchange of gifts: the speaker offers meaning and the listener accepts the offer. She says that "these illocutionary gestures of offering and accepting meanings create and sustain the social bond" (55). Young describes this movement as asymmetrical reciprocity because "I respond to your statement not by saying the same thing back to you, but my making another, different move in our language game" (1997, 55). While the difference between what the speaker says and what the listener says in response may be analogous to the difference between the marmalade and the bread: this difference is one of degree and not one of kind, especially if the speaker and listener are truly engaging in an open conversation. In that case, they are responding in kind out of generosity.

Young uses gift giving in order to avoid an economy of obligation. But without obligation, we do not have ethics. This is why while Lévinasian ethics is motivated by a primary and fundamental obligation, Young's notion of asymmetrical reciprocity does not carry any notion of obligation and therefore no motivation for ethical action.[1] While ethical obligation should not be conceived of as indebtedness—precisely the kind of obligation implicit in Young's gift giving model—it is necessary for ethics. Obligation to others, the obligation to be ethical itself, binds us to an imperative to continually question our relationships, our investments in relationships, our interpretations of situations—what we could call the transference that takes place in all interpretations and relationships.

In *The Alchemy of Race and Rights,* Patricia Williams raises the possibility of obligation without debt. Obligation itself need not put us within an economy of exchange, that is to say, an economy of property through which everything is translated into the same material currency. Only if obligation is conceived as debt does it need to propel us into an economy of exchange that levels differences through the use of common currencies. Williams argues that it is the economy of property through which everything becomes fungible that turns duty into debt (1991, 43). It is in an economy in which bread can be exchanged for marmalade that differences are erased and characteristics become owned or disowned as property. Gift giving itself need not bind us to an obligation as indebtedness within the economy of property that levels differences. Rather, gift giving breaks out of the economy of exchange when it provides necessary items for life, when it becomes a gift of life itself.[2]

For example, at one point in *Alchemy* Williams tells a story about feeding her godmother Marjorie when she was dying in the hospital. Williams says that "feeding the one who had so often fed me became a complex ritual of mirroring and self-assembly. The physical act of holding the spoon to her lips was not only a rite of nurture and sacrifice, it was the return of a gift" (229). She goes on to tell a story that she told her godmother about some neighbors who included her in their circle of barter (130). With this story it becomes clear that gift giving, even returning a gift, need not commit us to an economy of exchange that fills obligation with guilt and turns passion into an errand. Giving or returning the gift of life cannot be translated into some common currency that renders difference as the same and relationships between people as market exchanges, as much as we may try to do so. Williams describes this gift giving that becomes giving the provisions for life:

My value to the group was not calculated by the physical items I brought to it. These people included me because they wanted me to be part of their circle; they valued my participation apart from the material things I could offer. So I gave of myself to them, and they gave me fruit cakes and dandelion wine and smoked salmon and, in their giving, their goods became provisions. Cradled in this community whose currency was a relational ethic, my stock in myself soared. My value depended on the glorious intangibility, the eloquent invisibility, of my just being part of the collective—and in direct response I grew spacious and happy and gentle. (230)

Although Young's giving of jam and bread could be viewed as the giving of provisions, what Williams's text speaks to that Young's does not is the quality of giving that turns gift exchange into the interpersonal exchange that nourishes us and makes life meaningful. It is not the time between the receipt of one gift and the giving of another or the difference, however great or small, between one gift and another that takes gift giving out of an economy of market exchange. Rather, it is the nurturing bond, that basic provision of life, which is given as a gift that creates the relational ethic so powerfully described by Williams.

On the one hand, Young's notion of difference as that between what I give you and what you give me, or the difference between what you say and how I respond, doesn't account for the radical difference that she claims prevents one from taking the perspective or standpoint of another. If the only difference between us is temporal or the *strict* nonequivalence between what is given, then this difference does not explain why we cannot also exchange perspectives. On the other hand, Young's notion of difference still maintains the kind of self-contained identity supposed by Lugones; only now, language rather than imaginary identification plays the role of intermediary. Young suggests that language can bridge the gap between differences by expressing meaning in ways that can be understood by others if not claimed as their own. In Young's scenario, words, like gifts, create bonds between people who stand on either side of the abyss of difference crossed by understanding through communicative action.

While her goals are admirable, Young's theory leaves us with a kind of negative of Lugones's theory: with Lugones we have two people separated by the abyss between worlds that can be crossed through an identification; with Young we have two people separated by the abyss between differences that cannot be crossed through identification, but only through language. The problem with Young's theory is not that she posits language as a medium per se, but that she posits self-enclosed subjects, radically separated, such that with all the bread and jam in the world, any medium is ultimately doomed to failure.[3] Beginning with disconnected subjects and then trying to bring them together with jam or words always repeats the very symptom that this theory seeks to overcome by continually reasserting the impossibility of any communion even while it seeks community. If we start from the premise that we are in need of external connections, we never end up with the kinds of connections that can ground ethics.

Like Lugones, Young's theory presupposes fixed boundaries between people. While Lugones says that we can jump from one world to another, Young says that we can send gifts across borders. For both Lugones and Young perspectives are also fixed, tied to individuals, and what is at stake for both of them is whether or not we can adopt the perspective of another person: Lugones says yes, Young says no. Young talks about perspectives as if they are fixed entities that can only be relativized or enlarged by simply adding the perspectives of others:

> Through such dialogue that recognizes the asymmetry of others, moreover, people can enlarge their thinking in at least two ways. Their own assumptions and point of view become relativized for them as they are set in relation to those of others. By learning from others how the world and the collective relations have forged through interaction look to them, moreover, everyone can develop an enlarged understanding of that world and those relations that is unavailable to any of them from their own perspective alone. (1997, 59)

Neither Lugones nor Young, however, addresses the more fundamental questions of why identity and difference are positioned as opposites, or why subjectivity is taken as fixed or bounded. Only by starting with a conception of identity and difference that are not opposites, and a fluid conception of subjectivity, can we move from what Fraser calls mere affirmative remedies to transformative remedies.

Fraser prefers transformative to affirmative remedies because they treat the causes of injustice—not just the symptoms—and because they resolve what she problematically calls the redistribution-recognition dilemma.[4] She gives the example of homophobia. The affirmative remedy (gay identity politics) would be to give value to homosexuals as a group that is currently disrespected or devalued. Fraser argues that this remedy treats homosexuals as a "cultural positivity with its own substantive content . . . [which] is assumed to subsist in and of itself and to need only additional recognition" (1997, 24). The transformative remedy (queer politics) would be to destabilize the distinction between homosexual and heterosexual by explaining how they are dependent on each other. Although Fraser associates transformative remedies of recognition with deconstruction, she does not describe *how* deconstruction destabilizes identity and thereby changes everyone's sense of self. Since Judith Butler has developed probably the most thorough deconstruction of the heterosexual/homosexual opposition, it should be useful to turn to her theory to see how deconstruction might provide a transformative remedy for disrespect or lack of recognition. Does Butler's method reconceptualize our sense of ourselves as subjects such that we do not form our identities in opposition to others or the other and thereby transform our relationships?

3. Identity as Subordination, Abjection, and Exclusion

Subordinated Subject and Abjected Other

Like Taylor, Honneth, and Fraser, Judith Butler believes that recognition is essential to subjectivity. Unlike Taylor and Honneth, Butler claims that recognition is not conferred on a subject but is constitutive of its very being:

> It is not simply that one requires the recognition of the other and that a form of recognition is conferred through subordination, but rather that one is dependent on power for one's very formation, that that formation is impossible without dependency, and that the posture of the adult subject consists precisely in the denial and reenactment of this dependency. (1997b, 9)

Butler is concerned with how the subject becomes a subject in the first place, a subject who can be respected or disrespected, who can esteem itself or not. Taylor and Honneth seem to use *subject* to mean self or individual and insist that recognition is important to one's sense of self or well-being, whereas for Butler *subject* does not mean the self, the individual, or the active agent. Rather, she calls the subject "the linguistic occasion for the individual to achieve and reproduce intelligibility, the linguistic condition of its existence and agency" (1997b, 11).

For Butler, the subject is the result of subordination and dependency, both of which lead to a turning against itself that inaugurates the subject at the same time that it threatens the subject (1997b, 3, 10). This turning is enacted by social norms that work to foreclose certain types of desire. Bringing Foucault into dialogue with Freud, Butler argues that these social norms that form the subject do not operate according to a logic of *repression* through which the subject's preexisting desires are prohibited, but through a logic of *foreclosure* through which the subject's desire comes to be as a result of prohibition. Taking up this Lacanian distinction between repression and foreclosure, we could say that Taylor and Honneth are working within something like the logic of repression through which subjects become distorted and damaged in abusive social relations and by oppressive social norms. Butler, on the other hand, focuses on the ways in which the logic of foreclosure, repudiation, or disavowal sets desire in motion at its conception. Once again, Butler is concerned with how desire is produced, whereas Taylor and Honneth, we might say, are concerned with how an already formed desire is distorted.

While Butler's theory of subjection takes us further than Taylor's or Honneth's theories of recognition toward realizing the significance of the other in subjectivity, her theory continues to privilege the subject and to put the subject in an antagonistic relation with its others. By insisting that the structure of subjectivity is one of subjection and subordination, Butler builds oppression and abuse into the foundation of subjectivity. Moreover, she also maintains that subjective identity is the result of a logic of exclusion or repudiation of otherness. In *Bodies That Matter,* she says that

> this exclusionary matrix by which subjects are formed thus requires the simultaneous production of a domain of abject beings, those who are not yet "subjects" but who form the constitutive outside to the domain of the subject. The abject designates here precisely those "unlivable" and "uninhabitable" zones of social life which are nevertheless densely populated. (1993, 3)

In *The Psychic Life of Power,* she takes her analysis even further when she maintains that the subject is the condition of intelligibility, visibility, and existence (1997b, 11). Those who are foreclosed by social norms that constitute the subject are excluded as unintelligible, invisible, and nonexistent. To exist is to be intelligible and to be intelligible is to exist. In a strange sense, this conservative Hegelian formula drives Butler's analysis. Even while she is trying to shake the foundations of this exclusionary subject, Butler couldn't be more forceful in her own insistence that though the subject is dependent on that which is foreclosed, the foreclosed is all but annihilated.

Butler fine-tunes her use of *foreclosure* in *Excitable Speech,* in which she accepts the Lacanian conception that what is foreclosed is shut out completely with the modification that foreclosure is repeated continuously and "what is reinvoked by its continued action is precisely that primary scene in which the formation of the subject is tied to the circumscribed production of the domain of the speakable" (1997a, 139).[1] On the one side of the Lacanian bar of foreclosure is the speakable and on the other the unspeakable. This unspeakable acts as what Derrida calls the "constitutive outside" that forms the boundaries of subjectivity and the social (Butler 1997a, 180). The explicit assumption behind Butler's analysis of censorship in both "Sovereign Performatives in the Contemporary Scene of Utterance" (1997c) and *Excitable Speech* is "that no speech is permissible without some other speech becoming impermissible" (1997a, 139). Butler's bar of foreclosure necessarily sets up two mutually implicated but opposing sides constantly at war for the very right to exist.

In *The Psychic Life of Power* and *Excitable Speech*, Butler uses *foreclosure* and *disavowal* interchangeably. While the Lacanian notion of foreclosure suggests a permanent and irreversible exclusion from the realm of the symbolic or signification, the Freudian notion of disavowal suggests refusal/exclusion and acceptance/inclusion at the same time. Freud's notion of disavowal also and necessarily includes an avowal. Freud introduces the notion of disavowal in his discussion of fetishism, in which the male child both accepts and denies that his mother is castrated by substituting a fetish for her missing penis. In this way, the child accepts external prohibitions and satisfies his internal drive forces at the same time. This ambivalent relation to reality—both accepting and denying—is more flexible than any foreclosure. What is excluded through disavowal is also included on another unconscious level. What is excluded through disavowal is never excluded permanently or irreversibly. For this reason, the Freudian notion of disavowal would better serve to describe the kind of exclusion proposed by Butler. By taking over the Lacanian notion of foreclosure, her theory cannot allow for the possibility of including those who have been excluded within the symbolic or signification.

In her earlier work, Butler's theory of social exclusion was influenced by Julia Kristeva's theory of abjection. What Butler calls *foreclosure* in her latest work is related to what she calls *abjection* in her earlier work. In *Powers of Horror* Kristeva describes the abject in much the same way that Butler describes foreclosed desire: "Because it is excluded as a possible object, asserted to be a non-object of desire, abominated as ab-ject, as abjection, filth becomes defilement. . . . Defilement is what is jettisoned from the 'symbolic system.' It is what escapes that social rationality, that logical order on which a social aggregate is based" (1982, 65). For Kristeva, cultural abjection is the process of separation from animals, while personal abjection is the process of separation from the maternal body (1997a, 239). In both cases, nature or the body threatens to absorb culture and the psyche. Separation requires that the animal body, ultimately the maternal body, be abjected (made both horrible and fascinating) so that identity can be formed as a defense against it. Order and borders in culture and language are enacted through a separation from, and repression of, maternal authority, which constantly threatens with the in-between nature and culture, animal and human: "If language, like culture, sets up a separation and, starting with discrete elements, concatenates an order, it does so precisely by repressing maternal authority and the corporeal mapping that abuts against them" (1997a, 261). This abjection is necessary to found the borders of the speaking subject (1997a, 259). Like Butler, Kristeva also insists on a neo-Hegelian notion of identity founded on exclusion.

Whereas Butler talks about a foreclosed desire, Kristeva talks about a repressed desire and the return of the repressed. Just as Butler deconstructs Freud's distinction between mourning and melancholy, however, her distinction between repression and foreclosure could be subject to a similar deconstruction. In *The Psychic Life of Power* Butler argues: "There is no final reprieve from the ambivalence and no final separation of mourning from melancholia. . . . If ambivalence distinguishes melancholia from mourning, and if mourning entails ambivalence as part of the process of 'working through,' then there is no work of mourning that does not engage melancholia" (1997b, 193).

So, too, we could argue, there is no repression that does not engage foreclosure, at least within Butler's theory and perhaps also within Kristeva's. Butler describes the distinction between repression and foreclosure as the difference between desires that exist before prohibition and desires that are produced through prohibition. On the one hand, its seems that there would be no repression on Butler's account since there are no preexisting desires that are not produced through prohibition. On the other hand, it would seem that Butler's notion of foreclosure, insofar at it allows for a return of the foreclosed, operates more like a psychoanalytic notion of repression than foreclosure. Developed by Lacan, the notion of foreclosure does not allow for any return; the foreclosed is cut off forever from consciousness and is manifest only in symptoms. This Lacanian notion of foreclosure would prevent Butler from talking about any sort of social or individual transformation that involves renegotiating or resignifying what has been foreclosed. Given Butler's insistence on the ambivalence of desire, it becomes difficult to distinguish repression from foreclosure. Rather than take over the problematic notion of foreclosure, it is possible to distinguish between different types of repression: primary and secondary repression corresponding to Freud's notions of primary and secondary narcissism. Secondary repression operates as a prohibition that responds to desire while primary repression operates as a prohibition through which desire is created. Whether repressed or foreclosed, the excluded other of desire, as both Butler and Kristeva imagine, always continues to haunt the subject.

For Butler, the original trauma of what she calls inaugural alienation inherent in the subject's becoming a subject and entering into the social is repeated in subsequent traumas. Thus Butler prevents any effective distinction between types of alienation or subordination, which is necessary to identify unjust social practices such as discrimination, domination, slavery, torture, genocide, and so forth. For example, in *The Psychic Life of Power* Butler equates *dependency* and *subordination*: "If the effect of autonomy is conditioned by subordination and that founding subordination or dependency is rigorously repressed, the subject emerges in tandem with the unconscious" (1997b, 7). Although Butler does not explain what she means by *unconscious,* it seems that for her the unconscious is nothing more than the other side of the Lacanian bar, or that which has been foreclosed by socialization and subjectification. Subordination is foundational because the child can't help but attach to "those by whom she or he is subordinated" (1997b, 7). For Butler, then, primary attachments, dependency, and subordination all amount to the same thing. This, she says, "accounts in part for the adult sense of humiliation when confronted with the earliest objects of love—parents, guardians, siblings, and so on" (1997b, 8). Trauma is the essential feature of these formative familial relations that set up the possibility of subjectivity. It is the trauma of original subordination that is repeated in all performances of subjectivity: "It is not simply that one requires the recognition of the other and that a form of recognition is conferred through subordination, but rather that one is dependent on power for one's very formation, that that formation is impossible without dependency, and that the posture of the adult subject consists precisely in the denial and reenactment of this dependency" (1997b, 9).

In *Excitable Speech* Butler claims that language use is also always a repetition of this original trauma of subordination essential to subjectivity: "Social trauma takes the form, not of a structure that repeats mechanically, but rather of an ongoing subjugation, the restaging of injury through signs that both occlude and reenact the scene" (1997a, 36–37). She concludes that hate speech is "part of the continuous and uninterrupted process to which we are subjected, an on-going subjection *(assujetissement)* that is the very operation of interpellation, that continually repeated action of discourse by which subjects are formed in subjugation" (1997a, 27). These kinds of statements by Butler work to normalize hate speech and subordination. If "subordination," "pain," "trauma," "subjugation," "subjection," "vulnerability," "susceptibility," "violence," and so forth are all part of the normal and normalizing process of becoming a subject, then how can we distinguish between becoming a subject and being oppressed, abused, or tortured? How do we distinguish between the violence inherent in becoming subjects and the violence of domestic abuse, social abuse, or war? How do we distinguish between productive power and abusive power? In Butler's theory the latter is merely a repetition of the former. This normalization of violence makes it difficult to argue against unnecessary forms of abuse that could or should be outlawed or deemed unethical or at least unhealthy. Although Butler acknowledges that in order for her view to be persuasive she must "distinguish between kinds of injury that are socially contingent and avoidable, and kinds of subordination that are, as it were, the constitutive condition of the subject," she admits that such distinctions are difficult to make (1997a, 26). Indeed, she never adequately makes them.

Contra Butler, extreme forms of violence are not repetitions of the original trauma of subject formation; rather, extreme violence threatens the disintegration of subjectivity.[2] Instead of renewing subjectivity through the repetition of an original threat to it, extreme violence undermines the conditions of possibility for subjectivity, the possibility of dependence on another, which enables bearing witness to oneself and others. Extreme violence damages the internal witness born out of loving relations with others: the internal witness is necessary for innovative capacities or imagination that enables us to find meaning in life.

We could diagnose Butler's insistence on violence and the inability to distinguish productive power from abusive power as her Foucauldian rather than Nietzschean inheritance. Whereas Foucault, at least in his earlier works, seems to allow for only an oscillation of power between domination and resistance or trespass, Nietzsche makes a distinction between life-affirming and life-denying forms of power: those forces that expand life or produce excess are life-affirming, and those forces that conserve and limit life are negating. Whereas Foucauldian resistance/trespass is always a reaction to domination, Nietzschean life-affirming power is not reactionary but ultimately exceeds any mere oscillation within an economy of domination (Nietzsche 1967, bk. 1, sect. 10). Power need not be conceived within an economy of scarcity. Rather, power is generated in relationships. Social power is always greater than the sum of its parts. In this way, power can be produced in excess of the forces of domination.

Without the space for excess—whether it is power beyond domination, the unconscious out of bounds of social norms, or the imaginary that cannot be contained within the symbolic—there is no space for transformation or revolution. Rather, there is merely repeated revision or oscillations within the same economy of domination and subordination. Although Butler does sometimes talk of excess, she makes it clear that exceeding does not mean escaping the economy of domination: "To claim that the subject exceeds either/or is not to claim that it lives in some free zone of its own making. Exceeding is not escaping, and the subject exceeds precisely that to which it is bound" (1997b, 17). For Butler, then, excess is always circumscribed within the economy of subordination, and to imagine otherwise is to imagine the impossibility of a self-made subject escaping. Butler's theory itself can be read as an oscillation between the ideal of a self-made, self-possessed subject, and the constitutive/subjecting play of power itself.[3]

For Butler, because they are "not of our making," our primary relationships, our subsequent relationships, our relations to language, power, and society, are relations of subordination and subjugation. For all of her attempts to wean us from delusions of our own autonomous or sovereign agency through which we direct our world, Butler's angry and mournful eulogy to what we did not *make* and what is not our *own* sounds like nostalgia for the very notion of sovereign self-possessed subjectivity she insists we give up. Consider this passage from *Excitable Speech*: "There is no way to protect against that primary vulnerability and susceptibility to the call of recognition that solicits existence, to that primary dependency on a language *we never made* in order to acquire a tentative ontological status" (1997a, 26; my emphasis); or consider this passage from *The Psychic Life of Power*: "The desire to persist in one's own being requires submitting to a world of others that is fundamentally *not one's own*. . . . Vulnerability to terms that *one never made*, one persists always, to some degree, through categories, names, terms, and classifications that mark a primary and *inaugurative alienation* in sociality" (1997b, 28; my emphasis).

Butler's insistence that all alienation follows from, and is a form of, inaugurative alienation inherent in becoming social does not allow her to distinguish between different forms of alienation. Recall Fanon's description of the double alienation inherent in the subjective experience of victims of racism. Part of the alienation inherent in oppression is that those who are disempowered find themselves in a world not of their own making. Yet this "not of their own making" must be distinguished from Butler's inaugurative alienation. While it is true that all of us come into a world that preexists us, our positions in that world and our ability to "make the world"—to make meaning, perceptions, and truth—vary greatly according to our social class, race, ethnicity, culture, location, sex, and so on. And while it is possible that the trauma of double alienation or oppression recalls the trauma of inaugurative alienation, racist or sexist alienation does not follow from or necessarily resemble what Butler calls inaugurative alienation.

Butler's talk of ownership, and the alienation that comes from being in a world not of one's own making, presupposes the very self-possessed sovereign notion of subjectivity she argues against. To describe dependence on a world that is not of one's making as alienating and violent is to assume a self-possessed sovereign subject who has been violated. If the subject is inherently dependent on others, the world, and a language not of its own making, isn't it the illusion of autonomy itself and not the facts of dependency that produce alienation? And if the illusion itself does violence to the fundamental experience of dependency, then isn't it possible that exorcising the illusion of self-possession and embracing dependency can abate the violence suffered by the subject in its continual coming to be? Rather than avowing the loss of the other whose internalization constitutes one's sense of autonomy, as Butler suggests, we first need to avow our dependency on that other or those others before we can avow any loss of dependency (Butler 1997b, 195–96). Even then, as I have argued elsewhere (1997), it is only within the patriarchal imaginary that subjectivity need be bought at the price of losing our first relationships.

Why does dependency have to be figured as violent, alienating, subjugating, and dominating? Only if we start with the ideal of the self-possessed autonomous subject is dependence threatening. If, however, we give up that ideal and operate in the world with a truly interrelational conception of subjectivity, a subjectivity without subjects, then dependence is seen as the force of life, as the very possibility of change, rather than as the paradoxical life bought at the expense of violence and death (Oliver 1998). Subjectivity need not be the Faustian bargain struck by Butler.

If, however, Butlerian excess is always tied to the system of domination from which it tries but fails to escape, then violence is also inescapable. Without the ability to distinguish between necessary and unnecessary violence, we risk repeating, even justifying, unnecessary violence. In order to work through violence and move beyond it, we need to be able to interpret it as unnecessary. We need to analyze leveling comparisons that normalize violence to remember and acknowledge past violence in order to avoid repeating it in the future. We need to continually interpret our own investment in violence, in leveling comparisons, in order to acknowledge transferential relations with others. Only by acknowledging and interpreting our investments or transference can we begin to "work through" rather than repeat violence. "Working-through" is a profoundly ethical operation insofar as it forces us not only to acknowledge our relations and obligations to others— that is, the ethical foundations of subjectivity—but also thereby to transform those relations into more ethical relations through which we love or at least respect others rather than subordinate or kill them. By acknowledging power relations and our investments in them, we can change the structure of those relations. The difference between Kristeva's theory of the melancholy subject and Butler's will be instructive on the importance of interpretation to transformation.

Melancholy Subject and Lost Object

For Butler, and in some sense for Kristeva, repression and foreclosure are melancholy operations. One cornerstone of Butler's theory from *Gender Trouble* (1991) to her present work is an interpretation of Freud's notion of melancholy. Throughout her work, Butler develops the notion that the ego is produced through the incorporation of, or identification with, a lost love and the rage associated with it. Specifically, heterosexual gender identity develops through a melancholic relation to the loss of same-sex love; we become what we aren't allowed to desire, the foreclosed love object. According to Butler, the very possibility of the subjective turn is dependent on foreclosure. So not just the ego or gender identity but the subject itself is the result of melancholy foreclosed desire (1997b, 23). Melancholy is precisely the turning against the subject that inaugurates the subject; in this sense, melancholy is prior to subjectivity or the Freudian ego.

Compare this with Kristeva's theory of melancholy from *Black Sun* (1989). Kristeva also interprets Freud's theory of melancholy as a pre-Oedipal formative loss, ultimately associated with the maternal body. Not yet an object of desire for a subject, the maternal body becomes a "Thing" locked in the crypt of the psyche haunting subjectivity; this is especially true for females given prohibitions against homosexual desire, which complicate their love for the maternal body. For both sexes, the Thing is a matter of ambivalence because it is the underside of primary narcissism, a necessary prerequisite for subject and object formation. Like Butler, Kristeva describes melancholy as prior to, and productive of, the ego or subject. The melancholic Thing is what is abjected from one's own borders so that one can be a proper self:

> Never is the ambivalence of drive more fearsome than in this beginning of otherness where, lacking the filter of language, I cannot inscribe my violence in "no," nor in any other sign. I can expel it only by means of gestures, spasms, or shouts. I impel it. I project it. My necessary Thing is also and absolutely my enemy, my foil, the delightful focus of my hatred. The Thing falls from me along the outpost of signifiance where the Word is not yet my Being. (1989, 15)

Both Kristeva and Butler, then, extend Freud's theory of melancholy in the same direction when they suggest that melancholy is necessary to subjectivity and prior to the subject-object distinction.

For Kristeva, following Freud, the "cure" for melancholy is an interpretation and representation of the forbidden and inarticulate desire—that is to say, the ability to name it and thereby imagine it in order to unlock it and ultimately accept it. Butler's cure (in a rare moment when she suggests anything like a solution), on the other hand, involves rage: "Survival . . . requires redirecting rage against the lost other" and reexternalizing the aggression toward the other that has been internalized to form the ego (1997b, 193–94).[4]

Yet there are problems with Butler's theory that make it unclear what she means here. First, there are two different notions of the other, both of which are necessary to produce the subject, operating interchangeably in her text. It is unclear which other is the new object of rage. On the one hand, Butler says that "subjection exploits the desire for existence where existence is always conferred from elsewhere; it marks a primary vulnerability to the Other in order to be" (1997b, 20). Here *Other* refers to the "categories, terms and names that are not of [the subject's] own making," the "world of others that is fundamentally not one's own" (1997b, 20, 28). On the other hand, most of her work identifies a disavowed other whose foreclosure is the secret heart that beats in the subject. This other is the one who does not exist, cannot be seen, and remains unintelligible. This other is the underside of the social norm that subordinates the subject so that it might exist. The subject is, in a sense, the turning of the first of these others against the second other; or perhaps we could think of the subject as the thin lining between social norms and social foreclosures. Which of these others is the object of melancholic rage?

Given that Butler calls the object of melancholic rage the "lost other," it seems to be the foreclosed object of desire.[5] In this case, rage is to be directed against that which is already foreclosed by social norms, against those invisible, nonexistent, mute others who inhabit the margins of society. Can this really be what she means? If it is, then it seems that the "cure" is worse than the pathology. If, on the other hand, she means raging against the other of social norms that demands the sacrifice in the first place, in what sense is this other lost?

A second problem arises when we try to understand how reexternalizing aggression, which seems to assume a linear logic, would work, given Butler's theory of the circular logic of subjection. Can we simply undo the ego by directing aggression outward instead of inward? Moreover, given Butler's insistence that agency is a power that is produced through the inward turn of aggression, from whence does this redirection, or outward turn, come? More to the point, if in Butler's account all actions are reactions and all performance is reiteration or citation, then how does reexternalizing aggression "uncontain" the ego or free the subject (1997b, 193)? And a related question: what does Butler's insistence on performance as iteration imply for any attempt, including her own, to *elaborate* the logic of subjectivity? What, then, is the relationship between elaboration and resignification through performative repetition? What is the relation between critical analysis of the type that Butler only performs and that Kristeva endorses in her theory?

The Transformative Power of Working-Through

For Kristeva, we can learn to live with the specter of abjection by elaborating the process through which we become subjects. In general, Kristeva insists on elaboration and interpretation in addition to cathartic exercises (like art, religion, and literature), which discharge drive and affect associated with the repressed but do not name it (1989, 24). By *cathartic* Kristeva means to displace or dissolve what she calls the semiotic forces associated with repression, while interpretation or analysis names them (1981, 318).

Interpretation with its naming operations performs several transformative functions. First, interpretation provides metaphors that act as safety valves through which semiotic forces make their way into language. Second, interpretative metaphors create what Kristeva calls a "knowledge effect," which simultaneously bolsters confidence that transformation is possible and undermines any "authoritarian domination of à *Res externa,* necessarily divine or deifiable" (1987, 276–77). Interpretation, specifically psychoanalytic interpretation, allows us to treat both causes and effects as *symptoms,* always open to reinterpretation. An interpretation is "correct" or "true" only when it expands what is analyzable (1981, 309). In fact, Kristeva claims that in a successful analysis the analysand leaves with "a renewed desire to question all received truths" (1989, 58). The goal of analysis, then, is the search not for truth but for "innovative capacities," capacities that Kristeva laments are disappearing from contemporary culture, capacities that I maintain are born and reborn in and through our relations with others (Kristeva 1987, 15; Oliver 1995, 206–7).

Interpretation is impossible without imagination, which Kristeva associates with the ability to represent experience (1995, 207). It is this ability that allows us access to our bodies and ourselves and other people (1995, 205). I would modify Kristeva's formulation to say that the imagination fundamental to the ability to represent experience is inaugurated and nourished through relations with others. This is to say that we are psychically alive by virtue of our relations. And without acknowledging our fundamental ethical dependence on otherness through which we become ourselves, we lose our innovative capacities. Without imagination, that divine space created between people, we lose our ability to represent our experience. We lose our ability to find meaning in life.

Without the ability to represent, to imagine, to interpret, we suffer from what Kristeva calls the *New Maladies of the Soul* (1995, 207). But transformation is possible through imaginative interpretation: "We must realize that an imaginary deployment reconstructs the logic of the drive in order to free up the linguistic restrictions that ultimately govern our capacities as speaking beings. . . . The imaginary deployment thereby reveals itself as a privileged witness to the meaning of the drive that joins the signification of speech" (1995, 213). In *Sens et non-sens de la révolte,* Kristeva argues that the return of the repressed necessitates a revolt in imagination that can transform the logic of repression and repressed drives by reconnecting those drives and language (1996, 29–30). Representation or elaboration, based in imagination, restructures the logic of exclusion. The excluded can return to representation. It can become part of the representable, the visible, existence.

For Kristeva, imagination and what she calls "psychic space" are essential for any kind of transformation. Psychic space is the space between the human organism and its aims; it is the space between the biological and the social. It is the space of drives that move energy between these two interconnected spheres. It is within this psychic space that affects materialize between bodily organs and social customs. Our emotional lives depend on this space. Meaning is constituted in this space between the body and culture. Our words and our lives have meaning by virtue of their connection to affect. The meaning of words (in the narrow sense of the symbolic element of language) is charged with affective meaning (in the broader sense of the semiotic element of language) through the movement of drive energy within psychic space.

In *New Maladies of the Soul* Kristeva says that our souls *(psyche)* have been flattened and emptied by the rhythms and images of our culture, which are two-dimensional. Life takes place on the screen: movie screens, TV screens, computer screens. Yet these media images merely cover over the surface of the emptiness that we feel facing the loss of meaning. Psychotropic drugs and antidepressants also flatten the psyche. They relieve the feeling of crisis caused by a loss of meaning at the expense of a feeling of emptiness; they flatten or empty the patient's affects. Both drugs and media images provide only false or artificial selves that only temporarily smooth over the surface of an otherwise empty psyche. By substituting surface images for psychic depth, drugs and media images close up psychic space.

Psychic space and imagination are essential for life, for the life of the spirit that gives meaning to life: "Infinitesimal revolt, in order to preserve the life of the spirit and the species" (Révolte infinitésimale, pour préserver la vie de l'esprit, et de l'espèce) (1998a, 18). Although Kristeva suggests that political revolution in the sense of the French Revolution may no longer be possible, revolt has mutated into what she calls an intimate revolt or a psychic revolt. Against the mechanization of technological culture and the flashing pace of media-spectacle culture, Kristeva proposes a revolt as a return to an interior psychic space. This is not revolution on the grand scale, but a little revolt that can make all the difference to humanity. This infinitesimal and intimate psychic revolt requires interpretation, which is dependent on the imaginary. Our ability to imagine ourselves and the meaning of life is at stake in opening up psychic space. Indeed, for Kristeva, ethical and political transformation also hang in the balance:

> On the other hand, and doubtless following the psychoanalytic vision of the human being, the *imaginary* increasingly appears as an essential part of our psyches, but also, and above all, as the very site of the version of freedom I am in the process of defending before you. We are alive because we have a psychic life. The psychic life is that interior space, that *deep down inside* that permits us to take in attacks from both within and without—that is to say, physiological and biological traumas, but also political and social aggressions. The imaginary metabolizes, transforms, sublimates, and works these attacks: it supports us as living. (1998a, 107; cf. 27–28)[6]

Kristeva concludes that we must protect and guard our potential for psychic revolt by ceaselessly interpreting our experience through the powerful agency of the imaginary (1998a, 30–31; 1997b, 24).

A commitment to interpretation is also implicit in Butler's project since what she attempts to do in all of her writing is elaborate the process through which we become subjects; yet her method for avowing the other is explicitly very different from Kristeva's. Butler's theory suggests that there is no escape from social norms that promote the logic of exclusion, and therefore a Kristevan revolt in imagination that transforms representation seems questionable. Whereas Butler argues that "melancholia is a rebellion that has been put down, crushed [by] . . . the power of the state to preempt an insurrectionary rage," Kristeva maintains that every creative act requires revolt against, and incorporation of, authority (Butler 1997b, 190–91; Kristeva

1998a; 1998b, 103–5; 1997a; 1996, especially 32–40). Whereas Butler compares the "critical agency" of melancholy to the state's military power, Kristeva compares imaginary revolt to political revolt (Butler 1997b, 190–91; Kristeva 1998a, 1998b, 1996, 1997a, 1984).

For Butler, instead of revolt in the imaginary there is repetition in the symbolic. In "The Lesbian Phallus," a chapter in *Bodies That Matter,* Butler challenges the Lacanian distinction between the imaginary and symbolic. While her deconstruction of these two realms could be productively used in a theory of transformation, she does not use it to formulate a theory of transformation in her own work (1993). Instead, for Butler the subject is nothing more than the repetition of the conditions of power that produced it, which is to say subjection and subordination (1997b, 16). Similarly, gender identity is nothing more than the repetition of social norms: "Femininity is thus not the product of choice, but the forcible citation of a norm, one whose complex historicity is indissociable from relations of discipline, regulation, punishment" (1993, 232). All authority comes through citation and repetition and not through an individual's agency, will, or intention (1993, 227). But insofar as what is performed in repetition is also the disavowal that makes subjectivity possible, there is hope for transformation. This is to say that what is foreclosed, what is excluded by the social norms that make us subjects, is also repeated or reiterated in the repetition of those norms. So the repressed or foreclosed returns even in the performance of its prohibition.

Butler insists, however, that subversion of norms through the performance of the prohibited in the prohibition is not enough; there must also be a "resignification" of the foreclosed other (1993, 240). She maintains that this resignification comes through performance itself. In *Bodies That Matter* she gives the example of the resignification of the word *queer* through a performative reappropriation of the term by gays and lesbians. In *Excitable Speech* she explains that this unpredictable process works through repetition and the structure of social temporality "in which [performativity] remains enabled precisely by the contexts from which it breaks. This ambivalent structure at the heart of performativity implies that, within political discourse, the very terms of resistance and insurgency are spawned in part by the power they oppose" (1997a, 40). So for Butler it is not iterability itself but the temporal structure of performativity as a repetition of citations of authority that can go both ways, so to speak, that makes performativity transformative.

Thus the performative is transformative through repetition, says Butler. But it can't be just the repetition of the prohibited in the prohibition, or the repetition of the foreclosed desire in the foreclosure, because *every* instance of the social norm also repeats what it excludes and *still* the norms remain effective. To explain this in *Bodies That Matter*, Butler identifies chance as opening up the transformative in repetition (1993, 241). Her theory suggests that sometimes, by chance, the performance of the prohibited or foreclosed other dominates the constative operation of enforcing the social norms. In these cases the repressed other is seen and heard. Following Derrida, Butler suggests that the performative element of signification (how something is said) can undermine the constative element of signification (what is said). Derrida goes one step further and suggests that the power of this performance can transform the very structure of performance and iteration itself by performing and thereby displaying the process of subject construction and its dependence on what it excludes (Derrida 1992, 340). In my reading, the transformative power of the performative is similar to what Kristeva identifies as the revolutionary power of poetic language—power that comes by displaying the process through which identity is produced, which includes both repressed semiotic elements in dialectical relation to referential symbolic elements. The performative/constative distinction can be likened to Kristeva's semiotic/symbolic distinction. All signification operates on both levels simultaneously, and meaning is produced through the tension between levels. While the symbolic or constative describes meaning proper— referential meaning—the semiotic or performative describes another level of meaning, even nonmeaning, that motivates all attempts to refer.

The transformative power of the semiotic is the power of negativity. Kristeva distinguishes her conception of negativity from Hegel's when she suggests that negativity itself is the fourth term of the dialectic (1984). She emphasizes the role of a negativity that cannot be sublimated. Indeed, it is through the operations of semiotic negativity that signification is possible. Throughout her writings Kristeva identifies negativity with the motility of drive force and the power for transformation. In her earlier writings, negativity is associated with the semiotic drive force that can lead to the revolution in poetic language (1984). In her latest writings, negativity is associated with the power of the imaginary to lead to a psychic revolution (1998a, 1998b). For Kristeva, the transformative power of the performative comes from the force of negativity in all signification—the negativity identified with drive energy.

So, Kristeva takes us even one step further than Butler or Derrida when she insists that, although powerful in itself, this display of the process of identification or signification must be accompanied by an elaboration or interpretation in order to be transformative. The performance makes visible the subject's dependence on its other, but once seen this dependence must also be interpreted. This, in fact, is what Butler does in her work. We could say that her own performance of elaboration and interpretation challenges the constative level of her work, at which she insists that performance alone can resignify and thereby transform norms; in the spirit of her theory, we could say that her own performance both reiterates and challenges her theory of performance.

What elaboration or interpretation adds to the transformative power of performance is a reinscription—what Butler calls resignification—of the constative element of signification. If the performative and constative elements of signification affect each other, then not only can the performative challenge the constative but the constative can transform the performative. The relation is not Butler's one-directional impact of the performative on the constative. Rather, the interplay between these two allows for transformation and change, even changes in the very structure of signification. Interpretation configures and reconfigures the ways in which we conceive of ourselves and others and thereby adds transformative power to the mobility of meaning always opened up in the performative element of signification. But how can we distinguish between conservative and subversive resignifications? Which repetitions promote ethical, open, responsible relations, and which undermine them?

Freud's distinction between "acting-out" (merely repeating) and "working-through" can help answer this question. Butler's analysis of the continuous repetitions of the original trauma or subjection that constitute and maintain subjectivity is reminiscent of Freud's description of acting-out in "Remembering, Repeating, and Working-Through": "The patient does not remember anything of what he has forgotten or repressed, but acts it out. He reproduces it not as a memory but as an action; he repeats it, without, of course, knowing that he is repeating it" (1914, 150). While Butler's theory in its earlier and latest development embraces Freud's notion of acting-out or repetition of trauma, she never develops his notion of working-through.[7] This is why Butler's theory is useful and provocative, up to a point, but ultimately unsatisfying. Because Butler's theory includes neither a "thick" notion of the unconscious nor the Nietzschean notion of a life-affirming power in excess of Foucauldian oscillation between domination and resistance, her theory does not allow any space for transformation in the structure of the performative or the operations of power themselves. Without a notion of working-through, Butler's theory can never take us out of an us-versus-them approach to the relation between self and others, wherein we merely repeat original trauma suffered at the hands of others and react with rage directed at ourselves or others. A theory of the performative needs a notion of working-through in order to both ground ethics and explain how political transformation can be liberating rather than conservative.

For Freud, the goal of analysis is to turn acting-out into memory by providing interpretations and allowing the patient to "work-through" his or her resistances to interpretation (1914, 154–56). As Edward Bibring concludes in his elaboration of Freud's theory of repetition, acting-out alone does not lead to change (1943, 501). Bibring makes a distinction between defense mechanisms like acting-out, through which tensions are pushed aside, abreaction, through which tension is discharged directly, and what he calls "working-off," through which tensions are dissolved. He says that "working-off mechanisms of the ego are directed neither toward discharge [abreaction] nor toward rendering the tension harmless [acting-out]; their function is to dissolve the tension gradually by changing the internal conditions which give rise to it" (1943, 502). Although Bibring does not elaborate what internal conditions give rise to repetition or explain how working-off changes them, his theory is suggestive for the purpose of imagining how acting-out or iteration becomes structural change. Bibring's theory promises the reality of overcoming the repetition compulsion and breaking the cycle of repetition by changing the very conditions that make repetition possible. Building on Freud's theory that "working-through is undoubtedly a repetition albeit one modified by interpretation and—for this reason—liable to facilitate the subject's freeing himself from repetition mechanisms," Bibring emphasizes the role of interpretation in binding unbound psychic tension and thereby changing the structure of repetition (Laplanche and Pontalis 1973, 488; Freud 1914, Bibring 1943).

Daniel Lagache further develops Bibring's notion and describes various modes of working-off:

> The transition from the action of repetition to recollection by thought and word. . . : the transition from identification, where the subject fails to distinguish himself from his lived experience, to objectification, where he stands back from this experience; the transition from dissociation to integration; the detachment from the imaginary object, brought to completion with the change of object; that familiarization with phobic situations which replaces the anxious expectation of the traumatic and phantasy-dominated situation; the substitution of control for inhibition, of experience for obedience—in all these examples, the defensive operation [acting-out] is only neutralized in so

far as a working-off operation is substituted for it. (Quoted in Laplanche and
Pontalis 1973, 487)

We might also note that in all of Lagache's examples working-off is substituted for acting-out through the catalyst of interpretation. Through interpretation or diagnostic elaboration of acting-out, repetition is transformed from
compulsory behavior into more open possibilities.

In more recent work, Dominick LaCapra has argued that Freud's notion
of working-through is useful in thinking about social change as well as individual transformation. He argues that "the processes referred to by the basic
concepts of psychoanalysis undercut the opposition between individual and
society insofar as they involve social individuals whose relative individuation
or collective status should be a problem for inquiry and argument" (1994, 9,
173). Throughout his work, LaCapra argues that the psychoanalytic notion
of transference is not limited to clinical settings (1985, 1989, 1994). His focus
is on history and historians in particular, whom he argues enter transferential relations with the history they study. LaCapra loosely defines *transference*
as a "modified psychoanalytic sense of a repetition-displacement of the past
into the present as it necessarily bears on the future" (1985, 72). One of the
primary implications of his extension of transference to history is a sense of
both time and theory as repetition. Insofar as theorists or historians are necessarily involved in transferential relations with the object of their analysis, if
they are the least bit interested in their work, problems can arise if the transference is not acknowledged or interpreted: "Transference causes fear of possession by the past [or the object of study] and loss of control over both it
and oneself. It simultaneously brings the temptation to assert full control
over the 'object' of study through ideologically suspect procedures that may
be related to the phenomenon Freud discussed as 'narcissism'" (1985, 72).

LaCapra diagnoses two extreme reactions caused by transference: totalizing, controlling identification with the other; or total disassociation from the
other, who is seen as radically and completely different. Both the attempt to
completely assimilate the other (or the past, in the case of the historian) and
the attempt to deny any connection between the self and the other (the present and the past) are symptoms of an undiagnosed and uninterpreted transference. "The difficulty," says LaCapra, "is to develop an exchange with the
'other' that is both sensitive to transferential displacement and open to the
challenge of the other's 'voice'" (1985, 72–73). Just as in the clinical setting,
in order to make the transferential relation transformative there must be interpretative diagnoses that move the subject, group, or culture from acting-
out (mere repetition) to working-through (internal change).

LaCapra also argues that extreme theories of performative free play can lead to narcissistic obliteration of the other as other and the tendency to act-out one's own obsessions (1994, 34). For example, he diagnoses Lacan's insistence on the impossibility of overcoming the repetition compulsion, or what Lacan calls repetition automation, as acting-out. Lacan himself often describes his performance as one of acting-out the unconscious. LaCapra diagnoses these types of extreme theories as acting-out as denials of the possibility of the other as other. I see something like this tendency in Butler's insistence on repetition without the possibility of working-through.

In *Representing the Holocaust* LaCapra says that one common way to deny the significance of our relations to others and close off the possibility of working-through those relations is to engage in leveling comparisons. He argues that leveling comparisons can work to normalize trauma:

> The greatest danger at the present time, at least in the context of the historian's debate, is that certain comparisons may function as mechanisms of denial that do not enable one to "work through" problems. Indeed, they may misleadingly conflate normality with a leveling normalization. The seemingly balanced account of an unbalanced situation—particularly the appeal to comparisons that evenhandedly show the distribution of horror in history—may well be coded in a specific manner as mechanisms of denial that seek normalization and a "positive" identity through an avoidance or disavowal of the critical and self-critical requirements of both historical understanding and anything approximating "normality." (1994, 48)

We can place LaCapra's notion of leveling comparisons back into the context of my analysis of the performative in Butler's theory. Historical comparisons are not the only ones that can level and effectively normalize trauma. Structural comparisons are also in danger of leveling and normalizing trauma. As I have suggested, this danger is manifest in Butler's theory of repetition and power, especially in *The Psychic Life of Power*; and although she tries to qualify her theory in *Excitable Speech*, even there she does not escape the danger of leveling comparisons that effectively normalize trauma.

Before I can use LaCapra's analysis of leveling comparisons, however, I need to point out a telling normalization of trauma in LaCapra's own work. Throughout *Representing the Holocaust* there seems to be some originary trauma suggested in his analysis. This originary trauma becomes explicit in his endorsement of Eric Santner's comparison between the original trauma of separation from the mother and subsequent traumas (1994, 214–21). LaCapra quotes Santner's *Stranded Objects* at length, and I cite that quotation to make my point:

Both the child trying to master separateness from the mother and the trauma victim returning, in dream, to the site of a shock, are locked in a repetition compulsion: as effort to recuperate, in the controlled context of symbolic behavior, the *Angstbereitschaft* or readiness to feel anxiety, absent during the initial shock or loss. It was Freud's thought that the absence of appropriate affect—anxiety—is what leads to traumatization rather than loss per se. This affect can, however, be recuperated only in the presence of an empathic witness. In the case of the child playing fort/da it is the parent/observer, and in that of the trauma victim the empathic analyst, who co-constitute the space in which loss may come to be symbolically and affectively mastered. Homeopathy without appropriate affect becomes a purely mechanical procedure that can never lead to empowerment; without a social space in which this affect can be recuperated, the homeopathic operation becomes a sort of elegiac loop that must repeat itself endlessly. (Quoted in LaCapra 1994, 214)

While I agree with Santner's insistence that working-through requires the symbolization of affect, which can only be achieved in relation to an empathic witness, and I agree that this symbolization is effective only in a social context that supports it and makes it available, I am compelled to point out that his Freudian comparison between the child separating from its mother and trauma victims, and LaCapra's endorsement of that comparison, repeats the denial of differentiation that they warn against. First, this comparison assumes that weaning is traumatic without considering the social context within which weaning takes place. Some feminists have argued that weaning is in fact pleasurable for the child (see Willett 1995; Kristeva 1984, 1987; Benjamin 1988). And as I have suggested elsewhere, theories of the trauma of separation from the mother are based on a false notion of an antisocial mother-child dyad or unity that must be violently broken in order for the child to become social (Oliver 1995, 1997). Images of violence in the separation between mother and child serve a patriarchal notion of maternity as natural and antisocial. But if we consider that the context within which maternity and weaning take place is in fact patriarchal, then we must investigate the associations between the violence attributed to this situation and the patriarchal social context within which they are experienced and represented.

Second, by unquestioningly using the child's separation from the mother as an example of original trauma, Santner does not heed his own warning and examine the social space in which affects can or cannot be symbolized. The work of feminists such as Kristeva, Luce Irigaray, and Cynthia Willett (and my earlier work) makes a case for the need to refigure maternity and mother-child relationships as social relationships that don't require the violent intervention of paternal authority to socialize the child. This work is itself an attempt to make the social space in which maternal affects can be symbolized in order to demythologize the natural antisocial image of maternity upheld by patriarchy.

Third, the comparison between a child's separation from its mother and the trauma of Holocaust victims normalizes trauma in the very way that LaCapra warns against. Certainly, children "separating" from their mothers is an everyday occurrence. Whether or not it is traumatic, it is perceived as normal. To compare Holocaust victims, or other victims of trauma, to children being weaned is not only to dramatically oversimplify the situation but also to normalize torture and extreme trauma in ways that close off the social space necessary to symbolize affects toward working-through traumatic repetitions.

For LaCapra, the critical distance necessary for diagnostic interpretation that can lead to transformation is based in acknowledging transference and retrieving what has been repressed (1994, 175). In his own leveling move, it is the social nature of mother-child relationships that has been repressed, and the reduction of women as mothers to the realm of the natural has been repeated rather than worked-through by means of self-critical interpretation. Working-through requires interpretation born out of self-critical reflection and dialogue that works as an antidote to leveling comparisons and unacknowledged transference. In a sense, we could say that working-through is the process of acknowledging that our own subjectivity is not our own but the result of dialogic and transferential relations with others.

II. Witnessing

4. The Necessity and Impossibility of Witnessing

Shoshana Felman and Dori Laub's analysis of eyewitness testimonies of the Holocaust can enrich the notions of performance and elaboration or interpretation I have developed so far using Butler and Kristeva. Their theories of testimony enrich Freud's notion of working-through and begin to take us beyond a theory of identity based on recognition and exclusion toward a theory of subjectivity based on witnessing. Laub develops a notion of the inner witness, set up in dialogic relations with the other, necessary for a sense of one's self as a subjective agent. Extreme torture disintegrates the inner witness and thereby undermines subjectivity. Felman's theory emphasizes the importance of the performative and a version of what I am calling witnessing in order to both reframe subjectivity and diagnose the operations of extreme trauma and oppression. For Felman the paradoxes of witnessing the Holocaust point to the paradoxes inherent in any attempt to bear witness to one's own oppression. Moreover, the paradoxes inherent in bearing witness to one's own oppression teach us something about the dialogic nature of subjectivity. Subjectivity requires a responsible witness. The process of witnessing is both necessary to subjectivity and part of the process of working-through the trauma of oppression necessary to personal and political transformation. In addition, contra Butler, Felman and Laub's theory of the performative suggests that subjectivity is not formed through subordination, but, rather, that extreme forms of subordination destroy the witness necessary for subjectivity.

Felman's analysis suggests that there is a difference between the narration of historical facts by just anyone and the narration of history by those who lived through it. Historians and our legal system rely on eyewitness testimony for evidence uniquely available to witnesses—those who have firsthand knowledge through experience. Felman identifies the uniqueness of eyewitness testimony in the performance of testimony, which goes beyond the firsthand knowledge of the witness. The performance of testimony says more than the witness knows. And only the supplement of this more than knowledge can speak the truth of experience, a truth repeated and yet constituted in the very act of testimony. Felman asks, "What does it mean that the testimony cannot be simply reported, or narrated by another in its role as testimony? . . . What does testimony mean, if it is the uniqueness of the *performance* of a story which is constituted by the fact that, like an oath, it cannot be carried out by anybody else?" (Felman and Laub 1992, 205–6).

I began with an example of historians who discounted an eyewitness testimony because of its inaccuracy. The historians were listening for what was impersonal in the testimony, what could be repeated by anyone else. But, as Felman points out, if history is impersonal, then anyone should be able to testify to the truth of facts; eyewitnesses should have no privilege. Felman suggests, however, that there is something other than historical accuracy at stake in testimony. It is the *performance* of testimony, not merely what is said, that makes it effective in bringing to life a repetition of an event, not a repetition of the facts of the event, or the structure of the event, but the silences and the blindness inherent in the event that, at bottom, also make eyewitness testimony impossible. In other words, what makes testimony powerful is its dramatization of the impossibility of testifying to the event. What makes witnessing possible is its performance of the impossibility of ever witnessing the event. Discussing Claude Lanzmann's film *Shoah,* Felman says, "The *necessity of testimony* it affirms in reality derives, paradoxically enough, from the *impossibility of testimony* that the film at the same time dramatizes" (1992, 224).

The paradox between the necessity and impossibility of testimony, the paradox of the eyewitness, is the productive tension at the foundation of the notion of witnessing. The tension between history and testifying to what one knows from firsthand experience, on the one hand, and psychoanalysis and bearing witness to what is beyond knowledge or recognition, on the other, produces the possibility of getting beyond a mere repetition of either history or trauma. History and psychoanalysis, testimony and witnessing, are necessarily strapped together to create the tension that supports historical truth and the very structure of subjectivity itself. Witnessing means testifying to both something you have seen with your own eyes and something that you cannot see. We have both the juridical sense of bearing witness to what you know from experience as an eyewitness and the religious sense of bearing witness to what you believe through blind faith. Subject positions and subjectivity are constituted through the possibility of witnessing in this double sense. The tension inherent in witnessing is the tension between subject positions, which are historically determined, and subjectivity, which is an infinite response-ability.

Oppression and domination work on both levels of witnessing to restrict or annihilate the possibility of subject positions and to undermine or destroy the structure of subjectivity, both of which are necessary to a sense of agency. Oppression and domination succeed by undermining, damaging, or annihilating what Laub identifies as the inner witness necessary for the process of witnessing to support itself. The inner witness is produced and sustained by dialogic interaction with other people. Dialogue with others makes dialogue with oneself possible. In order to think, talk, and act as an agent, the inner witness must be in place. Address and response are possible because the interpersonal dialogue is interiorized. Having a sense of oneself as a subject and an agent requires that the structure of witnessing as the possibility of address and response has been set up in dialogic relations with others. The inner witness, then, is the structure of subjectivity as address-ability itself, the structure of witnessing.

The inner witness is the necessary condition for the structure of address-ability and response-ability inherent in subjectivity. This witnessing structure (subjectivity) is a necessary condition for assuming a subject position as active agent. The inner witness operates as a negotiating voice between subject positions and subjectivity. If one's subject position is the sociohistorical position in which one finds oneself, and one's subjectivity is the structure of witnessing as infinite response-ability, then the inner witness is where subject position and subjectivity meet. The inner witness is a necessary part of the structure of subjectivity as response-ability itself, and it is constitutive of one's subject position. On the one hand, if the inner witness is an incorporation of dialogic relations with others, of external witnesses, then its ability to create an enabling and empowering subject position is determined by the sociohistorical context of the dialogic relations with others. On the other hand, since subjectivity is itself the structure and process of witnessing, the place and function of the inner witness are also necessary to give the subject a sense of itself as agent.

The performative element of witnessing points to the structure of subjectivity itself, the unsaid in saying. To employ the Lévinasian distinction, we could say that the saying challenges the said, not just because the saying performs the unspoken conditions of the possibility of the said—or in Butler's terms, not just because the performance shows or displays the foreclosed condition of possibility of the reiteration of the social norm—but because the saying *enacts* the impossibility of really ever *having said* what happened. Vigilance and witnessing are necessary because of the impossibility of having said. Both are necessary, not in order to get at the truth but, more important, to maintain the possibility of the process of witnessing. Why is it necessary to bear witness to the impossibility of witnessing? Or, we could ask, why is it necessary to recognize the impossibility of recognizing otherness?

Subjectivity Requires a Witness

Thinking about what could be considered one of the limit cases of subordination and subjectivity, we could say that Felman and Laub's analysis of the Holocaust begins to answer these questions of why bearing witness to the impossibility of ever having said or of recognizing or understanding otherness is necessary for a theory of othered subjectivity. Indeed, from the limits of the intelligible, we might be able to think through the implications of the dialogic nature of subjectivity. If, as both Butler and Honneth maintain, "I" can say "I" only in *response* to an address from another, or as an addressee, it is also true that "I" can say "I" only by *supposing* an addressee, the one to whom I address myself. Without an addressee, without a witness, I cannot exist.

While I agree with Butler that subjectivity is dependent on address-ability, including my response to another, it need not be conceived as subordination to another. To conceive of any or all dependence on others as subordination is to discount degrees of subordination, which at their extreme can be forms of objectification and torture that jeopardize the possibility of subjectivity. Without acknowledging degrees of subordination, the tortures of war, subordination of slaves, domestic violence, and everyday child-rearing or socialization processes become the same. Moreover, while it is true that we become socialized by internalizing social norms that discipline us, our subjectivity develops only in relation to others who are much more than the officers of those norms. Subjectivity develops through address and address-ability from and to others. Without an external witness, we cannot develop or sustain the internal witness necessary for the ability to interpret and represent our experience, which is necessary for subjectivity and more essentially for both individual and social transformation. And if subordination is taken to the extreme of objectification, then the possibility of address, of witnessing, is destroyed and with it the possibility of subjectivity. Only when someone else listens to me can I listen to myself. If, as Butler argues, the subject is dependent on subjection and subordination in order to make the inaugural turn inward, then how do we explain that subordination taken to an extreme hinders the inward turn by destroying the possibility of a witness? Indeed, don't extreme forms of subordination teach us something about the nature of subordination in relation to subjectivity? I will suggest that what we learn is that subordination erodes the conditions of possibility for subjectivity.

There are of course degrees of subordination, degrees of objectification, and corresponding degrees of subjective erosion. As Axel Honneth argues, physical torture is the most extreme and most damaging to one's sense of self. Although I disagree with Honneth's implicit suggestion that subordination or disrespect is necessary to cause the conflict through which a subject comes to recognize itself, I agree that extreme forms of subordination lead not to subjectivity but to its destruction. Felman and Laub's analysis of the Holocaust persuasively shows how extreme subordination eliminates the conditions of possibility for subjectivity.

Both Felman and Laub conclude from their analysis of survivors' testimonies that the events of the concentration camps and mass murders constituted a holocaust because they annihilated the possibility of witnesses. Laub explains:

> The historical reality of the Holocaust became, thus, a reality which extinguished philosophically the very possibility of address, the possibility of appealing, or of turning to another. But when one cannot turn to a "you" one cannot say "thou" even to oneself. The Holocaust created in this way a world in which one could not bear witness to oneself. The Nazi system turned out therefore to be fool-proof, not only in the sense that it convinced its victims, the potential witnesses from the inside, that what was affirmed about their "otherness" and their inhumanity was correct and that their experiences were no longer communicable even to themselves, and therefore perhaps never took place. This loss of the capacity to be witness to oneself and thus to witness from the inside is perhaps the true meaning of annihilation, for when one's history is abolished, one's identity ceases to exist as well. (1992, 82; cf. 211)

As Felman points out, although there were eyewitnesses to the Holocaust, they could not really see what was going on. From the inside, victims were not only empirically annihilated as witnesses—murdered—but also cognitively and perceptually destroyed as witnesses because they were turned into objects and dehumanized. As inhuman objects they are unable to speak. Moreover, to speak, to bear witness to their dehumanization is to repeat it by telling the world that they were reduced to worthless objects. The Nazis made sure that the world from the outside did not see what was going on; they hid the death camps. And those involved in the killings were ordered with the threat of death not to refer to the victims as victims or people or even corpses but to call them *figuren* (puppets) or *Schmattes* (rags) (1992, 210). Even those who saw could not see, because it was impossible to grasp a world that was not a world, a world that was inhuman (1992, 232). For some of the soldiers in the Allied Forces, seeing the concentration camps meant going blind; they literally lost their sight at the sight of the incomprehensible world of the Holocaust.

What would it mean to bear witness to the Holocaust? asks Felman. To witness from the inside, from the experience of the victims? She argues that it would mean first bearing witness from inside the desire *not* to be inside (1992, 228). Also, it would mean testifying from inside the very binding of the secret that made victims feel as though they were part of a secret world (229). It would mean testifying from the inside of a radical deception by which one was separated from the truth of history even as one was living it (229). Moreover, it would mean testifying from inside otherness, bearing "witness from inside the living pathos of a tongue which nonetheless is bound to be heard as noise" (231). Felman concludes that it is impossible to testify from inside. From the inside the possibility of address and of an addressable other was eliminated. Yet in order to reestablish subjectivity and in order to demand justice, it is necessary to bear witness to the inarticulate experience of the inside. This is not the finite task of comprehending it; this is the infinite task of encountering it (268). It is the tension between finite understanding linked to historical facts and historically determined subject positions, and the infinite encounter linked to psychoanalysis and the infinite responsibility of subjectivity that produces a sense of agency. Such an encounter necessarily takes us beyond recognition and brings with it ethical obligation.

We are obligated to witness beyond recognition, to testify and to listen to testimony—to encounter each other—because subjectivity and humanity are the result of witnessing. That is to say, subjectivity and humanity are the result of response-ability. That which precludes a response destroys subjectivity and thereby humanity. As Dori Laub concludes, "The absence of *an addressable other,* an other who can hear the anguish of one's memories and thus affirm and recognize their realness, annihilates the story. And it is, precisely, this ultimate annihilation of a narrative, that, fundamentally, *cannot be heard* and of a story that *cannot be witnessed,* which constitutes the mortal [eighty-first] blow" (Felman and Laub 1992, 68).

Laub's analysis of his involvement with Holocaust survivors and their testimonies teaches us about all human relationships and the nature of subjectivity. As he points out, witnessing engages a joint responsibility. It takes two.

It is impossible to bear witness without an addressee. Response-ability is never solitary. In describing the Video Archive project at Yale, Laub says that

> the interviewer-listener takes on the responsibility for bearing witness that previously the narrator felt he bore alone, and therefore could not carry out. It is the encounter and the coming together between the survivor and the listener, which make possible something like a repossession of the act of witnessing. This joint responsibility is the source of the reemerging truth. (Felman and Laub 1992, 85)

The lesson of this limit experience is that without an addressee, without a witness, I cannot exist. I am by virtue of response-ability. And truth is itself a process of emergence and reemergence between response-able subjects.

Subjectivity requires the possibility of a witness, and the witnessing at the heart of subjectivity brings with it responsibility, response-ability, and ethical responsibility. Subjectivity as the ability to respond is linked in its conception to ethical responsibility. Subjectivity is responsibility: it is the ability to respond and to be responded to. Responsibility, then, has the double sense of opening up the ability to respond—response-ability—and ethically obligating subjects to respond by virtue of their very subjectivity itself. Reformulating Eva Kittay's analysis of relations of dependency, a subject who "refuses to support this bond absolves itself from its most fundamental obligation—its obligation to its founding possibility" (1998, 131). Response-ability is the founding possibility of subjectivity and its most fundamental obligation.

Although historical, this reemerging truth is not the truth of the historian. It is not accurate, because "accurate" cannot be a criterion for this type of truth. Although subject to repetition in the psychoanalytic sense, this truth is not one that can be simply reported or repeated by just anyone. As Laub maintains, "What ultimately matters in all processes of witnessing, spasmodic and continuous, conscious and unconscious, is not simply the information, the establishment of the facts, but the experience itself of *living through testimony,* of giving testimony" (Felman and Laub 1992, 85). The emphasis on living through testimony suggests not only the significance of living through this particular experience of testimony but also the fact that we live through witnessing. Yet it is this living through that historical facts conceal. Historical facts conceal the process of witnessing and the performance of testimony. As Felman argues,

> As the extinction of the subject of the signature and as the objectification of the victim's voice, "history" presents itself as anti-testimony . . . to make truth

happen as a testimony through the haunting repetition of an ill understood melody; to make the referent come back, paradoxically, as something heretofore unseen by history; to reveal the real as the impact of a literality that history cannot assimilate or integrate as knowledge, but that it keeps encountering in the return of the song. . . . We *"sing again"* what we cannot know, what we have not integrated and what, consequently, we can neither fully master nor completely understand. (Felman and Laub 1992, 276)

This is why the historians involved in the Video Archive project, looking for something comprehensible and accurate, could not hear any truth, anything valid or significant, in the eyewitness testimony of the woman who had been at Auschwitz.

What we could call the psychoanalytic truth, or the truth of performance, cannot be captured in historical facts. More specifically, the truth of trauma and victimization is lost even in the most astounding statistics. The experience of being othered and objectified is lost to history and regained only through the testimony of witnesses. As Laub notes,

> The testimony aspires to recapture the lost truth of that reality, but the realization of the testimony is not the fulfillment of this promise. The testimony in its commitment to truth is a passage through, and an exploration of, differences, rather than an exploration of identity, just as the experience it testifies to—the Holocaust—is unassimilable because it is a passage through the ultimate difference—the otherness of death. (Felman and Laub 1992, 91)

I would add the otherness of the inhuman, the otherness of the object. To various degrees, all experiences of objectification and subordination are the inarticulatable experiences of inhumanity that can only be repeated in testimony or performed in various ways but never fully reported in historical facts.

More important, it is through witnessing and reestablishing the inner witness who is damaged by objectification and subordination that we can move beyond repetition of trauma to elaboration and interpretation. The witness, ultimately the repair of the inner witness, allows someone to be both inside and outside her own oppression and victimization at the same time. And as Felman so forcefully argues, there is no voice from inside victimization. Testifying to a witness opens up the space to step outside. For this reason, it is in the process of testifying that the victim first comes to "know" his or her own experience, which is all the more reason why the process of witnessing is one of joint responsibility, for the very possibility of experience itself comes only through representation, elaboration, and interpretation (Felman and Laub 1992, 57). In addition, because witnessing is a process of reinventing experience, of making experience what it is, through witnessing the structure of the logic of repetition driving the psyche, particularly the psyche of victimization, is transformed. The performance of witnessing is transformative because it reestablishes the dialogue through which representation and thereby meaning are possible, and because this representation allows the victim to reassert his own subjective agency and humanity into an experience in which it was annihilated or reduced to guilt and self-abuse.

The Paradox of Bearing Witness to One's Own Oppression

Mae Gwendolyn Henderson describes the importance of testimony in the transformation from victim to agent in her essay "Speaking in Tongues: Dialogics Dialectics, and the Black Woman Writer's Literary Tradition" (1992). Henderson develops a notion of "speaking in tongues" in order to articulate what I call othered subjectivity or the subject position of those othered by oppression and domination. Her analysis of Mikhail Bakhtin's notion of inner speech or inner dialogue resonates with Laub's insistence on the possibility of an inner witness. Henderson concludes that "consciousness becomes a kind of 'inner speech' reflecting 'the outer world' in a process that links the psyche, language, and social interaction" (146). She argues that because of their marginal status in relation to both race and gender, for black women the negotiation of inner and outer voices is more explicit; the negotiation of voices or tongues is a project for black women in a way that it isn't for others for whom this negotiation is less necessary for daily survival.

Her notion of speaking in tongues brings together what she sees as Bakhtin's model of the multiplicity of speech in a dialogics of difference based on struggles and Hans-Georg Gadamer's model of a unity of understanding in a dialectics of identity based on consensus (150). She associates the dialogics of difference with social negotiations with others and the dialectics of identity with the inner voice; this voice marks a particular location in the social sphere that is *me* or *myself* or sometimes *we* or *us*. For Henderson, the negotiation between speaking different multiple languages and speaking secret inner languages makes us who we are. Moreover, she maintains that conceiving of identity and difference in a dialogic, dialectical relationship opens up the possibility of speaking in tongues, that is to say, speaking from the place of otherness, or what I am calling othered subjectivity:

In their works, black women writers have encoded oppression as a discursive dilemma, that is, their works have consistently raised the problem of the black woman's relationship to power and discourse. Silence is an important element of this code. . . . it is not that black women, in the past, have had nothing to say, but rather that they have had no say. The absence of black female voices has allowed others to inscribe, or write, and ascribe to, or read, them. The notion of speaking in tongues, however, leads us away from an examination of how the Other has written/read black women and toward an examination of how black women have written the other(s) writing/reading black women. (151)

Like Felman and Laub, Henderson discusses the difficulty of witnessing from inside the experience of oppression. Whereas Laub describes the way that oppression can destroy the inner voice or inner witness necessary for subjectivity and therefore necessary for any kind of witnessing, and Felman discusses the paradoxes of extreme oppression that render the inside speechless, Henderson describes a dialogic, dialectical relation of inside to outside that problematizes witnessing in a different way. As she describes it, black women experience two conflicting voices, inner and outer, which confound their sense of themselves as agents. In terms of my earlier analysis, we could say that the socially constrictive subject position of black women produces an othered subjectivity whose agency is on trial.

Henderson uses the example of Zora Neale Hurston's character Janie from *Their Eyes Were Watching God* to show how the position from which black women witness requires that they speak in tongues, that they "speak at once to a diverse audience about [their] experience in a racist and sexist society where to be black and female is to be, so to speak, 'on trial'" (148). Henderson argues that Janie's courtroom discourse in the trial scene at the end of the novel "emblematizes the way in which the categories of public and private break down in black women's discourse" (149). She says that in this scene "testimonial discourse takes on an expanded meaning, referring to both juridical, public, and dominant discourse as well as familial, private, and nondominant discourse. Testimonial, in this sense, derives its meaning from both 'testimony' as an official discursive mode and 'testifying'. . . in which the speaker gives verbal witness to the efficacy, truth, and power of some experience" (149).

Henderson's analysis suggests that black women's testimony is always on trial, that their testimony brings public, juridical standards to bear on private, familial, or domestic experiences. Her point is that black women survive by learning to speak in tongues, to speak differently to different groups.

In addition to speaking in tongues, when black women's discourse is continually put on trial, it forces black women into the paradoxical situation of both insisting on their legitimacy and the truth of their experience and doubting that their experience is legitimate or real. Certainly, one reason why the public and private cannot be neatly separated in the lives of black women is found in the ways in which public policy and juridical institutions affect their everyday private lives. Speaking in tongues may be as much a matter of negotiating different aspects of social, political, and cultural life in which inner and outer are always intertwined.

Like Felman and Laub, Henderson points to an aspect of testifying or witnessing that takes us beyond the juridical notion of testimony or eyewitness. And it is this aspect of witnessing beyond recognition that in a sense reconnects inner and outer voice, or private and public discourse, even as it problematizes that distinction. Although they employ the distinction between inner and outer in different ways and in different contexts, Felman's, Laub's, and Henderson's insistence on the split between the two raises some of the same questions. How can we translate from inner to outer in order to bear witness to our experience? In the case of the Holocaust, how is any witnessing possible if either the inner voice is destroyed or it is impossible to witness from the inside? How does the inside become outside? In the case of Henderson's analysis of black women's experience, how can what she calls the secret language of inner experience ever be articulated? Isn't the very notion of speaking in tongues associated with an inarticulate other who cannot testify to his or her own experience?

Analyses by Felman, Laub, and Henderson suggest that bearing witness to extreme experiences of oppression, subordination, and objectification leaves the victim/survivor in a paradoxical relation to such witnessing. Bearing witness to your own oppression is as paradoxical as it is necessary. The heart of the paradox is that oppression and subordination are experiences that attempt to objectify the subject and mutilate or annihilate subjectivity, that is, your sense of yourself, especially your sense of yourself as an agent. Rendered an object, the victim of oppression and subordination is also rendered speechless. Objects do not talk. Objects do not act. Objects are not subjects or agents of their own lives.

Even in Hegel's master-slave dialectic, objectification is the antithesis of subjectivity. Hegel's description of self-consciousness in *Phenomenology of Spirit* points up the dangers of objectification (1977). While in the end Hegel maintains that enslavement or objectification is necessary for self-consciousness, the stakes of the lord-bondsman struggle are objectification and thingness. When one self-consciousness encounters another, the other appears first as an object like any other: "Appearing thus immediately on the scene, they are for one another like ordinary objects, *independent* shapes, individuals submerged in the being or immediacy of *Life*—for the object in its immediacy is here determined as Life" (1977, 113).

The lord and bondsman become certain of their own self-consciousness only by negating Life or the immediacy of being both in themselves and in the other. This is why they must risk their own life and also risk the life of the other. Life itself must be negated. Recognition requires abstracting from the immediacy or being/Life. It requires a negation of being to become for itself, that is to say, consciousness becomes an *object* for itself. But they can become objects for themselves only by retaining the other as an independent object. This is the lord's problem: he makes the bondsman a dependent object, and therefore he himself remains a dependent object. From the beginning Hegel points out that the object's dependence on the subject is what makes certainty a problem (113).

Even though self-consciousness requires a struggle to the death, death renders self-consciousness impossible. Upon death, self-consciousness becomes a lifeless immediacy. It becomes "like things" (1977, 114). Things can't engage in the process of recognition, which requires activity/action. Lifeless things are inanimate. The process so far is one where the self-conscious individual experiences himself as a simple "I"; his first experience of the other is as a thing that exists for him. Both the recognizer and recognized are essential moments of self-consciousness:

> Since to begin with they are unequal and opposed, and their reflection into a unity has not yet been achieved, they exist as two opposed shapes of consciousness; one is the independent consciousness whose essential nature is to be for itself, the other is the dependent consciousness whose essential nature is simply to live or to be for another. The former is lord, the other is bondsman. (115)

The lord is the recognizer and the bondsman is the recognized. The lord is active, the bondsman passive. The lord is subject, the bondsman is object, "consciousness in the form of thinghood" (115). The first stage of recognition is unequal because it requires a recognizer and a recognized. Someone must take the place of the self-consciousness and the other must take the place of its object: "At first, it will exhibit the side of the inequality of the two, or the splitting-up of the middle term into the extremes which, as extremes, are opposed to one another, one being only *recognized*, the other only *recognizing*" (112–13).

To become self-certain, self-consciousness must become active, the recognizer and not just the recognized. Consciousness must leave the realm of ordinary objects to assert its self-consciousness. Yet this is what the bondsman fails to do. The lord's triumph over the bondsman is precisely his ability to render the bondsman an ordinary object or thing. The lord's triumph is a triumph over things:

> The lord is the consciousness that exists for itself, but no longer merely the Notion of such a consciousness. Rather, it is a consciousness existing *for itself* which is mediated with itself through another consciousness, i.e. through a consciousness whose nature it is to be bound up with an existence that is independent, or thinghood in general. The lord puts himself into relation with both of these moments, to a *thing* as such, the object of desire, and to the consciousness for which thinghood is the essential characteristic. (1977, 115)

The lord makes the thing dependent on himself; it is a thing for him. For the bondsman, the thing remains independent. The lord annihilates the thing/object by making it his own. But since the bondsman merely works on it, the thing retains its independence. The lord is lord over the thing and achieves (so he thinks) absolute negation of it: "The latter's [the lord's] essential nature is to exist only for himself; he is the sheer negative power for whom the thing is nothing. Thus he is the pure, essential action in this relationship, while the action of the bondsman is impure and unessential" (116). The lord is active and master of the thing, while the bondsman is reduced to thingness.

Of course, the lord doesn't gain recognition through his mastery of the thing, because the thing is not independent, and because it is a thing and not a self-consciousness. As a thing, it cannot recognize him. It is passive and not active (1977, 116–17). The bondsman, on the other hand, is transformed into a truly independent consciousness because it is a "consciousness forced back into itself" (117). It is a thing forced to see itself as thing or object, and thereby it takes itself as its own object. That is to say, its own consciousness becomes its own object, and that is the birth of self-consciousness: "For in fashioning the thing, the bondsman's own negativity, his being-for-self, becomes an object for him only through his setting at nought the existing shape confronting him" (118).

Insofar as the thing remains independent for the bondsman, he can see himself as independent, too: "It is in this way, therefore, that consciousness, *qua* worker, comes to see in the independent being [of the object] its *own* independence" (118). Through the doubling of his thingness, through his consciousness as thingness turning back on itself, the bondsman becomes no-thing: "Now, however, he destroys this alien negative moment, posits *himself* as a negative in the permanent order of things, and thereby becomes *for himself,* someone existing on his own account" (118). Through his "formative activity" he escapes the world of things. Self-consciousness must become master of the whole of objective being, life, by realizing itself as the activity of negativity.

Thingness, or the status of thing, then, is what is at stake in the struggle for recognition. And bearing witness to the ways in which one was or is rendered a thing or an object is paradoxical in that things and objects cannot testify. While the act of witnessing itself is a testimony to one's subjectivity, the narrative of oppression tells the story of one's objectification and silence. How, then, can we speak the silence of objectification?

This paradox takes us back to Derrida and his use of J. L. Austin's distinction between the performative and the constative so crucial to Butler's theory. In the case of bearing witness to your own oppression, the performative is in special tension with the constative element of speech. The performance is one of a human subject in a dialogic relation with another human subject while the constative element—what is said—tells the tale of dehumanization and objectification. The content of testimonies of oppression reinscribes the survivor as victim and object even while the act of testifying restores subjectivity to the experience of objectification.

It is the paradoxical nature of witnessing oppression that makes it so powerful in restoring subjectivity and agency to an experience that shamefully lacks any such agency. The act of witnessing itself can help restore self-respect and a sense of one's self as an agent or a self, even while it necessarily recalls the trauma of objectification. Witnessing enables the subject to reconstitute the experience of objectification in ways that allow her to reinsert subjectivity into a situation designed to destroy it. Even so, the paradoxical nature of bearing witness to your own oppression makes it difficult and painful to testify.

Although bearing witness to torture or enslavement may be necessary for working through the trauma and avoiding the repetition compulsion, witnessing your own oppression and degradation also recalls the trauma of that experience. Along with the pain of remembering physical abuse and torture, there is a special pain involved in recalling the ways in which you were made into an object. Most victims of torture and abuse are ashamed to tell their stories; Holocaust survivors, rape survivors, and survivors of slavery all report the shame of the experience and the shame of bearing witness to it. But what is the source of this feeling of shame? The shame comes from becoming an object. Even in a situation where you had no choice, where you were not strong enough to resist, the experience of becoming a mere object for another produces feelings of shame. So along with the memories of physical pain and torture, witnessing recalls memories of being objectified, of losing one's sense of self as agent, of losing one's subjectivity and ultimately one's humanity. The shame involved in experiencing and testifying to one's own oppression is the result of being something not human, an object for another. The experience of testifying to one's oppression repeats that objectification even while it restores subjectivity. In addition to the more obvious reasons why it is painful for victims of violence and degradation to testify to their experiences, there is also the paradox of subjectivity inherent in bearing witness to one's own oppression. Therefore, insofar as on the constative level witnessing makes one an object over again, the act of witnessing can also produce shame.

In a significant sense, however, it is impossible to bearing witness to becoming an object, since objects have nothing to say. Becoming an object means becoming inarticulate. Only by testifying, by witnessing objectification, can survivors reinscribe their subjectivity into situations that mutilated it to the point of annihilation. So far I have described three ways in which bearing witness to your own oppression is paradoxical: (1) the performance of witnessing, which reinscribes subjectivity, is in tension with the constative description of becoming an object; (2) the process of witnessing, which restores subjectivity, also recalls the shame and pain of becoming an object; (3) in an important sense, the experience of becoming an object cannot be described, since it is the experience of becoming inarticulate.

There is a fourth paradox articulated by Henderson as the way in which testimonies of those oppressed (by sexism and racism) are always "on trial." If testimonies of oppression are presented from within the oppressive culture, then the dominant culture judges those testimonies; their credibility is always at issue. As Henderson argues, testimony of personal experience is put on trial in a way that renders all testimony juridical as well as personal. She says that the testimony of black women in a sexist and racist culture is always on trial, always put to a test, always suspect. This will be true of the testimony of any form of oppression, subordination, or objectification as long as the culture within which one speaks continues its oppressive practices.

Henderson's description of the way that black women's testimony is always on trial resonates with Fanon's description of the ways that colonization requires those colonized to seek approval and legitimation from their colonizers. Colonized or oppressed subjects are delegitimized, even dehumanized, so that their legitimacy and humanity are controlled by their colonizers. The right to speak, the right to claim agency or subjectivity, the right to claim humanity are made the prerogatives of the dominator. This is what I identified earlier as the pathology of recognition. Demands for recognition from the oppressed are the result of their being put on trial by their oppressors.

When testimony is put on trial and personal experience is judged as credible or not by public institutions, then the speaker is in the paradoxical position of justifying her status as subject. Once again, the performance of speaking proves subjectivity even while the social context calls it into question. This kind of questioning and the continual call to legitimate yourself as a self, to legitimate your right, or ability, to speak, make witnessing your own oppression even more painful and problematic. The right or ability to speak is accorded to those who have been accepted as legitimate subjects. To speak from the position of othered or oppressed flies in the face of a culture that silences people by making them the other and reducing them to inarticulate objects.

Perhaps the paradoxes of bearing witness to oppression will take on new life if we analyze their expression in Harriet Jacobs's 1861 testimony to her experience as a slave in the southeastern United States. Jacobs's story expresses the tensions involved in witnessing her own oppression and slavery. Jacobs is constantly concerned with maintaining her self-respect and dignity in the face of testifying to the loss of self-respect and dignity. Her narrative is an attempt to reinscribe dignity and self-respect into the experience of slavery. Yet in an important sense Jacobs seems aware that the performative element of her narrative is in tension with the constative element, that testifying to the ways in which she was objectified risks making her into an object over again for her readers. This is complicated by the fact that she is writing for white women in the North whom she hopes will become more involved in freeing slaves.

Jacobs's testimony is surrounded by an introduction and an appendix from her white supporters that pledge the veracity of her account; they felt the need to reassure those who would judge her that her story is true and her character sound. The editor, L. Maria Child, introduces the narrative by claiming that

> the author of the following autobiography is personally known to me, and her conversation and manners inspire me with confidence. During the last seventeen years, she has lived the greater part of the time with a distinguished family in New York, and has so deported herself as to be highly esteemed by them.

This fact is sufficient, without further credentials of her character. I believe those who know her will not be disposed to doubt her veracity, though some incidents in her story are more romantic than fiction. (Quoted in Jacobs 1861, 337)

And after Jacobs's testimony, the editor includes statements from others as to the veracity of the story and the credibility of its witness. These character witnesses on behalf of Jacobs frame her testimony with a juridical tone.

It seems clear from Jacobs's own narrative that she feels *on trial* writing for the white women of the North. She begins her testimony, "Reader, be assured this narrative is no fiction. I am aware that some of my adventures may seem incredible; but they are, nevertheless, strictly true" (335). She not only continually asserts the veracity of her testimony, which she must feel is on trial, but she repeatedly justifies her own actions, decisions, and morality. She asks her readers not to judge a slave woman by the same standards as one would a free woman. Although she could not freely marry or control the future of her children, she feels guilty in spite of this lack of choices. She calls her plans to free herself and her children "wrong" because she hated her master and because she became pregnant out of wedlock by another man hoping that her master would sell her to him.

Her narrative often reads as juridical testimony defending her actions as if she were literally on trial and being judged by her reader. For example, in one of the most striking passages expressing her concern over her reader's judgment, Jacobs writes:

Pity me, and pardon me, O virtuous reader! You never knew what it is to be a slave; to be entirely unprotected by law or custom; to have the laws reduce you to the condition of chattel, entirely subject to the will of another. You never exhausted your ingenuity in avoiding the snares, and eluding power of a hated tyrant; you never shuddered at the sound of his footsteps, and trembled within hearing of his voice. I know I did wrong. No one can feel it more sensible than I do. The painful and humiliating memory will haunt me to my dying day. Still, in looking back, calmly, on the events of my life, I feel that the slave woman ought not be judged by the same standards as others. (386)

The feeling of being judged is obviously painful for Jacobs. Throughout her narrative she is concerned about being judged not only by her readers but also by her family. She is humiliated that her parents or children should know of the humiliations that she suffered. In this case, she is as concerned with the pain and humiliation it would cause them as their judgment of her.

She is aware that they too will share her shame at being made an object for another.

In several places, Jacobs describes the pain she feels in retelling her objectification and enslavement. She describes the way in which bearing witness to her own oppression and subordination recalls the shame of being made into an object:

> I have not written my experiences in order to attract attention to myself; on the contrary, it would have been more pleasant to me to have been silent about my own history. (335)

> And now, reader, I come to a period in my unhappy life, which I would gladly forget if I could. The remembrance fills me with sorrow and shame. It pains me to tell you of it; but I have promised to tell you the truth, and I will do it honestly, let it cost me what it may. (384)

> It has been painful to me, in many ways, to recall the dreary years I passed in bondage. I would gladly forget them if I could. (513)

Repeatedly, Jacobs mentions how painful it is for her to testify to her own degradation and objectification.

Even Amy Post, the suffragette who finally convinced Jacobs to record her life enslaved, remarks on the pain Jacobs experienced in retelling her story:

> Though impelled by a natural craving for human sympathy, she passed through a baptism of suffering. Even in recounting her trials to me, in private conversations. The burden of these memories lay heavily upon her spirit— naturally virtuous and refined. . . . Even in talking with me, she wept so much, and seemed to suffer such mental agony, that I felt her story was too sacred to be drawn from her by inquisitive questions, and I left her free to tell as much, or as little, as she chose. (Quoted in Jacobs 1861, 514)

Jacobs makes it clear that it is the shame of her bondage that she suffers in the retelling. That shame, I propose, comes from the experience of becoming an object, especially a sexual object. Her memory of becoming a passive object in moments where resistance was impossible causes her to suffer even in recounting the events.

Jacobs also speaks to the inarticulate position of one who is objectified by the degradations of slavery: "No pen can give an adequate description of the all-pervading corruption produced by slavery" (382); "He came every day; and I was subjected to such insults as no pen can describe. I would not describe them if I could; they were too low, too revolting" (405). It is telling that

Jacobs uses the expression "no pen can describe" since in a literal sense a pen is not a subject capable of describing anything. Jacobs says that she cannot describe the degradation of slavery, which is more than the reader would willingly believe: "The degradation, the wrongs, the vices, that grow out of slavery, are more than I can describe. They are greater than you would willing believe" (361). The world of slavery is not a world of humanity or of subjective articulation, but a world beyond description. It is a world where both slaves and masters are inhumane; masters because of their cruelty and inhumanity, slaves because they have been rendered less than human objects.

In spite of the hardship of testifying, in spite of the paradoxical position into which it put her, Harriet Jacobs eloquently told her story. By so doing, she reinscribed self-respect into the experience of slavery. She talks about the ways in which she maintained her self-respect throughout the degradation of slavery. She describes the dignity, humanity, and intelligence of her grandmother and her parents. In addition to writing the story of self-respect back into her story of slavery, she describes her self-respect as a type of resistance to her owner: "My strongest weapon with him was gone. I was lowered in my own estimation, and had resolved to bear his abuse in silence" (388–89).

Jacobs's autobiography is a testimony to the ways in which slavery, subordination, and oppression work to dismantle self-respect by mutilating one's sense of oneself as a subject or agent. Her testimony expresses the paradoxes of witnessing one's own oppression and degradation. Yet she refuses to allow slavery to define her or her life. Through her descriptions of the ways in which she resists objectification and of the loving community to which she belongs, she reinscribes her subjectivity into an institution designed to strip her of it. Even the title of her narrative, "Incidents in the Life of a Slave Girl," refuses to define her life in terms of slavery; unlike other slave narratives, she resists calling hers "the life of" or "the history of."[1]

On a symbolic level, her use of the alias "Linda Brent" signals her refusal to be defined by her experience of slavery. More than that, it can be read as a sign of the paradoxical position of one witnessing her own slavery and objectification insofar as she uses the alias to distance herself from her experience of objectification. The fact that the alias was necessary to protect her, those close to her, and those who helped her from the "bloodhounds" who could track her down makes the risks involved in witnessing one's own oppression more physically dangerous but not necessarily greater. On the other hand, the greatest benefit of witnessing is working through the trauma of oppression, degradation, and slavery.

In her testimony Jacobs bears witness to the necessity of having someone to listen. She refused to write her autobiography until Amy Post became the sympathetic listener who did not judge or put her testimony on trial. Inside the experience of slavery, Jacobs did have her family, especially her grandmother, who was capable of listening to her without judging. Jacobs ends her narrative by saying that in spite of the pain of recounting her story, "the retrospection is not altogether without solace; for with those gloomy recollections come tender memories of my good old grandmother, like light, fleecy clouds floating over a dark and troubled sea" (513). In some sense, then, Jacobs's is also the story of those witnesses to her life and her testimony who enabled her to maintain her subjectivity even as she was objectified by slavery.

Along with other slave narratives, Harriet Jacobs's *Incidents in the Life of a Slave Girl* shows how subjectivity and agency are produced through witnessing. In his introduction to *Bearing Witness: Selections from African-American Autobiography in the Twentieth Century,* Henry Louis Gates Jr. describes the importance of bearing witness to one's subjectivity:

> Through autobiography, these writers could, at once, shape a public "self" in language, and protest the degradation of their ethnic group by the multiple forms of American racism. The ultimate form of protest, certainly, was to register in print the existence of a "black self" that had transcended the limitations and restrictions that racism had placed on the personal development of the black individual. (1991, 3)

Yet, as Gates points out, it is through bearing witness itself that the black self is created and re-created against slavery. He proposes that

> if the individual black self could not exist before the law, it could, and would, be forged in language, as a testimony at once to the supposed integrity of the black self and against the social and political evils that delimited individual and group equality for all African-Americans. The will to power for black Americans was the will to write; and the predominant mode that this writing would assume was the shaping of a black self in words. (1991, 4)

Gates quotes Barbara Mellix's description of the self-creative power of language: "I came to comprehend more fully the generative power of language. I discovered . . . that through writing one can continually bring new selves into being, each with new responsibilities and difficulties, but also with new possibilities. Remarkable power, indeed, I write and continually give birth to myself" (in Gates 1991, 8). Gates concludes that the black autobiographies that he has gathered "endure as chronicles not merely of personal achievement, but of the *impulse to bear witness*" (9). Bearing witness re-constitutes the inner witness even as it is addressed to an external witness. The process of bearing witness begins to repair address-ability and response-ability damaged through slavery and oppression. Bearing witness works-through the trauma of objectification by reinstituting subjective agency as the ability to respond or address oneself.

Gates's description of the process and effects of bearing witness lends support to the thesis that address-ability and response-ability are the conditions for subjectivity. The subject is the result of a response to an address from another and the possibility of addressing itself to another. Oppression, domination, and torture undermine subjectivity by compromising or destroying response-ability necessary for subjectivity. Witnessing can restore subjectivity by restoring response-ability. Restoring response-ability is an ethical responsibility to our founding possibility as subjects.

This notion of subjectivity begins to go beyond the categories of subject and object, self and other, which work within scenarios of dominance and subordination. Like Derridean undecidables—pharmakon, hymen, supplement, and so forth—the notion of witnessing with its double sense opens up the possibility of thinking beyond binaries: subject-object, psychoanalysis-history, constative-performative. The relation between historically determined subject positions and infinitely response-able subjectivity insists that we reconceive of history, objectivity, and the constative in relation to subjectivity, psychoanalysis, and the performative. The double meaning of witnessing, as both eyewitness testimony based on firsthand knowledge and testifying to something beyond recognition that cannot be seen, is at the center of subjectivity, which is maintained in the tension between these two meanings. The oppositional pull between the force of historical facts and the force of historical (psychoanalytic) truth both positions the subject in history and necessitates the infinite responsibility of subjectivity. Subjective agency is produced between knowledge and truth. The double meaning of witnessing can be exploited as the productive tension at the center of subjectivity, the tension between historically determined subject positions and infinitely response-able subjectivity. Insofar as this productive tension between forces opens up the possibility of subjectivity itself, it should not be conceived as a rigid binarism.

Bearing witness to one's own oppression works through—both operationally and in the psychoanalytic sense of working-through—the forces whose oppositional pull makes subjectivity possible and ultimately ethical. Subjectivity is held together by the tension between forces of finite history and infinite responsibility. The paradoxical forces of witnessing are not the forces of oppression and domination that pull subjectivity apart and undermine agency. On the contrary, the paradoxical forces of history and analysis, of historically determined subject positions and infinitely response-able subjectivity, of the constative and performative, provide the productive tension that moves us beyond the melancholic choice between dead historical facts or traumatic repetition.[2] The paradoxical forces of witnessing maintain subjectivity through their equilibrium, which is never static and only precariously stable.

By taking othered subjectivity as a point of departure, perhaps we can begin to establish and reestablish the conditions of address-ability and response-ability that make subjectivity and human experience possible and ultimately ethical. Realness and reality are experiential categories that refer to a phenomenological truth rather than a purely historical truth. Witnessing and responding, testifying and listening transform our reality, the realness of our experiences. As Laub suggests, experiences are constituted and reconstituted in the process of witnessing. Reality and experience are themselves processes continually transformed through witnessing. In fact, both individual and social change are possible through the transformative power of witnessing, the power to (re)inscribe humanity and subjective agency into both social and psychic life.

If recognition is necessary to subjectivity, it isn't the kind of recognition identified by Taylor through which we recognize others only when we have understood them and passed judgment on them. It is more than Honneth's conferring respect on others. And it can't begin from Butler's or Kristeva's logic of exclusion or repudiation. To recognize others requires acknowledging that their experiences are real even though they may be incomprehensible to us; this means that we must recognize that not everything that is real is recognizable to us. Acknowledging the realness of another's life is not judging its worth, or conferring respect, or understanding or recognizing it, but responding in a way that affirms response-ability. We are obligated to respond to what is beyond our comprehension, beyond recognition, because ethics is possible only beyond recognition.

5. False Witnesses

Issues of realness and responsibility raise the question of false witnesses. There are many ways of denying responsibility. Refusing to acknowledge one's own response-ability is also to deny one's responsibility. It is possible to tell stories that cover over one's responsibility for social injustice; people do it all the time. What are we to make, for example, of racists testifying to their suffering from "reverse discrimination" or men testifying to their suffering from male privilege? Is it possible to engage with these testimonies in productive ways that don't discount racism or sexism, on the one hand, and don't undermine the significance of testimony, on the other? Can we make distinctions between true and false witnesses?

In *The Alchemy of Race and Rights,* Patricia Williams considers a version of this question when she analyzes the relationship between ownership and testimony. She is concerned with the problems of testimony in a culture where words are a type of currency like money; they "function as the mediators by which we make all things equal, interchangeable" (1991, 31). Image, meaning, and reality are bought and sold as commodities whose value is entirely determined by the market. Williams cites the example of actress Jessica Lange's testimony to Congress on the economic condition of farmers on the basis that she had played the role of a farmer's wife in one of her movies. Williams asks, "What on earth does 'testimony' mean in that context?" (30–31). Williams concludes that the harm is that "it puts reality up for sale and makes meaning fungible: dishonest, empty, irresponsible" (30). At the same time, however, it points up the way in which reality is in fact the effect of various relationships and dialogue.

If reality can be bought and sold, if individuals or groups of people can be disenfranchised from reality itself, then what does it mean to recognize the reality or realness of another person's experience in spite of the fact that we may not comprehend it? Does the reality of Jessica Lange's suffering in the fictional role of a farmer's wife obligate a response, even though her experience of that suffering may be beyond comprehension? My earlier analysis suggests that it is not the reality of one's experience that obligates a response. Rather, it is subjectivity as response-ability itself that obligates a response— not just any response, but a response that nourishes the possibility of response. Only a response that opens rather than closes the possibility of response is a responsible response. And while a responsible response begins in acknowledging another person's reality, it also *performs* the dialogic constitution of reality itself. This is not to deny that there is testimony that closes off the possibility of response, or that there are responses that attempt to deny the subjectivity of the witness. The question is how to respond to these false witnesses in a way that reopens the possibility of witnessing, of responsibility. The process through which reality becomes real is itself hidden in the notion that what is real is what can or will be seen by the eyewitness.

Yet what is real or reality is intimately linked to what Williams calls "subject-position." Williams always insists on interpreting the dynamics of subject positions in any situation. For Williams, the subject position seems to be the social position in which one finds oneself. Considering and interpreting subject positions help distinguish between "true" and "false" witnesses. While Williams makes it clear how not considering subject positions can lead to injustice, Dominick LaCapra's analysis of subject positions in *Representing the Holocaust* makes it clear how truth may be connected to subject positions. LaCapra defines a subject position as a "partial, problematic identity . . . intricately bound up with the other subject-positions any social individual occupies" (1994, 12). Subject positions are social positions that can become overwhelming or totalizing in extreme circumstances of violence or victimization. In these situations, the roles of perpetrator or victim can take over subjective identity, and one's present becomes the compulsive repetition (acting-out) of past instances of perpetration or victimization. LaCapra argues that in order to overcome the repetition compulsion driving totalizing subject positions, it is crucial to critically reflect on subject positions in their relations and social context. "This process," he says, " is not purely individual or psychological but linked, in however undogmatic and mediated a manner, with ethical, social, and political concerns" (12).

A crucial factor in the ability to transform totalizing subject positions into more fluid and response-able subjectivity is an acknowledgment of the differences in power and authority in different social positions. While our subjectivities are the result of witnessing and dialogic relationships, and therefore at their core a matter of ethics and responsibility, in our day-to-day interactions dialogues always take place within concrete political situations that constitute differential relations between participants.

Addressing the problem of false witnesses requires attention to political or power differentials in our relationships to one another. It requires attention to the difference in our subject positions. In the context of discussing historical representations of the Holocaust, LaCapra concludes that "certain statements or even entire orientations may seem appropriate for someone in a given subject-position but not in others. (It would, for example, be ridiculous if I tried to assume the voice of Elie Wiesel or of Saul Friedlander. There is a sense in which I have no right to these voices.)" (46). Historical, political, social, and economic circumstances govern what subject positions are available to whom. Of course, these circumstances and interpretations of them can change such that subject positions and their availability change, too. The point that LaCapra makes is that he has no right to speak as a Holocaust survivor because he isn't one. He does not occupy that subject position, and to pretend to do so is certainly to become a false witness.

LaCapra's notion of appropriate subject positions again echoes his continual insistence throughout his work on critical reflection and attention to social relationships and transference. It is only by attending to social context and subject positions in relation to their social context that we can begin to talk about appropriate subject positions. Identifying false witnesses begins with critically examining and interpreting the social context within which we speak. But, as LaCapra warns, subject positions are never totalizing unless they are caught in the self-destructive world of the repetition compulsion. For LaCapra this means that we must continually complicate our ideas about who we are and how we relate to others. Our relationships are never as simple as they might seem. Moreover, our self-identity is always formed in relation to others, even—maybe especially—those we claim to disregard.

Another implication of LaCapra's analysis is that false witnessing is associated with acting-out or the repetition compulsion. Recall my earlier discussion of the difference between acting-out and working-through. False witnesses act-out the falsity of their testimony even as they testify to its truth. Testimony is false if it is merely acting-out rather than working-through the ways in which the indebtedness to others is repressed. While acting-out is unavoidable, as we have seen, there are ways of overcoming the repetition compulsion. On the other hand, there are ways of denying or closing off the possibility of working-through. This type of acting-out or repetition can be especially painful to blacks and women, for example, insofar as it is a repetition of the denial of their experiences; and it is certainly frustrating for anyone committed to response-able dialogue. These testimonies that repeat discrimination and oppression by denying differential subject positions and different social situations work to close off the social space necessary for symbolizing affects in an effort to work-through the suffering of being othered and dehumanized.

Recall Eric Santner's thesis that working-through is possible only when there is the social space and symbols available with which to articulate the trauma of oppression in a way that binds affects to words. Binding affects to words, as Kristeva also emphasizes, is necessary in order to work-through trauma. Kristeva argues that it is through imaginative interpretation or elaboration that we can bind words and affects and heal wounds. And while she diagnoses the ways in which contemporary culture flattens the psyche and prevents such healing interpretations, there is still the possibility of psychic revolt within our specular media culture. Santner goes further than Kristeva in suggesting the connection between social and psychic space. As we also learned from Fanon, psychic space must be nourished by social space in order to flourish. Following Freud, Santner maintains that trauma prevents the appropriate affect—anxiety. The trauma is repeated compulsively because the affect is not bound to the experience. The missing affect can "be recuperated only in the presence of an empathic witness . . . who co-constitute[s] the space in which loss may come to be symbolically and affectively mastered" (Santner 1990, 25). Santner emphasizes, however, that in order to bind affects and words this witnessing requires social space and symbols: "Homeopathy without appropriate affect becomes a purely mechanical procedure that can never lead to empowerment; without a social space in which this affect can be recuperated, the homeopathic operation becomes a sort of elegiac loop that must repeat itself endlessly" (Santner 1990, 25).

Judith Butler uses Santner's analysis of the need for social spaces when she points to the lack of social spaces in which to grieve for people dying from AIDS (1997b, 148). Because AIDS is associated with homosexuality and drug use, and these activities are marginalized, a socially acceptable space for grieving does not exist. Butler describes how grief becomes compounded without a socially acceptable outlet: "Insofar as the grief remains unspeakable, the rage over the loss can redouble by virtue of remaining unavowed. And if that rage is publicly proscribed, the melancholic effects of such a proscription can achieve suicidal proportions. The emergence of collective institutions for grieving are thus crucial to survival, to reassembling community, to rearticulating kinship, to reweaving sustaining relationships" (1997b, 148). Bell hooks speaks to the need for public space for collective grieving when she discusses the despair felt by black people after the deaths of civil rights leaders:

> Wounded in that space where we would know love, black people collectively experience intense pain and anguish about our future. The absence of public spaces where that pain could be articulated, expressed, shared meant that it was held in—festering, suppressing the possibility that this collective grief would be reconciled in community even as ways to move beyond it and continue resistance struggle would be envisioned. . . . a life threatening despair took hold in black life. (1994a, 245)

Affect can be deadly without a socially sanctioned space in which, and symbols available with which, to express it.

Affirmative Action Debates and the Repetition of Racism

The connection between social and psychic space can be seen in the current controversies over affirmative action and "reverse discrimination." Santner's and LaCapra's extensions of psychoanalysis to social problems are instructive when applied to the vexed problem of affirmative action. Freud's analysis of acting-out or repetition and remembering or working-through, along with LaCapra's applications of Freud's notion of transference and leveling comparisons, is helpful in thinking about recent shifts in attitudes toward affirmative action. LaCapra's analysis of misleading comparisons that work to normalize horror and level differential circumstances is useful in thinking about how testimonies of reverse discrimination and suffering from one's privilege, which may appear to be balanced accounts of discrimination and suffering, actually work to deny oppression and minimize instances of discrimination and suffering. LaCapra describes "leveling comparisons" as the tendency of historians to compare one trauma or disaster to another and thereby "evenhandedly show[ing] the distribution of horror in history" (1994, 48). In the case of testimonies of "reverse discrimination," the harms of allegedly being denied admission into professional school on the basis of being white are compared to the documented harms of slavery and racist discrimination. Testimonies of reverse discrimination have the effect of normalizing suffering rather than working-through racist or sexist attitudes that perpetuate suffering. Rather than critically and self-critically reflecting on differences in social positions, these testimonies act-out or repeat the refusal to value differences, which gives rise to racism and sexism. Of course, LaCapra's analysis indicates that connections and distinctions between racism and sexism, between the experience of blacks and women, and especially black women and white women, are necessary in order to avoid the very leveling discourse he warns against.

In this section, I will diagnose the shift in affirmative action debates from discussions of past discrimination and retribution to discussions of "reverse discrimination" and a color-blind society, using psychoanalytic notions of repetition, transference, and projection. I will use two principles already discussed: Freud's notion that we repeat what we don't remember, while we remember only what we have worked-through by means of self-critical interpretation, and LaCapra's notion that unacknowledged transference or leveling comparisons can result in either assimilation or denial of the past.

Recent debates over affirmative action are displays of symptomatic forgetfulness and repetitions of discrimination, leveling comparisons and unacknowledged transference, rather than working-through. Across the country, affirmative action policies in hiring, contracting, and admission to higher education are being challenged in the name of a color-blind society. The argument is that considerations of race or sex are always forms of discrimination, and that we can't uphold the principle of equality if we acknowledge that race or sex makes a difference. Equality must be defended by insisting that differences don't make any difference, that we are, or should be, a color- and gender-blind society. The powerful rhetoric of the civil rights movement—rhetoric of equality, civil rights, and an end of discrimination—has been reappropriated by conservative forces to overturn affirmative action policies and legislation. While this example supports Butler's analysis of the transformative power of the performative, it is an example not of an ethical transformation but of a reactionary formation, which in fact undermines the possibility of ethical relations. Ethical relations are engendered through self-critical interpretative analysis in which repressed transferential identifications and disassociations are opened to question and diagnosed. In Butler's work, the very performance of such critical interpretive diagnoses supplements and challenges the constative level of her work, namely, the thesis that the performative itself is transformative.

Through an analysis of recent affirmative action legislation and court cases I hope to support Butler's theory that rhetoric is a repetition of operations of citation that can either subvert or conserve dominant discourse. And while this analysis supports Butler's thesis that performative repetitions can work to resignify words within different contexts, it also gives a powerful example of how the resignification process itself can be either subversive or conservative. In the case of affirmative action, however, it is not simply that dominant discourse is subverted or conserved but, rather, that dominant discourse is refigured to serve conservative rather than liberatory ends. This suggests that Butler's theory of performative resignification needs to be supplemented with a theory that can explain how to distinguish between conservative and liberatory resignifications. I have argued that a notion of working-through as an ongoing process of self-critical interpretation in which the self is conceived as fundamentally dialogic and relational rather than sovereign is necessary to make a theory of the performative work as a political theory.

While Butler has persuasively shown that the sovereign conception of the self is an illusion produced through dependence on others, her one-sided insistence on the pain and domination of that dependence prevents us from adequately distinguishing between necessary and unnecessary oppression and domination. Butler describes the internalization of social norms that makes subjectivity possible as a process of subordination and subjection akin to Hegel's insistence that subjectivity requires enslavement. But if domination and enslavement are necessary in order to become subjects, then can we even imagine compassion, peace, or justice? If, as Butler insists, social existence means necessarily killing off the other and maintaining it as socially dead, can we get beyond murder and sacrifice (1997b, 27)?

My analysis of affirmative action also suggests that the notion that empowering one means disempowering another or that recognizing one means annihilating another, is itself a conservative conception of individual or group relationships. This notion of a fixed oscillation of power—a simple movement between domination and transgression—works against the idea that power is not something we possess. Butler's repeated turns to the rhetoric of ownership and alienation unintentionally return us to a discourse of self-made and sovereign subjects. It is this discourse that fuels the fires of hate speech and the conservative turn in recent affirmative action debates. The idea that identity is bought at the expense of others, that empowering one group means disempowering another, can only lead to war and violence, the standard tools of conservative forces.

In a world where more people confront more differences than maybe ever before, how can we theorize relations to difference that both explain current identity struggles over sexual, ethnic, racial, cultural, or national identities and open up the possibility for transforming hostile relations into peaceful relations? Perhaps with Butler, before we can talk about peace, we need to ask about power. But how can we transform oppressive relations into empowering relations? How can we transform abusive power relations into ethical ones?

While performative repetitions can resignify words and practices, changing the structure or terms of performative repetition itself requires critical self-analysis and interpretation that acknowledge our transferential investments in others and otherness. Changing the structure of performative repetitions is crucial to the possibility of ethical relations in an era when relations are seen as struggles for recognition at best and hostile attempts to annihilate difference at worst. We need to reconceive of power relations such that empowering one is not disempowering another. In order to imagine and create democratic political relations, ethical social relations, and compassionate personal relations, we need to work-through performative repetitions of us-versus-them notions of subjectivity and identity toward conceptions of subjectivity and identity that acknowledge not only the ways in which our dependence on others causes pain and subordination but also the ways in which our dependence on others gives birth to and nourishes our imaginative and innovative capacity to find meaning in life.

A look at affirmative action debates will be instructive in how the lack of self-critical interpretation leaves us with conservative repetitions of racism. In the name of preserving a color-blind society, affirmative action policies are being overturned in courts and voted out at polls. Affirmative action policies are now called policies that grant "preferential treatment." Appeals to affirmative action as a remedy for past discrimination and racism fall flat in courts and on street corners in an era when affirmative action policies are themselves viewed as racist discrimination. Opponents of affirmative action argue that current affirmative action policies discriminate against whites and men. They also argue that past discrimination has no effect in the present, that racism and sexism are things of the past, and therefore that affirmative action policies only undermine the goal of a color- and gender-blind society. In these debates, in a leveling move, past discrimination is irrelevant to the present, and present "reverse discrimination" is equated with past discrimination. The past is thereby both assimilated into the present and denied any connection to that present. This double performance of assimilation and denial, however, merely repeats racist and sexist discrimination in a new form.

The Rhetoric of Preference and the Projection of Racism

The language of preferential treatment that has taken over affirmative action debates is a performance of the symptomatic forgetting of a history of preference for white men and the projection of that preference onto women and people of color. The success of the rhetoric of preferential treatment was demonstrated in California with Proposition 209 and more recently in Washington with Initiative 200. On November 3, 1998, Washington voters overwhelmingly passed I-200, modeled on California's Proposition 209. Called the Washington State Civil Rights Act, it reads: "The state shall not discriminate against, or grant preferential treatment to, any individual or group on the basis of race, sex, color, ethnicity, or national origin in the operation of public employment, public education, or public contracting." The language of Initiative 200, the language of preferential treatment that has replaced the language of affirmative action, promotes the unhealthy idea that we are enemies and that the survival of one means the death or exclusion of the other. More than this, the language of preferential treatment repeats racism and sexism.

First, the language of granting preferential treatment assumes a kind of either-or logic that turns all difference into opposition. At the heart of I-200 and this language is an exclusionary conception of difference that presumes that to prefer one is to exclude the other, to prefer one is to reject the other without reason. When differences between people are seen as oppositions, then people are positioned as antagonists, even enemies, in the end, fighting for their right to be themselves. But if we start from the assumption that anything or anyone different from ourselves is a threat, then we can never imagine compassionate personal relations, peaceful social relations, or democratic political relations.

The language of preference presupposes this kind of oppositional model and thereby reinscribes racial and gender hierarchies. Preference is always at another's expense. In the case of Initiative 200, when preferential treatment is granted on the basis of race or sex—that is, granted to people of color or women—the presumption is that it is taken away from whites and men. Initiative 200 is intended to protect whites and men from that type of exclusion. The language of preference paints the picture in black versus white, women versus men. With this rhetoric, affirmative action policies become mere preferences for blacks or women over white men. The language of preference is a symptom of this unhealthy us-versus-them conception of difference. The power of the rhetoric of exclusion, however, is demonstrated by the fact that public opinion polls show that people reject "preferential treatment" even while they accept affirmative action (*Seattle Times* Web site, October 27, 1998, 3).

Behind the rhetoric of assimilation, that we are all equal, that we live in a color-blind society, is an oppositional notion of race and gender. This oppositional dynamic is an example of the kind of antagonistic structure that underlies Honneth's struggle for recognition (and that of other theorists of recognition). Honneth presupposes fully formed antagonists struggling to gain mutual recognition. Yet his theory assumes an antagonism that prevents one from ever achieving the goal of mutual recognition. The language of preference in affirmative action debates displays the same kind of self-defeating logic. In the name of a color-blind society and equality, opponents of affirmative action make race and gender into oppositional categories that force people to take sides for or against one race or one gender in a struggle for recognition. In so doing, racist and sexist discrimination is merely repeated in another form.

The rhetoric of preference in affirmative action debates reflects the current hysteria over *undeserving* people of color, women, or foreigners taking jobs and positions that rightfully belong to *deserving* white men.[1] Underlying this rhetoric is the prejudice that white men are deserving and have a right to jobs and education while people of color, women, and foreigners are undeserving and don't have a right to jobs and education. The statement for Initiative 200 in the State of Washington Voters pamphlet (written by conservative talk-show host John Carlson and two Republican state senators, Scott Smith and Jeannette Hayner) expresses this hysterical notion that affirmative action programs give jobs to people of color, women, and foreigners who are less qualified and therefore less deserving than white men: I-200 prohibits "those programs that use race or gender to select a less qualified applicant over a more deserving applicant for a public job, contract or admission to a state college or university" (14). Thus I-200 is seen as a remedy for programs that supposedly give preference to less qualified and less deserving women and minorities.

The pamphlet uses an example of a young woman who grew up in poverty, worked her way through community college and then the University of Washington, and was denied admission to the university's law school in spite of good grades and test scores. Against protests from the dean of the law school, the statement claims that this dean said that the young woman would have been admitted if she were black. The pamphlet concludes that "it's time for government to get out of the discrimination business" (14). This example is telling because the proponents of I-200 use it to imply that less qualified applicants are being admitted to law school. Yet what the dean supposedly said is that if the young woman were black, having the exact same qualifications, the same test scores and grades, she would have been admitted. As an example of using race to "select a less qualified applicant over a more deserving applicant," this case suggests that being black in itself makes one less qualified and less deserving, and being white makes one more deserving and more qualified. In the pamphlet this covert racism is put forth using the civil rights rhetoric: "Our Laws Should Be Colorblind" and "Equal Treatment, Regardless of Race" (14).

In this context, however, the rhetoric of equal treatment and color blindness operates to normalize whiteness. White is not considered a color, and equal treatment is used to cover up important and relevant differences between people, a cover-up that leads to unjust treatment. Take the example from the voter's pamphlet: although we find out that the young woman denied admission to the law school is not black, she is not racially marked, so we are to assume that she is white.

The rhetoric of preferential treatment promotes a false assimilation by perpetuating the normalization of whiteness and maleness through both overt and covert sexism and racism. First, initiatives like I-200 are *not* intended to apply to white men. This is obvious in the case of I-200 since the only groups covered by state affirmative action programs not targeted by the initiative are groups made up of mostly white men, veterans, and people with disabilities. The *Seattle Times* reports in its Web site that "white men were included [in affirmative action statistics] because they make up about 70 percent of the veterans and about half of the disabled" (October 27, 1998, 7). Ironically, now that I-200 has passed, the state will continue practicing affirmative action for groups that are largely composed of white men.

In addition to the obvious ways that white men are protected from I-200, there are less visible yet more dangerous ways in which white men are protected from and by the rhetoric of preferential treatment. White men are not considered the beneficiaries of preferential treatment, in spite of the fact that civil rights legislation and affirmative action policies were originally instituted because white men were almost exclusively preferred to people of color and women when it came to employment, admission to higher education, and government contracts. By denying the racist and sexist past that gave preference almost exclusively to white men, and projecting preference onto women and people of color, opponents of affirmative action propel us into the vicious cycle of repeating the past, of merely acting-out, instead of interpreting the past and working-through racism and sexism in order to change the future.

In the contemporary discourse, when we talk about preferential treatment, we are talking about granting preference to people of color and women over white men and not vice versa. Why is that? Why don't we talk about granting preference to white men? There are at least two reasons why white men are not the targets of initiatives to overturn affirmative action even if they are the beneficiaries. First, *white* and *male* operate as invisible norms or unmarked categories within our culture, and norms are not considered preferences but natural facts. Second, the rhetoric of preference connotes a lack of standards or qualifications because preference suggests subjective choice rather than objective standards; white men are presumed to have qualifications and meet standards, so they don't need to be granted preferential treatment.

The fact that contemporary discussions of preferential treatment operate as if they only apply to people of color and women is telling. The discourse of preference reflects the fact that in our culture only blacks and other people of color are racially marked and only women are sexually marked or gendered. This is why when a black person or a woman occupies a position normally held by a white man, he or she is often referred to as a "black lawyer" or a "lady lawyer," a "black doctor" or a "woman doctor." Gender is specified when a woman occupies a position normally held by a man or vice versa, and race is only specified when referring to nonwhites. Even the seemingly politically correct phrase *people of color* operates as if white is not also a color.

So, too, when we talk about culture, we talk about Black culture, Asian culture, Latino culture, but not White culture. This is *not* because there is no White culture. Rather, it is because whiteness operates as an unmarked culture, a culture not marked by race, the norm, the standard, regular culture. All the other cultures, all the other races, they are different while white culture is the same, the invisible norm. Whites are not seen as different. Difference itself has become a racially marked and sexed category.

In *White Women, Race Matters: The Social Construction of Whiteness* sociologist Ruth Frankenberg interviews more than thirty white women and concludes that, with the exception of Jewish women, most do not consider themselves racially or culturally marked (1993). Frankenberg quotes extensively from interviews to substantiate her conclusion that whiteness operates as an invisible norm. One example stands out: a woman describes her first experience noticing racial differences when one of her friends started dating a Mexican American: her friend's boyfriend listened to "Mexican" music while they all listened to "regular" music (1993, 67). *Regular* of course meant white Anglo American music.

Whiteness and maleness are not considered different but normal. If it is normal to hire or admit whites and males over blacks and females, then it cannot be seen as a preference. Norms do not operate as preferences but as institutional standards or natural facts. Norms only work to normalize insofar as they hide the fact that they are preferences. The language of preference covers over the assumption that white and male operate as the norms against which everything else is defined as different; and difference is seen as a threat. The language of preference assumes an exclusionary notion of difference that fosters an us-versus-them attitude. And the language of preference assumes that preferences are only given to minorities and women.

In addition to identifying racial and sexual differences with people of color and females rather than with whites and males, in this context the word *preference* also connotes undeserving and unqualified. If someone is chosen on the basis of preference, then there are no objective criteria or standards used to make the choice. Preference is seen as something subjective, justified by tastes or whims. This is why people of color and women can be admitted or hired on the basis of preference while whites and males are not considered the beneficiaries of preference. Because the language of preference suggests undeserved benefits, many women and people of color voted against I-200; they wanted their qualifications and hard work acknowledged. Recall the example from the voters' pamphlet that implied that being black made an applicant to law school less qualified and less deserving than a white applicant with the exact same credentials. We talk of preferences in reference to people of color and women but not white men, in spite of the fact that this country was built on the government granting preferential treatment to white men. Of course, rhetorically, the government could not grant preference to white men, since they are presumed to be deserving and qualified. Preference for white men has become normalized into so-called standards and objective criteria.

If the word *preference* is suspect because it presumes an exclusionary or oppositional notion of difference and because it smuggles in racist and sexist notions of qualifications, standards, and deserts, the word *grant* is suspect because it reinscribes the very racial power imbalance that affirmative action programs were designed to correct. Indeed, in the name of color-blind laws, it reinscribes racial hierarchies. Granting is the privilege of those in power who have the sovereignty to give to those who are powerless. In the case of I-200 the state government is the sovereign; the granting in question, however, is not done by some abstract government but by those people invested with the authority to grant. The language of I-200 suggests that those who have the power to grant are not women and people of color. Indeed, women and people of color are placed in the position of receiving the bounties given to them in their powerlessness by those more powerful. The grantors are in the active subject position, while the grantees—people of color and women— are in the passive object position. The very rhetoric of "granting preference to" renders people of color and women passive objects and then implies that because they are passive objects, they are undeserving. In the circular logic of affirmative action opponents, those who are powerless are so because they are undeserving. Like the rhetoric of preference, the rhetoric of granting reflects the hysterical notion that undeserving blacks and women are being given jobs that should go to more deserving white men.

The most obvious problem with the language of I-200, however, is that if you voted no on I-200, then you were voting not only to permit the state to grant preferential treatment on the basis of race, sex, color, ethnicity, or national origin, but you were also voting to permit the state to discriminate against people on the basis of race, sex, color, ethnicity, or national origin. The initiative reads: "The state shall not discriminate against, or grant preferential treatment to. . . ." By combining the language of discrimination against and preferential treatment to, the authors of I-200 put proponents of affirmative action in a sort of double bind.

At this point, I would like to turn from the language of I-200 to the principles behind it: "Our laws should be color-blind" and "Equal Treatment, Regardless of Race." The way that these principles have been reappropriated and deployed both assimilates the past into the present and denies any connection between the past and present. Principles of formal equality so powerful in the civil rights movement are being used to overlook important differences between people—physical, cultural, historical, and social. In the contemporary context, people are not being treated equally: people are being discriminated against on the basis of race, sex, and national origin, so the use of principles of equal treatment in this context actually perpetuates real inequalities because they are employed without consideration of past injustice and differences in social position. To illustrate my point, I will discuss three examples of court cases in which the judges' use of the principle of equal treatment works to deny historical differences between race, class, and gender and thereby repeats racism, classism, and sexism. In these cases, the rhetoric of equality is employed toward unjust ends because obvious real-world inequalities and differences in social position are ignored in the name of an abstract formal principle of metaphysical equality.

First, let's look at the 1989 Supreme Court case *City of Richmond v. J. A. Croson Co.* After determining that discrimination resulted in less than 1 percent of city construction contracts going to minority contractors in a city whose population is more than 50 percent black, the City of Richmond set a goal of 30 percent for city contracts with minority contractors (cited in Williams 1991, 104–5).

The Supreme Court ruled that:

> We, therefore, hold that the city has failed to demonstrate a compelling interest in apportioning public contracting opportunities on the basis of race. To

accept Richmond's claim that past societal discrimination alone can serve as the basis for rigid racial *preferences* would be to open the door to competing claims for "remedial relief" for every disadvantaged group. The dream of a Nation of equal citizens in a society where race is irrelevant to personal opportunity and achievement would be lost in a mosaic of shifting *preferences* based on inherently unmeasurable claims of past wrongs. Courts would be asked to evaluate the extent of the prejudice and consequent harm suffered by various minority groups. Those whose societal injury is thought to exceed some arbitrary level of tolerability then would be entitled to *preferential* classification. We think such a result would be contrary to both the letter and the spirit of a constitutional provision whose central command is equality. (109 S.Ct.706 [1989], 730; my emphasis)[2]

What is striking is that the Court justifies ruling against affirmative action by alluding to the overwhelming numbers of disadvantaged who have suffered the harms of prejudice: there are just too many for the court to deal with. The numbers are too great and the harms are beyond calculation ("inherently unmeasurable"), yet this huge harm to huge numbers becomes the reason to do nothing, in the name of equality. Using the kind of leveling comparison analyzed by LaCapra, the court equates the harms of any sort of disadvantage or prejudice and thereby renders remediation impossible. The court then dismisses those harms by calling them "arbitrary," ignoring the statistical data confirming racism in municipal contracting in Richmond.

Like the authors of I-200, the Supreme Court reduced affirmative action to "rigid racial preferences," "a mosaic of shifting preferences," and "preferential classification," which it claims go against the principle of equality. It is the rhetoric of preference that allows the court to suggest that both claims of harm from discrimination and their remedies are arbitrary. This language has the arbitrariness of mere subjective tastes or whims built into it. Using the language of preference, the dream of a Nation in which race is irrelevant becomes the justification for a racist status quo, where a city like Richmond can have a majority of black residents and still give city contracts to almost exclusively white contractors. By denying a past in which race was relevant to success in business, the court promotes a false assimilation of past and present in order to deny the present effects of our racist past and render race irrelevant to the present. Is race really irrelevant in the city offices in Richmond? Aren't we living in a dream world completely out of touch with reality if we blind ourselves to racism in the name of a color-blind society? Because it is a precedent-setting case that has been cited over and over in recent affirmative action decisions, *Croson* has become a very important example of how the rhetoric of equality is employed to justify and perpetuate real inequalities.

Another example is the so-called *Matter of Baby M,* the most famous child custody suit involving surrogacy. Here the inequities are not based on racism, but on classism and sexism.[3] Here again the rhetoric of equal rights covers over and perpetuates real inequalities by denying differences in social position. The *Matter of Baby M* is the appeal that Mary Beth Whitehead made to the New Jersey Supreme Court to challenge the earlier superior court decision that her surrogacy contract with William Stern was valid and that custody of Baby M should go to Stern, the contracting father. The original contract between Whitehead and Stern was signed in February 1985. In March 1986, Baby M was born, but Whitehead refused to relinquish the baby to Stern. Early in 1987, Stern sued Whitehead for custody of the baby and sought the enforcement of the surrogacy contract. Custody of the baby was awarded to him. The New Jersey Supreme Court overturned the superior court's decision that the surrogacy contract was valid but awarded custody of the baby to Stern anyway.

The *Matter of Baby M* was argued as a battle between the biological mother's and father's equal rights: Whitehead's right to the companionship of her child and Stern's right to procreate. But debates over equal rights gloss over important gender, class, race, and social differences that make the surrogacy contract possible and appealing in the first place. In other words, there are inequalities built into a surrogacy contract that are overlooked by the courts when these contracts are discussed only in terms of equal rights. First, the surrogacy arrangement demands different investments from the biological father and the biological mother. The father provides his sperm; the mother provides not only her egg and womb but also nine months of her life and the pain of childbirth. If the parties to the contract were truly equal, then men wouldn't need women to birth their babies. Second, very few women would agree to a surrogacy arrangement without payment for their services. Most women who engage in paid surrogacy are poor or in debt. Most men who contract surrogates are considerably more financially secure than the women whom they hire. This factor becomes crucial in deciding custody, although it is never discussed in terms of this built-in financial inequality.

In this case the lower court Judge Sorkow noted that the Whiteheads' house was too small and that Whitehead's concern for her daughter's education was suspect in light of her own lack of education. In contrast, the judge pointed out that the Sterns had a new house and could provide the child with "music lessons," "athletics," and a certain college education (*Stern v. Whitehead* 1987, 74–75). Supreme Court Justice Wilentz also noted the financially superior position of the Sterns, whose "finances are more than adequate, their circle of friends supportive, and their marriage happy," while Whitehead's "finances were in serious trouble" (*Matter of Baby M* 1988, 1258–59). The court was concerned about Whitehead's "omniscient" attitude toward her child since she claimed to know what her cries meant; as a result, the court concluded that the Sterns would give the baby more independence than Whitehead.

All of these factors are the result of differences built into the arrangement. College education and music lessons are possible only for those who are financially secure. Gender stereotypes and biases mean that the surrogacy contract itself makes the mother suspect because she is "willing to sell her child," while the same contract makes the father more capable of "raising an independent child." The contract sets up the mother as an evil woman who would give away—worse, sell—her baby, while the father comes to the child's rescue. The discourse here creates the illusion that the parties are equal before the law and have equal rights, but in reality social inequalities ensure the outcome before the litigants even enter the courtroom.

One final example that brings out the absurdity of the principle of formal equality in the face of real differences is the 1972 case of *Gilbert v. General Electric*. General Electric's employee health insurance policy excluded pregnancy-related disabilities. Women employees sued, arguing that GE's health insurance policy discriminated against them. The court ruled that the policy did not discriminate against women since pregnancy-related disabilities were equally excluded for men, too. In the name of equality, the court denied the most obvious, if not significant, difference between men and women—that women get pregnant and men don't.[4]

This kind of thinking is analogous to the statement in the Washington State Voters' pamphlet in support of I-200: "The government should not use race or gender to treat applicants for employment or education opportunities differently. Why? Because *all* Americans deserve protection from race or sex discrimination" (14). All Americans, that is, except for those who do in fact suffer from race or sex discrimination. Since Washington State already has civil rights legislation that prohibits discrimination on the basis of race or sex, *all Americans* in this context must mean racially and sexually unmarked white men. Ruth Frankenberg concludes from her interviews in *White Women, Race Matters* that like *white*, *American* also operates as a racially and culturally unmarked category (1993, 229). Americans are assumed to be white, and when they aren't the word *American* is qualified with *Mexican, Asian, African* to signify difference from "regular" Americans.

Just as the court ruled that if pregnancy-related disabilities aren't covered for *men or women* at GE, then we are all treated equally, or if *men like women* freely choose to take birth control pills or not and suffer the consequences of their choice, then we are all really the same, I-200 implies that if white men aren't discriminated against, then all Americans are treated equally. We might as well say that if the black contractors in Richmond were white, then they too would get the city contracts. Or if Mary Beth Whitehead had been Stern, then she too would have gotten custody of Baby M.

This logic is symptomatic of what LaCapra identifies as the assimilation of differences that results from unacknowledged and unexamined transference in relation to others and our past. Unacknowledged transference leads to false identifications that become the catalyst for repetitions of past discrimination in the guise of equality. This reverse logic, the logic of arguments against so-called reverse discrimination, raises the question: when we talk of being equal, equal to whom? Once again whites and males appear as the standard, the norm. *Equality* in this context means equal to white men. This is not to say that blacks and females will receive equal opportunities or equal distribution of wealth, as we have seen from these three court cases. On the contrary, it means that they will have to compete with white men in spite of the social inequalities that prevent them from benefiting from equal opportunities or equal distribution of wealth. The reverse logic of this type of rhetoric of equality is that if they were white men, then they too would receive the same benefits. Of course, this logic completely ignores the fact that they are not white men; it ignores the reality that blacks and women are still subject to statistically verifiable as well as more qualitative social inequalities in almost every aspect of life.

"Reverse Discrimination" and Leveling Differences

I was teaching at the University of Texas at Austin (UT) when the Fifth Circuit Court was hearing the *Cheryl Hopwood v. the State of Texas* case. In the March 1996 case, the court ruled that the affirmative action admission policy used by the university's law school was discriminatory. In the immediate wake of the decision there was turmoil in the administration at UT. The *Hopwood* decision was reached in early spring, just before the next year's students were to be admitted to the university. For fear of being sued again, in the middle of undergraduate and graduate admissions the administration had to find an immediate way to erase race from consideration for admissions or fellowships. The provost's office acted quickly to send out a memo giving us, especially those involved in admissions selections, detailed instructions on how to use *white-out* to cover over all mentions of race on application forms or application materials. The use of white-out (indeed, in this case an apt name for an office-supply item) to cover any mention of race can be seen as a metaphor for the conservative reappropriation of the civil rights rhetoric of a color-blind society and equal treatment regardless of race, rhetoric that in this context works to level differences and normalize whiteness.[5]

In March 1996, affirmative action policies in admissions were eliminated in the University of Texas system after the Fifth Circuit Court ruled in *Hopwood* that the affirmative action admission policy used by the law school was discriminatory. Four white students sued the university, arguing that minority students with the same or lesser credentials were given preferential treatment. In 1994, the Texas district court had ruled that although affirmative action policies were justified on the grounds of remedying past discrimination and for the sake of educational diversity, the specific segregated system used at the UT law school was unconstitutional since minority and nonminority candidates were never directly compared to each other in the admissions process. Relying heavily on Chief Justice William Powell's opinion in the Supreme Court decision *Bakke v. the Regents of the University of California,* the Texas district court ruled that as long as candidates were all evaluated together, race and ethnicity along with GPA and test scores could be viewed as criteria for admission. In *Bakke* Justice Powell concluded that race and ethnicity could be "pluses" that tipped the scale in favor of a candidate just as long as they weren't the only reason for admission and all candidates were evaluated together using the same criteria. As an aside, one interesting implication of Powell's statement is that so-called objective criteria like GPAs and test scores could be seen as the same kind of criteria as race, ethnicity, background, and any other factors a university might consider relevant to admissions or questions of quality or qualifications. In *Hopwood* the court concluded that the plaintiffs would not have gotten into UT law school even if race had not been used in the admissions policy. They ruled that although UT's segregated admissions policy is unconstitutional, affirmative action policies in general are justified. The court awarded the plaintiffs $1 each in damages.

Backed by conservative organizations looking to overturn affirmative action and hoping for more damages, the plaintiffs appealed the case to the U.S. Fifth Circuit Court. The case was heard by three of the seventeen judges serving the circuit court. The majority opinion written by two judges agreed with the lower court that the law school's admissions policy was unconstitutional, but they went much further when they concluded that Justice Powell's opinion in *Bakke* was not precedent setting, that affirmative action policies cannot be justified on the general basis of remedying past discrimination (after *Croson v. the City of Richmond*) or for the sake of educational diversity (after *Adarand v. Metro Broadcasting*). Seven of the justices thought that the court in *Hopwood* had gone too far in overturning Supreme Court precedent rather than following the law of the land as set by the Supreme Court; the motion to have the case heard again and decided by the entire panel of seventeen justices was rejected by a majority vote of 10–7. The Fifth Circuit also shifted the burden of proof from the plaintiffs to the defendant, so UT had to prove that the students would not have been admitted anyway. And they reopened the question of damages, which, they said in a perverse echo of *Croson*'s "unmeasurable harms," "opens a panoply of potential relief" (32). A panoply of relief and potential damages is a scary prospect for any university employing affirmative action policies (even those like the University of Texas, which was originally ordered to develop such policies by the U.S. Department of Health, Education, and Welfare).

In the face of a backlash against so-called preferential treatment, proponents of affirmative action have appealed to diversity as a social ideal, especially in educational institutions. And although the appeal to the rhetoric of diversity has not captured the public imagination in the way that the appeal to the rhetoric of preferential treatment has—evidenced by the success of anti–affirmative action ballot measures in California and Washington—until recently, with Justice Powell's opinion in *Bakke* as precedent, it had legally succeeded in protecting affirmative action programs in educational institutions, if not in the workplace (see *US v. Fordice* [1992]; *Podberesky v. Kirwan* [1992]). The precedent set by the Fifth Circuit Court's decision in *Hopwood*, however, destroys the diversity defense for affirmative action policies, even in education. *Hopwood* put another nail in the coffin of arguments for affirmative action based on past discrimination and completely destroyed the use of diversity arguments to justify affirmative action policies.

> The majority opinion in the *Hopwood* appeal states that the use of race, in and of itself, to choose students simply achieves a student body that looks different. Such a criterion is no more rational on its own terms than would be choices based upon the physical size or blood type of applications. . . . Accordingly, we see the case law as sufficiently established that the use of ethnic diversity simply to achieve racial heterogeneity, *even as part of the consideration of a number of other factors,* is unconstitutional. (No. 94-50569 *Hopwood et al. v. State of Texas et al.* 1994, 17; my emphasis)

The court also makes a persuasive argument that race and gender are not determinant of an individual's beliefs and viewpoint and that "to believe that a person's race controls his point of view is to stereotype him" (18). The court concludes that "if the law school continues to operate a disguised or overt racial classification system in the future, its actors could be subject to actual and punitive damages" (34–35).

It becomes clear in the court's statement that the university will risk damages by even mentioning race at all. The court concludes that

> We recognize that the use of some factors such as economic or educational background of one's parents may be somewhat correlated with race. This correlation, however, will not render the use of the factor unconstitutional if it is not adopted for the purpose of discriminating on the basis of race. As Justice O'Connor indicated in *Hernandez v. New York,* based upon the prosecution's strike of potential jurors who spoke Spanish: "No matter how closely tied or significantly correlated to race the explanation for a preemptory strike may be, the strike does not implicate the Equal Protection Clause unless it is based on race." (53)

The court's view on race and the Equal Protection Clause implies that as long as race is not mentioned, other correlated factors can be considered. Any mention of race, however, is strictly outlawed.

The Equal Protection Clause, designed to protect people of color from racism and discrimination, was used in *Hopwood* to argue against "reverse discrimination" of whites. The *Hopwood* court concluded that individual rights should not be sacrificed for group rights. That is to say that individual white students should not be denied admission to professional schools for the sake of the rights of any group. The court maintained that there is no such thing as group harm in the case of racism. In the end, the court insisted on individual harms and individual rights only, justified by the Equal Protection Clause. A closer look at *Hopwood,* however, reveals a double standard in the use of group harms to justify redress or retribution. There is a slippage between individual and group identity and rights in the *Hopwood* decision. The majority opinion both discounts group identification in the name of individual protection in order to assert Cheryl Hopwood's rights and uses an argument from group identification to assert the harm to Hopwood, that she was discriminated against because of her race. This is to say that Hopwood's individual rights as they are argued in the case are in fact based on her membership in a group, whites or Caucasians. The court recognizes the harm to whites as a group from "reverse discrimination" in admissions policies at the

University of Texas but does not recognize any harm to people of color as a group from racism at the university or anywhere else.

On the issue of remedying past discrimination, the court maintained that "a state does not have a compelling state interest in remedying the present effects of past societal discrimination.... Accordingly, the state's use of remedial racial classifications is limited to the harm caused by a specific state actor" (21). The court ruled that the hostile environment for minorities at the law school and the law school's reputation of racism are the effects of societal discrimination and not discrimination at the law school per se (cf. 25).[6] Although the court admits that remedying present effects of past discrimination is the only grounds on which affirmative action programs can be justified legally, they limit the remedy so that it applies only to past discrimination by state agencies against the *actual* victims of discrimination and not social groups or classes (56). This means that state institutions cannot respond to racism in society or racism in the state or in its institutions, but only to specific instances of racism; then the response can be directed only at those particular individuals harmed by that specific instance of racism. Also, the court in *Hopwood* exacted such a narrow definition of present effects, past discrimination, and the actors involved, that in essence present effects of past discrimination become legally nonexistent. After *Hopwood*, it becomes virtually impossible to prove any present effect of past discrimination.

LaCapra's analysis of transference can be productively applied to the strange configuration of past, present, and future in *Hopwood*. The case displays what LaCapra identifies as "the fear of possession by the past." The *Hopwood* court engaged in both extremes of transference onto the past: totalizing, controlling identification with the past, and total disassociation with the past through the attempt to deny any connection between the present and the past (LaCapra 1985, 72–73). In the name of the future, the *Hopwood* court forgot the past. The lesson we learn from psychoanalysis is that forgetting the past does not lead to a better future but in fact ensures the return of that very past from which we want to disassociate ourselves. Only by interpreting the past with a vigilant attention to the relationship between present and past can we hope for a better future as a result of working-through rather than merely repeating past discrimination.

The *Hopwood* court and current debates over reverse discrimination engage in totalizing identifications with the past that level social and historical differences. The *Hopwood* court concluded that giving preference to blacks and Mexican Americans works to the detriment of whites and nonpreferred minorities (2). The court equated the University of Texas's system for discriminating between applicants with racial discrimination against whites (34). Treating all forms of discrimination as the same, however, conflates past and present and levels significant differences in the physical, emotional, and material effects of racial discrimination. The belief that white students not admitted to law schools or medical schools are victims of reverse racial discrimination is a symptom of the kind of false assimilation, or leveling, of past and present that LaCapra claims results from unacknowledged transference. White students identify with blacks and others who were/are the victims of racial discrimination, and the suffering of the victims of so-called reverse discrimination is equated with the suffering of victims of racial discrimination. Being denied admission to professional school is equated with being denied the right to vote or own property, with being enslaved, lynched, and denigrated through segregation. The harms of racial discrimination are transferred to the beneficiaries of that very discrimination while the responsibility for racial discrimination is projected onto proponents of affirmative action and people of color who allegedly steal jobs and places in professional schools away from more deserving whites.

The *Hopwood* court's use of the distinction between present effects of societal discrimination and present effects of past discrimination is symptomatic of the view of the past diagnosed by LaCapra, which blindly insists on a disassociation between past and present. Denying any connection between past and present allows us to refuse responsibility for past discrimination or its present effects, both effects on whites who benefit from a history of racial discrimination and blacks and others who continue to be disadvantaged by past and present racial discrimination. The *Hopwood* court legislates forgetting the past for the sake of a color-blind future. The effect, however, of forgetting the past, and then forgetting/denying that we have forgotten, is to repeat the very past from which we so ardently disassociate ourselves. This forgetting that we have forgotten is what Edward Casey calls "double oblivion" (1992).

The phenomenon of double oblivion can be seen, for example, in the *Hopwood* court's use of a Fourth Circuit Court decision that struck down the use of race-based scholarships, which were intended to change the university's "poor reputation within the African-American community" because "the atmosphere on campus [was] perceived as being hostile to African-American students" (*Podberesky* 152; *Hopwood* 26). The Fourth Circuit Court concluded that the school's poor reputation was the result of knowledge of its past admission policies excluding African Americans: but "mere knowledge of historical fact is not the kind of present effect that can justify a race-exclusive remedy. If it were otherwise, as long as there are people who have access to history books, there will be programs such as this" (cited in *Hopwood* 26). This reasoning seems to suppose that history is a set of discrete facts that can be known or not known, written in history books, and discontinuous with the present. Historical facts are treated as things that reside in a separate memory compartment that is roped off from current events, beliefs, or attitudes. Past oppression, exclusion, and slavery have no effect on present events because they are not themselves seen as events but as things/facts whose discreteness protects us from their continued effects. The present effects of oppression, exclusion, and slavery are reduced to the effects of schooling—learned history—rather than the lived effects of continued racism in the United States.

With *Hopwood*, racism can no longer be seen as the result of the past but, rather, the result of what the court calls "present societal discrimination," for which there is no legal remedy. Appealing to abstract principles of equality and individual rights, the Fifth Circuit Court applies laws formulated to protect individuals from being discriminated against on the basis of race—laws designed to outlaw racism—in order to eliminate programs designed to address what the court calls "societal discrimination" or racism. It is absurd to think that Cheryl Hopwood and the three other white male students denied admission to the law school were not admitted because they were white when hundreds of white students are admitted and awarded degrees every year. It is equally absurd to argue that Hopwood et al. were not admitted because they were not black, or not Mexican American, when so few blacks and Mexican Americans are admitted and awarded degrees every year. Hopwood et al. were not the victims of racism or discrimination because of their race. If anything, they were "discriminated against" because they didn't have high enough GPAs and LSAT scores.

Calling the denial of admission to medical or law school to white students "discrimination against" or "reverse discrimination" is an example of what LaCapra calls a leveling comparison. In effect, intent, and lived experience, "reverse discrimination" has very little in common with the experience of one who is the object of racism. By denying that the past has present effects, and by conflating present "discrimination" with past discrimination, current court precedent engages in Casey's "double oblivion"—forgetting that the past has been forgotten by "denial, projection, displacement, obfuscation, mystification, and obliteration" (1992, 292). The double movement of this forgetting of forgetting works to annihilate the difference of the past by forgetting "not merely the detail of the memories no longer communally articulated at leisure but of the very sense that this other world exists as importantly different" (295). This is why Casey concludes that collective memory

> is on the verge of *forgetting that it has forgotten* the very fact of the otherness that surrounds and delimits it. The hubris of collective remembering of a monocultural (and usually mono-lingual) sort goes hand in hand with the double oblivion in which cultural differences sink into the obscured and self-obscuring waters of Lethe. (296)

Hopwood's projection of victimization onto whites; the denial of present effects of past discrimination; the assimilation or leveling of any form of discrimination without distinguishing between benign, necessary, or racist forms; and the refusal to see worlds of difference between discrimination against people of color and so-called reverse discrimination toward whites—all of these are symptomatic of double oblivion. In this type of oblivion, cultural differences are forgotten and then remembered through the double movement of forgetting the forgotten for the sake of a monolithic collective memory—in the case of *Hopwood,* a memory of a country founded on equal justice for all regardless of race. Racism is obliterated in the collective memory (of the white court system) for the sake of a future that is not like the past. Yet, as I have argued, forgetting the past through the double oblivion of forgetting what has been forgotten almost guarantees that we will repeat rather than work-through past racism.

Working-through racism requires continually reinterpreting and elaborating our relations to racial difference. We need to continually reinterpret and reanalyze our performance of race relations. What is race? What are race relations? How and why do we conceive of ourselves as raced or not raced? Why are so many people advocating color blindness at this moment in history? This process of interpretation must be a process of witnessing in the sense that we acknowledge our dependence on each other, not just physical but also psychic dependence. Once we acknowledge that our very sense of ourselves as agents, and the subjectivity on which that agency rests, is the result of witnessing relationships to others and otherness, then, and only then, will we feel compelled by the ethical obligation inherent in subjectivity.

What this means in terms of affirmative action is that rather than deny or forget the past, we must continually reinterpret it. We have an ethical obligation rooted in our very subjectivity for the response-ability of others. We must be vigilant in opening up dialogue and responding to others and otherness in ways that open up the possibility of response rather than closing it down. As a society, we must open up social spaces in which otherness and differences can be articulated. Projecting racism on the victims of racism, blaming the victims, denying or willfully forgetting our racist past and its effects on the present, and leveling differences between types of "discrimination" all work to close off responses from people of color.

6. History, Transformation, and Vigilance

One lesson that the repeal of affirmative action should teach us is that neither the mobility or negativity generated by the performative nor the transformative power of interpretation or elaboration alone is sufficient for opening ourselves onto otherness. Working-through is a continual process, and vigilance is also necessary. Vigilance in self-elaboration, self-analysis, self-interpretation is also necessary. That is to say, vigilance in elaborating, analyzing, and interpreting the process through which *we* become who *we* are, the process through which *we* become subjects and those othered. Vigilance in performance, in testifying and witnessing, vigilance in listening for the performance beyond meaning and recognition. Vigilance in listening to the performance not just as a repetition of the law of exclusion but as a repetition of an advent of what is impossible to perform. Vigilance in listening to the silences in which we are implicated and through which we are responsible to each other. The combination of performance, elaboration, and vigilance makes openness to otherness possible. Vigilance is necessary to "recognize" the unrecognizable in the process of witnessing itself, to recognize that you cannot expect to recognize otherness. To demand vigilance is to demand infinite analysis through ongoing performance, elaboration, and interpretation. Infinite analysis is the affirmation of the process of witnessing that makes subjectivity possible. The demand for vigilance as the demand for infinite analysis is the ethical imperative of subjectivity conceived in witnessing beyond recognition.

This is the vigilance that Lévinas, and Derrida in his more Lévinasian moments, insists on

> Performativity is necessary but not sufficient. . . . The deconstruction I am invoking only invents or affirms, lets the other come insofar as, while a performative, it is not only performative but also continues to unsettle the conditions

of the performative and of whatever distinguished it comfortably from the constative. This writing is liable to the other, opened to and by the other, to the work of the other; it is writing working at not letting itself be enclosed or dominated by that economy of the same in its totality. (Derrida 1992, 342–43)

Performativity alone is not sufficient. But neither is elaboration. Vigilance is also crucial.

The Necessity of Vigilance

Vigilance is defined by the *Oxford English Dictionary* in terms of watchfulness, alertness of observation, wakefulness, insomnia, from *vigilant*, which is defined as wakeful and watchful, keeping steady, on the alert, attentively or closely observant. Following Lévinas's thoughts on insomnia, I would like to suggest a second, radically different, meaning for *vigilance*. Just as witnessing can mean both seeing and not seeing, vigilance can mean both observing or keeping watch and responding to something beyond your own control. Whereas keeping watch or observing is something that one intends to do, the wakefulness of insomnia is not intended but, rather, appears as a response to something or someone beyond one's self. Insomnia is not the vigilance of a self-possessed watchman but the vigilance of a self opened onto otherness itself. Otherness keeps me awake. Vigilance as insomnia is a response to the demands of otherness. This is vigilance as response-ability.

As Lévinas says, the vigilance or wakefulness of insomnia is

> not equivalent to *watching over.* . . , where already the identical, rest, sleep, is sought after. . . . Insomnia—the wakefulness in awakening—is disturbed in the core of its formal or categorical *sameness* by the *other,* which tears away at whatever forms a nucleus, a substance of the same, identity, a rest, a presence, a sleep. . . . The other is in the same, and does not alienate the same but awakens it. (1993, 156)

Lévinas describes this awakening as a demand from the other. In vigilance the response to this demand is neither self-destruction nor the destruction of the other. As Lévinas says, "Insomnia . . . does not get inscribed in a table of categories from a determining activity exercised on the other as given by the unity of the same (and all activity is but the identification and crystallization of the same against the other, upon being affected by that other)" (156). Rather, Lévinas explains, the relationship between the self and other is one of response-ability in which vigilance is a response to the other. In order to avoid this language of subjects and others that leads Lévinas to talk about

hostages, I would say that subjectivity is a responsiveness to o
vigilance is a movement beyond ourselves toward otherness.

Derrida takes over the Lévinasian notion of vigilance whei
the future of justice. As Derrida's work suggests, justice is a process that
never ends, not because human limitations keep us from our goal or because time is infinite, but because justice is never within the realm of the
possible. In "Psyche: Invention of the Other," Derrida says that "deconstruction loses nothing from admitting that it is impossible . . . for a deconstructive operation *possibility* would rather be the danger, the danger of becoming
an available set of rule-governed procedures, methods, accessible approaches" (1992, 327–28). Justice is response-ability itself, the infinite need to respond, which can never be fulfilled once and for all in history. In *Otherwise
Than Being*, Lévinas maintains that justice and responsibility are inherent in
the saying that makes the said possible: "It will be possible to show that
there is question of the said and being only because saying or responsibility
require justice" (1991, 45). History is precisely what the vigilance inherent in
demands for justice must continually call into question. History is of the
past while justice is of the future. History is of the actual while the future is
of the possible, or in Derrida's terms, the impossible. Whereas the historians
work in past tenses—it was, it had been—justice works in the future anteri-
or—it will have been. It will have been in the past so that it might become in
the future. The future anterior blurs the distinction between past and future
and suggests that time does not just flow in one direction from past to future but also from future to past.

This is not to say that we can or should ignore the past. This is not an endorsement of *Hopwood*'s conflation of past, present, and future in order to
deny the effects of past harms in the present. This is not an endorsement of
the logic of *Hopwood* by virtue of which future justice exists only by forgetting the past. On the contrary, future justice exists only by vigilantly returning to the past, reinvestigating the past over and over again in order to find
places and moments of resistance to oppression that might open up a better
future. Contrary to the logic of *Hopwood*, we must continually acknowledge
the effects of the past on the future. This is why it is also crucial to find the
seeds of future justice in the past. In Derridean fashion we could say that the
future determines the past because the past determines the future. This is to
say, justice demands that the future determines the past because the past determines the future.

Following Lévinas, Derrida talks about a future yet to come, always deferred, in which the impossible becomes possible. This is why in order to

open up different possible futures, more particularly to open up a future in which it is possible to think the impossible, we need to rethink history. Rather than embrace the historian's past as actual, we need to rethink that past as possible. In other words, we need to find the conditions of possibility for justice—for the impossible to become possible in the future—in the past. This implies a reverse causality whereby the future affects the past. The image of a better future affects the past that makes it (the future) possible. In a sense, we revisit the past for the sake of a different future. And only by reading the conditions of possibility of that future into the past (it will have been) can we open up alternatives to the present. In order to imagine the present impossibilities becoming possible in the future, we need to imagine them as possible in the past: the future opens onto otherness only insofar as the past does too. But this requires a vigilance, an insomnia that refuses to sleep the dogmatic slumber of historical facts inhabiting a determinant past in a world where the past has already caused the future and the future is just like the past. This refusal of "facts" is what Dori Laub says the psychoanalysts saw in the testimony of the woman who reported four chimneys blown up in the Jewish uprising at Auschwitz; what she "saw" is a testimony to the existence of Jewish resistance at Auschwitz, which is evidence that resistance was possible. This is what Patricia Williams insists on when she continually recalls the inconsistencies of past and present injustice in order to open up the possibility of alternatives.

In *Archive Fever*, Derrida argues that history, or the archive, is more about the future than the past. The meaning of history is always in the future, determined by the future, never determined by the past, which implies that its meaning is open and never closed (Derrida 1996, 36). He says of the archive, "It is a question of the future, the question of the future itself, the question of a response, of a promise and of a responsibility for tomorrow" (36). Derrida's analysis suggests that there are at least three ways in which the past or archive is determined by the future. First, archive fever or the passion for keeping records is driven by a responsibility for tomorrow, a responsibility to remember for the sake of the future. Second, history is always interpreted after the fact, which is to say in the future. For this reason, the meaning of history or the archive of history is always deferred. Third, the archive or recorded history must repeat the process of archivization over and over again: "The archivist produces more archive, and that is why the archive is never closed. It opens out of the future" (68).

The performance of archivization inscribes the archivist and his future into the past that he or she interprets. In the context of analyzing Freud, Derrida says,

The strange result of this performative repetition, the irrepressible effectuation of this *enactment,* in any case what it unavoidably demonstrates, is that the interpretation of the archive ... can only illuminate, read, interpret, establish its object, namely a given inheritance, by inscribing itself into it, that is to say by opening it and enriching it enough to have a rightful place in it. (67)

Derrida insists that what is at issue in this performative repetition is not the past but the future, more precisely, an affirmation of the future to come (68).

Dominick LaCapra takes a similar tack when he argues that what he calls "repetitive temporality" necessitates an open future and open debates over the status of the past. He maintains that "a psychoanalytical informed notion such as repetitive temporality (or history as displacement) ... counteracts historicist teleology and redemptive or messianic narratives, and it has a hypothetical, revisionary status that is always in need of further specification and open to debate" (1994, 9). As we have seen, LaCapra complicates the notion of history by insisting on the transference or displacement relationship between theorist or historian and the past.

Derrida further complicates the relationship between past and future by insisting that history is not of the past but of the future. Turning a corner with Derrida's analysis, we could say that the performative repetition of the archivist is an attempt to inscribe the future into the past so that the conditions of possibility necessary for the future desired by the archivist are available from the past. Imagining otherness, then, is a matter of archiving the other into history so that causality between past and future becomes reversible. Derrida warns, however, that insofar as this history is always the history of the One, archiving the other within this history is always paradoxical, if not impossible: "As soon as there is One, there is murder, wounding, traumatism" because the one is the result of a continuous repetition of its own instituting violence (1996, 78, 79). In Derrida's reading of psychoanalysis, the relation between the One and others is bound to be violent. Derrida criticizes Freud for repeating the violence of patriarchal authority by assuming the certainty of maternity operating in the realm of the sense (47) and by reinstating the father as ultimate authority (95). Derrida wonders if within the patriarchal logic of Freudian psychoanalysis sons can ever speak in their own names and if daughters are ever more than specters (95). Yet he does not suggest any other alternative. Like so much of his work, *Archive Fever* leaves us with the dismal prospect of repeating originary violence in every attempt to overcome it.

But perhaps in his own insistence on originary violence, Derrida too is repeating the patriarchal logic—not of patricide but of matricide. Derrida's discussion of originary violence and its constitutive repetitions mirrors the psychoanalytic discussion of the originary and constitutive violence involved in separating oneself from one's mother. As I have argued elsewhere, this pre-Oedipal scene is imagined as a violent battleground in which the child must commit imaginary matricide in order to become autonomous (Oliver 1995, 1997). This is to say that in order to become One, the child must kill off the (m)other. If, however, we reconceive of the relationship between mother and child as a social relationship and not a natural unity, then this violent break in order to become One is not necessary. And while theories that represent or presuppose weaning as originary violence make ethical relationship impossible, theories that re-present maternity and relations between mother and child as primarily ethical provide a more useful and promising future than Derrida's aporias.[1]

In spite of his own patriarchal repetitions, Derrida's insistence on the connection between justice and the future anterior—what will have been, and what I read as the reversibility of the past and future—is useful in thinking of the time of otherness. But just as we have to imagine that the future can change the past and that the past is a matter of possibilities, vigilance demands that we imagine the present as past. Chandra Talpade Mohanty suggests that in order to work for social change it is necessary to imagine a future in which present injustice is past. Both Derrida's and Mohanty's analyses of the relationship between past, future, and justice require imagination, perhaps something like what Kristeva calls the revolt in imagination necessary for any individual or social transformation (1997b, 1998a).

Imagining Otherwise

For Mohanty, although this future is yet to come, which is the nature of the future, political and social activism requires imagining the determinant future in which our present becomes a history lesson. She concludes her essay "Feminist Encounters: Locating the Politics of Experience" by insisting that the place from which we seek to know what is just and from which we work for social change must be an imaginary encounter with a possible future in which we see the present as already past, as the future anterior (will have been):

> I *know*—in my own non-synchronous temporality—that by the year 2000, apartheid will be discussed as a nightmarish chapter in Black South Africa's history, the resistance to and victory over the efforts of the U.S. government and multinational mining conglomerates to relocate the Navajo and Hopi reservations from Big Mountain, Arizona will be written in elementary-

school textbooks, and the Palestinian "homeland" will no longer be referred to as the "Middle-East question"—it will be a reality. But that is my preferred history: what I hope and struggle for, I garner as *my* knowledge, create as the place from where I seek to know. (1987, 42)

When Mohanty talks about "*my* knowledge," she is not proposing that she or anybody else can assume a position of transcendence in relation to justice. In fact, she is insisting that all knowledge and understanding are positional in relation to sociopolitical and economic histories. She argues that it is this positionality that is not addressed by traditional notions of history as linear and teleological, moving, as they do, between the two poles of origin and end. Following Shiv Visvanathan, Mohanty suggests that the "diagnostic classification[s] along the linear, irreversible continuum of Time/Progress" is itself a position determined by its own historical conditions (1987, 30). Using Visvanathan's analysis of the museum, Mohanty describes how the notion of history as an irreversible continuum assumes a Eurocentric notion of evolution from more primitive to civilized, where "progress is defined as the ordained linear movement across this sequence" and "as a result, other civilizations or tribal cultures are seen as 'contemporary ancestors,' the past the West has already lived out" (30). Within this Eurocentric history, the poles of origin and end correspond to subject and other insofar as the other is the primitive origin of the Western subject who occupies the position of telos.

Mohanty points to a difference between history and historicity. Whereas history operates according to a "Eurocentric law of identical temporality" and is in some sense always already written, historicity can never be written in that sense, because it is the dynamic process through which the positions or perspectives that make writing history possible are negotiated. These negotiations can be contestatory or conciliatory, but in either case they are made possible by the response-ability of subjectivity. And the categories of subject, object, and other perpetuated by traditional notions of history are complicated by analyses of the historicity of the categories themselves. Mohanty, along with Joan Scott and others, has argued that opening history to otherness requires more than writing alternative histories of cultures or groups. In addition, opening history to otherness requires historicizing notions of identity and difference both in the abstract and in their particular embodiments.

Strangely resonant with Lévinas, Mohanty quotes Bernice Reagon's contribution to *Home Girls: A Black Feminist Anthology*: "The only way you can take yourself seriously is if you can throw yourself into the next period beyond your little meager human-body-mouth-talking all the time" (in

Mohanty 1987, 40). Mohanty argues that "we take ourselves seriously only when we go 'beyond' ourselves, valuing not just the plurality of differences among us but also the massive presence of the Difference that our recent planetary history has installed. This 'Difference' is what we see only through the lenses of our present moment, our present struggles" (40). While in Reagon's analysis this going beyond ourselves seems to be working for a better future for future generations, for Mohanty going beyond ourselves means an encounter with Difference that takes us beyond identity politics and the history of struggles toward a historicity of identity and difference that begins when we bring temporality back into discussions of history, identity, and difference. She maintains that

> the notion of a temporality of struggle defies and subverts the logic of European modernity and the "law of identical temporality." . . . It suggests an insistent, simultaneous, non-synchronous process characterized by multiple locations, rather than a search for origins and endings which as Adrienne Rich says, "seems a way of stopping time in its tracks." (41)

For Mohanty, we take experience as a given, and we risk stopping time in its tracks if we are not vigilant about the temporality of experience. Only by attending to the temporality of experience can we restore historicity to history. Only this vigilance will prevent us from overlooking the social contexts and subject positions from which we experience identity and difference—the historicity of notions of identity and difference themselves. Temporality, then, is what both enables and challenges history.

For Butler, following Derrida, temporality is what makes performative iterations potentially transformative: no two iterations of social norms are the same because of the differences in their temporal positionality. In some sense, in Shoshana Felman's analysis what is unique or disruptive about the signature of the voice of a witness is the way in which testimony returns temporality to history. And for Lévinas it is the temporality of saying that is lost in the said. We might say that the performative operates in the realm of temporality while what is performed, the constative, operates in the realm of history. The tension between performative temporality and historicity, and constative time and history, makes transformation and change possible. The experience of time or the movement of time is the temporality that both makes time possible for us and challenges linear time. The historicity of our experience of time, which is to say the individual-social context and subject positions that make any historical perspective possible, also challenge historical facts as universal. The performative element in any activity, that is, the doing of it, both enables and challenges the constative element, what is done or said. It is the tension between our historical positions, which may be fixed at any one moment, and the process of history or experience that makes transformation possible. Subjective agency is the result of the tension between subject position at any one moment and the infinite responsibility that is subjectivity.

This analysis suggests that what is transformative about the performative is not just the differences that result from performing at time 1 (t1) and then again at time 2 (t2). Rather, it is by returning temporality to time and historicity to history that the performative becomes transformative. Performativity destabilizes history by showing that the constative element central to historical truth is dependent on the process of temporality, which is always in tension with the constative element. The tension between the process and the momentary results of the process works together to give us a sense of our own agency and the power to transform history. Echoing Mohanty, we could say that interpretation of how the performative challenges the constative or how temporality challenges history returns the historicity of struggles over social norms to history.

In *Otherwise Than Being*, Lévinas makes a distinction between history and temporality as a lapse of (linear, historical) time, or immemorial time. He characterizes this distinction as one between diachronic and synchronic elements of time, which correspond to the saying and the said:

> For the lapse of time is also something irrecuperable, refractory to the simultaneity of the present, something unrepresentable, immemorial, pre-historical. Before the synthesis of apprehension and recognition, the absolutely passive "synthesis" of aging is effected. Through it time passes *(se passe)*. The immemorial is not an effect of a weakness of memory, an incapacity to cross large intervals of time, to resuscitate pasts too deep. It is the impossibility of the dispersion of time to assemble itself in the present, the insurmountable diachrony of time, beyond the said.... Need temporization signify only by letting itself be understood in the said, in which its diachrony is exposed to synchronization? If saying is not only the correlative of a said, if its signifyingness is not absorbed in the signification said, can we not find beyond or on the hither side of the saying that tells being the signifyingness of diachrony? (1991, 38)

Attending to historicity requires a vigilance in bearing witness to the process, the saying, the response-ability (or lack of it), which creates the conditions of possibility for the construction of historical evidence in the first place. Attention to the temporality of the performative along with interpretation of performance and vigilance in insisting on the impossibility of ever fully recognizing otherness are three elements that open subjectivity onto otherness. My analysis of performance, interpretation, and vigilance in developing a theory of open subjectivity and othered subjectivity is itself intended as a testimony to the necessity of witnessing subjectivity.

In a discussion of temporality and the move away from subject-centered philosophy, it is impossible not to gesture toward Heidegger's analysis of temporality as the fundamental characteristic of Being and therefore of *Dasein*'s relation to Being. In fact, Heidegger's association of the moment with an *Augenblick* takes me back to my discussion of the eyewitness.[2] *Augenblick* connotes the blinking of the eye. We might say that the moment takes place in the blink of an eye. But, as Heidegger points out, insofar as the present moment takes place in the blink of an eye, we are not its eyewitnesses. Rather, it is the blinking of the eyes that prevents us from seeing what is happening at every instant. It is the *Augenblick*, the temporality of the moment, that makes us unreliable eyewitnesses. And it is only a vigilance in investigating our blindness—what is for us beyond recognition—that keeps us aware of our response-ability, of our need to respond to what for Heidegger is calling. In a Heideggerian move, vision gives way to hearing, time gives way to temporality, history gives way to historicity, and the historian's eyewitness is blind to as much as he sees. The blink challenges the link between vision and history. Perhaps we could say that for Derrida and Butler, Heidegger's blink becomes a wink, a parodic performance that displays the importance of blinking—not seeing—to witnessing.[3]

Eyewitness Testimony and Historical Evidence

While eyewitness testimony is distilled into the facts that make up historical evidence, the process of witnessing itself defies assimilation into the evidence of history. In a sense, vigilance is necessary to avoid the reduction of history to its evidence and facts. Traditionally, the eyewitness is privileged by historians because, as Joan Scott points out, they presume that "knowledge is gained through vision; vision is a direct, unmediated apprehension of a world of transparent objects.... Seeing is the origin of knowing. [And] writing is reproduction, transmission—the communication of knowledge gained through (visual, visceral) experience" (1992, 22–23). Scott argues that when experience is taken as an origin and evidence is based on eyewitness testimony or the vision of the individual, then questions about how that experience is produced are left aside (25). Echoing Mohanty, Scott claims that even progressive historians who want to make visible the experience of those traditionally made invisible merely reproduce the terms through which the visible and invisible support each other: "Making visible the experience of a different group exposes the existence of repressive mechanisms, but not their inner workings or logics; we know that difference exists, but we don't understand it as constituted relationally. For that we need to attend to the historical processes that, through discourse, position subjects and produce their experiences" (25). The processes of subjectivity and experience are left out of a notion of evidence that presumes that eyewitnesses have direct access to an experience that exists in itself and can be translated directly into testimony.

Even philosophers who complicate any notion of an unmediated connection among experience, the eyewitness, and testimony still privilege vision—seeing with one's own eyes. Along with historians, philosophers of recognition have also traditionally privileged vision. For example, Plato privileges vision because of its relation to beauty. Hegel describes the onset of subjectivity as a reaction to the sight of another just like one's self. For Freud, sexual difference and self-identity are the result of seeing the genitals of the other sex. Lacan's mirror stage couldn't make the role of vision more prominent in self-recognition, or misrecognition, as he has it. Even Butler discusses subjectivity in terms of visibility and invisibility (e.g., 1997b, 11).

In order to rethink notions of identity based on recognition, I want to emphasize the ways in which the notion of witnessing that I am developing challenges the traditional notion of vision, which is at the foundation of theories of recognition. First, it is important that the witness is testifying to something that cannot be seen (subjectivity and the loss of subjectivity that comes from extreme oppression). In this sense, the witness is bearing witness rather than testifying as an eyewitness. Second, it is significant to remember that this experience does not exist in itself; it is not available for the witness or anyone else to access. Rather, the experience is constituted and reconstituted as such for the witness through testimony. In addition, insofar as the addressee of the witness, or the witness of the testimony, responds to the performative element of testimony and insofar as the unseen of history is shown through performance, our sights are directed beyond the visible world of the eyewitness. Finally, what the process of witnessing testifies to is not a state of facts but a commitment to the truth of subjectivity as address-ability and response-ability. Witnessing is addressed to another and to a community; and witnessing—in both senses as addressing and responding, testifying and listening—is a commitment to embrace the responsibility of constituting communities, the responsibility inherent in subjectivity itself. In this sense, witnessing is always bearing witness to the necessity of its process and to the impossibility of the eyewitness.

III. Visions

7. Seeing Race

In contemporary discussions, recognition is often accompanied by visibility as its political partner. Demands for recognition are also demands for visibility. Marginalization and enfranchisement are discussed in terms of visibility and invisibility. In a Foucauldian vein, theorists like Judith Butler, Iris Young, and Patricia Williams, among many others, point out that certain groups of people and their problems and suffering remain invisible within mainstream culture. In this vein, visibility is a matter of power. Those empowered within dominant culture are visible, and visibility itself empowers. Those disempowered are rendered invisible, which is a means of disempowering.

The intersection of one's subject position, political convictions, and the metaphysical presuppositions that support both is belied by a type of ideological Rorschach test of what one sees and does not see. Are most welfare recipients black or white? Are single mothers responsible for the decay in moral fiber or are they the victims of patriarchal values? If young black men are at greater risk of being murdered than young white men, is it because they are criminals, because they are victims of police brutality, because racism limits their options, and so forth? What we see when we look around us is politically charged and manipulated by the media. The phrase "seeing is believing" takes on new meaning if what we see is influenced by what we believe. And experiencing what is eye-opening is not necessarily a result of opening or closing our eyelids. What we recognize and what we see are the result of much more than opening our eyes and looking.

Visibility and Property

The complications of the relation between vision and visions—visions of the past, visions for the future—become apparent, if not resolved, in the work of Patricia Williams. Her work turns around issues of visibility, invisibility, and hypervisibility in relation to issues of property and ownership. Williams is looking for a way for blacks and women to be seen without being spotlighted or made into spectacles. Somewhere between invisibility and hypervisibility is the kind of recognition equality demands. Yet this place of perfect vision may not be imaginable until we interrogate our very notions of recognition, vision, and visibility. Using Williams's suggestion that our conceptions of ourselves are marinated in the economy of property and therefore are heirs to slavery, I argue that our notions of recognition and visibility are symptoms of what she calls alternatively the owned or disowned world. By examining the productive tension in Williams's work between her criticisms of the economy of property—with its ownership and the possibility of disowning—and her use of the rhetoric of visibility, recognition, and seeing, we can see how the rhetoric of visibility plays into the economy of property. The play between recognition/visibility and property/ownership must be "seen" before there is hope of imagining another vision beyond recognition and beyond property.

Williams's analyses of legal decisions, media culture, university dynamics, and her own experiences lead her to conclude that visibility is a complicated issue when it comes to race:

> If race is something about which we dare not speak in polite social company, the same cannot be said of the viewing of race. How, or whether, blacks are seen depends upon a dynamic of display that ricochets between hypervisibility and oblivion. Blacks are seen "everywhere," taking over the world one minute; yet the great ongoing toll of poverty and isolation that engulfs so many remains the object of persistent oversight. If, moreover, the real lives of real blacks unfold outside the view of many whites, the fantasy of black life as a theatrical enterprise is an almost obsessive indulgence. This sort of voyeurism is hardly peculiar to the mechanics of racial colonization, of course: any group designated the colorful local, the bangled native, or the folksy ethnic stands to suffer its peculiar limitation. (1998, 17)

Throughout her work, Williams critically points to examples of these forms of "being seen" or "unseen" that variously stereotype, ignore, or make a spectacle of people marginalized and oppressed by dominant culture. In her analysis there is an undercurrent that blacks and other marginalized people need to be made visible in ways that empower rather than stereotype and objectify. There is a sense of a good visibility and a bad visibility. The good visibility is "a recognition of individuality that includes blacks as a social presence" (1991, 121). An example of good visibility is affirmative action as "an act of verification and vision, an act of social as well as professional responsibility" (1991, 121). Good visibility is characterized as responsible vision that does not stereotype by group but recognizes individuality yet includes blacks as a group with social presence or importance. Bad visibility has various forms including invisibility, unseeing, hypervisibility, stereotyping, making a spectacle, and other types of exaggerated seeing. Examples of bad visibility include the ways that homeless people become invisible in public policy and in everyday experience, the ways that television and films make racist stereotypes entertainment, the ways that even white liberals approach black culture as spectacle.

Yet what is a recognition of individuality that includes blacks as a social presence? How is good visibility distinct from bad? In fact, aren't these two faces of visibility merely symptoms of a problematic notion of vision that confounds attempts at anything like mutual recognition? As Williams observes, "There is great power in being able to see the world as one will and then to have that vision enacted. But if being is seeing for the subject, then being seen is the precise measure of existence for the object" (1991, 28). It follows that if being is seeing for the subject, then being seen as a measure of one's existence renders subjects into nothing more than objects. The seeing/ being seen dichotomy mirrors the subject/object dualism that is symptomatic of oppression. The seer is the active subject while the seen is the passive object. Being seen, like recognition, is a goal created by the pathology of oppression.

Oppression makes people into faceless objects or lesser subjects. The lack of visage in objects renders them invisible in any ethical or political sense. In turn, subjectivity becomes the domain of domination. Subjectivity is conferred by those in power and empowered on those they deem powerless and disempowered. The desire to be seen, to be recognized is the paradoxical desire created by oppression. It is the desire to become objectified in order to be recognized by the sovereign subject to whom the oppressed is beholden for his or her own self-worth. Bell hooks describes this dynamic:

> Often when black subjects give expression to multiple aspects of our identity, which emerge from a different location, we may be seen by white others as "spectacle." For example, when I give an academic talk without reading a paper, using a popular, performative, black story-telling mode, I risk being seen by the dominating white other as unprepared, or just entertainment. Yet their mode of seeing cannot be the factor which determines style of representation or the content of one's work. Fundamental to the process of decentering the oppressive other and claiming our right to subjectivity is the insistence

that we must determine how we will be and not rely on colonizing responses to determine our legitimacy. We are not looking to that Other for recognition. We are recognizing ourselves and willingly making contact with all who would engage us in a constructive manner. (1990, 22)

So it is not merely being seen, or being recognized between spectacle and oblivion, that makes for an ethical or just relation. Rather, Williams, along with hooks, describes the oscillation between invisibility and hypervisibility as a matter not so much of being seen but of making one's world: "I know that my feelings of exaggerated visibility and invisibility are the product of my not being part of the larger cultural picture. I know too that the larger cultural picture is an illusion, albeit a powerful one, concocted from a perceptual consensus to which I am not a party; and that while these perceptions operate as dictators of truth, they are after all merely perceptions" (1991, 56). What is a stake, then, is not visibility per se but being a party to the perception making that shapes our world, being as seeing in addition to being as being seen. Echoing Frantz Fanon's concern for meaning making and the alienation that results from being denied the making of one's own meaning, Williams is concerned with who has the power to make meaning and truth. The split between subject and object, seeing and seen, presupposes a split between those involved in perception making for their own benefit and those subjected to it for the benefit of others.

Sometimes Williams describes this difference as that between the self-possessed and the dispossessed. The self-possessed enjoy the sense of entitlement to exercise control over themselves and their bodies, while the dispossessed are denied a sense of entitlement. The dispossessed are subject to laws and policies governing their bodies and behaviors. The dispossessed are those whose bodies have been dispossessed by culture and thereby become alien to themselves. They are the victims of the double alienation described by Fanon. Williams claims that the self-possessed are those who also possess other material property and therefore buy the right to their privacy, while the dispossessed have been ostracized and thrown into public scrutiny without basic rights, including privacy (1991, 21–26, 68–69). Those who own property are seen as virtuous while those who do not, especially those who inhabit public spaces, are seen as harmful. Homelessness is seen as a vice, and those dispossessed are seen as vicious.

For example, Williams's analysis of the beating of three black men by a group of white men in Howard Beach suggests that public space is becoming privatized and that the presence of those who do not "'own' something specific" is seen as harmful (1991, 68). Dispossession is possible in an owned

world in which possessions bring with them entitlements and lack of possessions leads to disenfranchisement:

> In this nation there is, it is true, relatively little force in the public domain
> compared to other nations, relatively little intrusive governmental interfer-
> ence. But we risk instead the life-crushing disenfranchisement of an entirely
> owned world. Permission must be sought to walk upon the face of the earth.
> Freedom becomes contractual and therefore obligated; freedom is framed by
> obligation; and obligation is paired not with duty but with debt. (1991, 43)

Freedom, rights, entitlements, and our very sense of ourselves are permeated
by the market economy.

Subjects are capable of ownership, of having their own, of having "ownness," while those who are not capable of ownership become objects to be
seen or not by propertied subjects.[1] In this scenario, you either own property
or you are disowned. Williams discusses ownership in terms of the connection, or disconnection, between privacy and intimacy and the way in which
the private-public split works to split people into subjects (the haves) and
objects (the have-nots). Williams suggests that the public-private split is
used to deny the proximity of others and otherness. The private realm is an
illusory haven against otherness. As space becomes privatized and owned,
otherness becomes disowned.

An incident in Amarillo, Texas, in 1997 points to the connections between ownership, space, entitlements, and language. Because they spoke
Spanish, Ester Hernandez and Rosa Gonzales were hired at Allied Insurance
Agency, "a small store-front office in the Barrio, a heavily Hispanic neighbor-
hood in south Amarillo," "where many customers speak Spanish as their primary language" (*New York Times,* September 30, 1997, A10). But in July 1997
they were fired from their jobs for "chatting" to each other in Spanish after
the owner of the agency, Pat Polk, presented them with a pledge to speak
only English in the office, which they refused to sign.

The handwritten pledge began, "Linda has asked that this be an English
speaking office except when we have customers who can't speak our language. All of our Employees do speak English." Linda, Polk's wife and co-
owner of the agency, "said the women's chatting in Spanish was 'almost like
they were whispering to each other behind our backs.'" The *New York Times*
report quotes Polk as saying that

> it's been made into me belittling the Spanish people, and it's not that way....
> They're trying to make this a racial thing, and it's not.... Our office is a four-
> employee office.... We had three Spanish and one Caucasian woman working

for us. The Spanish women were chatting in Spanish a great portion of the day amongst themselves, while I, my wife, and the other woman were left out of the conversations, as we don't understand Spanish.

The third employee fluent in both English and Spanish, Edna Mobley, agreed to sign the pledge to speak English only in the office "to which a beaming Mr. Polk beckoned to a visitor and said, 'That's one sharp little Mexican girl right there!'" The fact is that the so-called "sharp little Mexican girl," the "Spanish women," the "Caucasian woman," and the Polks are also all Americans, born in the Texas Panhandle.

Most of the people in the community who supported the Polks argued that since they owned the business, their employees should obey their rules. This idea that the Polks own the space in which their employees speak—the linguistic space itself, the space that connects coworkers to each other—is a symptom of what Williams identifies as the privatization of public space. The Polks seemed to presume that since they owned the business, that they also owned the space and relations and everything that went on within the walls of the office in which their business operated. Language itself is presumed to be something that can be owned—and certainly, in the case of the Polks' relationship to Spanish, disowned. The very identities of people and their interpersonal relationships become fungible. Rosa Gonzales—one of the women fired for the very reason she was hired—realized that her identity was at stake, when she said that in response to Polk's demand to sign the pledge, she "told him no. This is what I am; this is what I do. This is normal to me. I'm not doing it to offend anybody. It just feels comfortable." With this example, self-possession is equated with literal ownership.[2]

Presuming to own the space in which people speak, or to own or possess language itself, restricts rather than opens up dialogue. The idea that linguistic space is divided between owners and workers plays off of a capitalistic subject-centered notion of human relationships that ignores the fundamental responsibility that comes with subjectivity, a responsibility to respond and open up the possibility of response from others. This presumption to own linguistic space disowns those who are not allowed the self-possession of either their own linguistic space or language itself. As Williams suggests, we live in an entirely owned world where only those who have property, material, linguistic, or otherwise, are subjects and everyone else becomes disowned property.

In *The Rooster's Egg: On the Persistence of Prejudice* Williams argues that the notion of self-possession takes on new meaning when bodies and body parts can be bought and sold on the market. Williams claims that slavery makes the notion of self-possession take a literal turn when the slave does not own her own body and yet all she does own is her own body (1995, 231). In addition, she points out that the notion of self-possession turns against the self when individuals can, or must, sell or rent their body parts for profit in order to survive. Here again freedom is linked with ownership. Subjectivity itself becomes a matter of property, and agency becomes a matter of property control. Even while Williams talks of "owning the self in a disowned world," she is suspicious of the ways that the economy of property has taken over our self-conceptions (1991, 181).

Williams is vigilant in tracing the legacy of slavery in our present conceptions of ourselves (1995, 232). Slavery divided human beings into two categories: property and the owners of property. Williams argues that the Civil War did not emancipate the slaves but merely "unowned" and "disowned" them by thrusting them outside of the market, the labor market and the marketplace of rights, and placed them beyond the bounds of value (1991, 21). Freed slaves were no longer property, a change in status that did away with their value as chattel, the only value they had as slaves. Because they were still disenfranchised from the making of value, from perception making or meaning making, and because they had been valued as only property by the slave-owning culture, emancipation left them without social value, disowned.

Williams sees the echoing repercussions of turning people into property and valuing them only as property in various aspects of contemporary culture. The legal precedents and rhetoric around women's reproduction, eugenics, and organ transplants are some of Williams's examples. She warns that

> it is with great care, therefore, that we should look for its [slavery's] echoing repercussions in our world today, for 1856 is not very long ago at all. It is with caution that we must notice that with the advent of a variety of new technologies, we presumed free agents are not less but increasingly defined as body-centered. We live more, not less, in relation to our body parts, the dispossession or employment of ourselves constrained by a complicated pattern of self-alienation. (1995, 232)

This pattern of self-alienation extends beyond new technologies. Williams's work suggests that the self-alienation inherent in slavery, in making property of people, pervades not only our legal system but also our culture and imaginations.

It is not just our material possessions and our bodies and their parts that are seen as property but also our characteristics as well. Our properties have become property. And some properties (certain looks, physiques, accents, styles, genders, races, ethnicities) are valued more than others. Williams asks, "At what cost, this assemblage of the self-through-adornment, this sifting through the jumbled jewelry box of cultural assets, selected body parts, and just the right accessories?" (1995, 242). Difference itself has become a property (1991, 212).

Williams concludes that "'black,' 'female,' 'male,' and 'white' are every bit as much properties as the buses, private clubs, neighborhoods, and schools that provide the extracorporeal battlegrounds of their expression. . . . possessions become the description of who we are and the reflection of our worth" (1991, 124). Even *I* or the self becomes a property such that Williams can talk of owning the self in a disowned world. *I* or *myself* becomes my prized possession, especially if I am battling against the disowned status of those marginalized within racist and sexist culture (1991, 128). As Williams points out, this commodification of human beings puts us beyond humanity and into the world of things, objects, products, to be used, even disposed of (1991, 39, 227). More than this, it recalls slavery in all of its contemporary incarnations, which, perhaps without the bill of sale, continue to treat people as property—owned or disowned, self-possessed or dispossessed.

Williams argues in favor of self-possession for those who have been dispossessed—those whose sense of self is compromised by oppression and domination—yet she criticizes the connections between the rhetoric of self-possession and the economy of property; she attempts to make visible those disenfranchised within dominant culture, yet she is critical of modes of visibility that make people into spectacles and stereotypes. She uses identity politics when it suits her purposes and deconstructs identity when it doesn't. It might be fair to say that she even uses a form of spectacle in her own writings when she puts herself, her experiences, and her emotions on display in her text. Her explicit strategy is analyzing truth and facts as rhetorical events in order to short-circuit the naturalization process through which ideologies become reality (1991, 10–11). What is at stake, it seems, is not so much (good) visibility or (good) self-possession, but reassessing reality—what is considered normal and what is considered natural. The struggle for recognition is really the struggle to be accepted as normal or natural rather than different and therefore abnormal. The struggle is to make difference normal and natural without making it the same or homogeneous.

Williams interrogates the norms that define reality by "acknowledging, challenging, playing with these [rhetorical truths] as rhetorical gestures,"

which she insists is "necessary for any conception of justice. Such acknowl-
edgement complicates the supposed purity of gender, race, voice, boundary;
it allows us to acknowledge the utility of such categorizations for certain
purposes and the necessity of their breakdown on other occasions" (1991,
10–11). For her, rhetorical gestures are tied to subject positions, which must
be acknowledged in order to denaturalize discourse and expose its ethical
and political dimensions. Disregarding subject positions is common practice
in most scholarly discourse, including law and medicine; and yet, as she
points out, obscuring subject positions "hopelessly befuddles" ethical and
political agency and responsibility. She proposes that

> one of the most important results of reconceptualizing from "objective truth"
> to rhetorical event will be a more nuanced sense of legal and social responsi-
> bility. This will be so because much of what is spoken in so-called objective,
> unmediated voices is in fact mired in hidden subjectivities and unexamined
> claims that make property of others beyond the self, all the while denying
> such connections. (1991, 11)

Williams's concern with truth as rhetorical event or gesture resonates
with my analysis of witnessing as performance. What Williams's emphasis
on subject position adds is a concern for the historical-social context of the
performance. Williams tries to present complex analyses of events by combining an attention to the historical context along with the realization that
history is contextualized through interpretation and rhetorical gestures. In
other words, Williams's work re-creates history by writing a history aware of
itself as rhetorical event. The tension in Williams's work between a call for
recognition, visibility, and self-possession on the one hand, and her challenge to identity politics, hypervisibility, and property on the other, is a vi-
bration of the tension inherent in witnessing: the tension between subject
positions, which are historically determined, and subjectivity, which is an infinite response-ability. By attending to both subject positions and the rhetorical events that produce them, Williams opens up the possibility of thinking
through ethical, political, and social responsibility as inherent in one's very
sense of oneself as an agent or subject.

Williams prefers the metaphor of investment instead of possession to
convey social relations and their incumbent responsibility. Imagining a more
optimistic future, she says: "What a world it would be if we could all wake
up and see all of ourselves reflected in the world, not merely in a territorial
sense but with a kind of nonexclusive entitlement that grants not so much
possession as investment. A peculiarly anachronistic notion of investment, I

suppose, at once both ancient and futuristic. An investment that envisions each of us in each other" (1998, 16). If we can acknowledge our investment in others, then perhaps we can imagine relationships outside of an economy of property; perhaps we can see beyond self-possession or possession of the other toward mutually implicated investments in self and other.

Envisioning identity and relationships beyond an economy of property entails vision beyond vision, imagining what we do not yet see with our eyes. This investigation of what we see takes us beyond eyewitness testimony by raising the question of how we come to see what we see. Only by interrogating our perceptions, meanings, and truths—what we see—can we imagine a vision of something beyond domination and slavery in any of its forms. This kind of vision is itself an investment in a just future. For Williams, this investment is a matter of imagining the world otherwise: "Just the momentary, imaginary exercise of taking to mind and heart the investment of oneself in another, indeed the investment of oneself as that other" (1998, 69). This imaginary exercise brings with it responsibility and obligation, not as debt but as ethical duty to oneself and others in interconnection. Seeing investments in each other should prevent what Williams calls "pornographic seeing," which makes the other into an object or spectacle, there for the viewer's pleasure, possessed by the subject's gaze.

As we have seen, even as she uses metaphors of vision, Williams's analysis complicates notions of visibility and seeing race. Yet what of the notion of vision or seeing itself? Is there a relationship between the pornographic seeing of race and a pornographic notion of vision that permeates our cultural imaginary? Just as we must analyze the truth of experience as rhetorical gesture or event, so too we must analyze the truth of vision as rhetorical event. If, as Williams suggests, "for better or worse, our customs and laws, our culture and society are sustained by the myths we embrace, the stories we recirculate to explain what we behold," then vision, how we behold, is also sustained by myths and stories we recirculate to explain how we see the world (1991, 16). Pornographic seeing of race is symptomatic of racism, but pornographic seeing itself is symptomatic of a particular rhetoric of vision—a rhetoric produced in conjunction with an economy of property and therefore not far removed from the ideology of slavery.

Fredric Jameson begins *Signatures of the Visible* by claiming that "the visual is *essentially* pornographic, which is to say that it has its end in rapt, mindless fascination; thinking about its attributes becomes an adjunct to that, if it is unwilling to betray its object" (1992, 1). More optimistic than Jameson perhaps, later I will argue that it is not the visual itself that is pornographic but indeed our thinking about the visual, our conceptions of what it is to see. Pornographic seeing is voyeuristic looking that treats the seen or looked at as an object for one's own pleasure or entertainment. The seer considers only his own interests and maintains a willful ignorance about the subject positions of those he watches. The seer also maintains a willful ignorance about the interconnection or interrelationship between himself and what he sees. His gaze is one-way since he discounts the other's ability to see. For him, the other is to be seen and not subject enough to look. Except insofar as it relates to his own pleasure, the voyeur is not concerned with the effect of his watching on his object. This type of seeing or vision divides the world into seers and seen, subjects and objects. The seer remains in control of the scene of sight, while the seen is there *for* him.

Williams gives an example of this type of disinterested or self-interested pornographic seeing when she describes the many tours of black churches in Harlem, where in spite of some churches' disapproval of being on display, hundreds of tourists flock to watch Sunday services (1998, 22; 1991, 71–72). These tourists are not there to engage in the joy and communion of Sunday services but to watch, to be entertained, to see a spectacle, without regard for the congregations' relationship to their religious practices. For the tourist, the churchgoers are not subjects expressing their faith or sense of community but objects to be watched and filmed. Williams describes various ways that these tourists disrupt and undermine Sunday services and the ways that they demonstrate total disregard for their effect on those whom they watch.

The myth that the relationship to the seen is as an object of sight, even a spectacle there for one's own enjoyment, denies the interconnection between the seer and the world seen and ignores the responsibility of seeing. Seeing is an activity that like any other brings with it responsibilities. When it involves other human beings, then it brings with it ethical, social, and political responsibilities. Pornographic seeing denies the seer's responsibility for seeing by ignoring the seer's connection to what he sees. Pornographic seeing treats others as objects for the subject, as the subject's rightful property. The subject is entitled to treat the other as spectacle; his freedom and rights guarantee that he can take others as objects. This logic of seeing as possessing or enjoying one's property became apparent to me when a student in an introduction to women's studies class defended the tourists in Williams's example by asserting that it is a "free country" and "churches are public property," so the tourists have a "right to be there watching the show." This view of rights, freedom, property, and looking presupposes an autonomous subject disconnected from the world in which he acts. Myths of property, and human beings as property, cannot be separated from our notions of vision, visibility, and what it means to see.

Another of Williams's examples makes the politics of vision explicit. She recounts an experience of her friend "C.," who was surrounded by police in Florida when she refused to pay for the sour milk she had repeatedly asked the waitress to take back (1991, 56). In an all-white restaurant, a black woman was ordered at gunpoint to pay for sour milk. C. demanded that the police officer taste the milk himself, but C. said "no one was interested in whether or not I was telling the truth. The glass was sitting there in the middle of all this, with the curdle hanging on the sides, but nobody would taste it because a black woman's lips had touched it" (57). Williams comments on the scene, with "the police with guns drawn, battlelines drawn, the contest over her contestation; the proof of the milk in the glass inadmissible, unaccounted for, unseen" (57).

As Williams suggests, recognition is a matter of seeing. What is unrecognized is unseen. Yet the connection between recognition and seeing is precisely the problem with theories of recognition. As Williams's illustration points up, the glass of milk was not really the issue. The issues of the relationship between power and identity, subjects and those othered, the process through which positions curdled and solidified cannot be recognized by the eyewitness; they cannot be seen. The stakes are precisely the unseen in vision—the process through which something is seen or not seen.

Color Blindness and the Pathology of Racism

Recent rhetoric of a color-blind society raises the question of what it means to see or not to see. With the metaphor of a color-blind society, the connection between vision and politics becomes explicit.[3] The connections between entitlements, freedom, property, and vision become even more apparent when we analyze the rhetoric of a color-blind society. Seeing and not seeing or blindness become political acts. When not seeing race is mandated by the courts, it is time to examine the eyes of our culture. The choice of a physical limitation, color blindness, as the metaphor for racial justice is curious, to say the least. It may be useful to analyze this color blindness as a hysterical symptom. As Freud suggests in his analysis of hysterical blindness, "Excitations of the blind eye may have certain psychical consequences (for instance, they may produce affects) even though they do not become conscious. Thus hysterically blind people are only blind as far as consciousness is concerned; in their unconscious they can see" (1910, 212). Whether or not color is "seen," it produces socially and psychically significant affects in relation to

race and political effects. The rhetoric of a color-blind society denies and ignores the affective effects of seeing race in a racist society.

With good intentions people say, "I don't care whether he is black, white,
green, or purple; color doesn't matter." As utopian as this sentiment is, it denies the social significance of color and the history of racism by treating socially meaningful colors on par with colors without a social history and
meaning.[4] Indeed, it trivializes the meaning of color and racism in our society by comparing what we take to be real skin colors with impossible skin colors. By appealing to a fantasy world of green and purple people, this rhetoric
denies the reality of the world of racially meaningful colors in which—for
better or worse—we actually live.

In addition, the conflation of ought and is in the rhetoric of a color-blind
society covers over and perpetuates current social injustice. Even if we were
to accept that we ought to have a color-blind society, that doesn't mean that
we have one now. And to act like we do when we don't is to ignore or discount both the most violent and the most pedestrian types of racism and
sexism that are still part of our everyday experience. Pretending to live in a
color-blind society when we don't blinds us to social injustice and the history and reality of racism and sexism. The notion of a color-blind society levels
historically meaningful differences and denies the connection between past
racism and sexism and the present.

In *Seeing a Color-Blind Future* Patricia Williams tells an anecdote about
her son's experience in a predominantly white nursery school. Three of the
nursery schoolteachers told Williams that her son was color-blind. But when
she took him to have his eyes tested, the ophthalmologist said that his vision
was fine. Williams describes how she started listening to what her son said
about color and discovered that he didn't confuse one color with another; instead, he resisted identifying colors at all: "'I don't know,' he would say when
asked what color the grass was; or, most peculiarly, 'It makes no difference'"
(1998, 3). So it wasn't that he couldn't see and identify the greenness of the
grass but that he insisted that its greenness made no difference. After some
investigation, Williams realized that her son's refusal to identify color or give
it any meaning was the result of his teachers assuring the children that color
makes no difference, that "it doesn't matter . . . whether you're black or white
or red or green or blue" (3). But Williams reports that "upon further investigation, the very reason that the teachers had felt it necessary to impart this
lesson in the first place was that it *did* matter, and in predictable cruel ways:
some of the children had been fighting about whether black people could
play 'good guys'" (3).

In her first book, *The Alchemy of Race and Rights,* Williams describes another case of when students seem to be arguing over whether or not black
people can "play good guys." She analyzes an incident at Stanford University
where a black student argued with a white student about whether or not
Beethoven was mulatto; the white student maintained that it was "preposter-
ous" that Beethoven was black. The *Stanford University Campus Report* describes what happened: "The following night, the white students said that
they got drunk and decided to color a poster of Beethoven to represent a
black stereotype. They posted it outside the room of Q.C., the black student
who had originally made the claim about Beethoven's race" (quoted in
Williams 1991, 111). After the incident, the white student who instigated the
poster, the one who had argued with Q.C. the night before, did some reading
and found that Beethoven was indeed mulatto: "This discovery upset him, so
deeply in fact that his entire relation to the music changed: he said he heard
it differently" (112). His excuse was that he didn't know and that it was an
innocent mistake. He wasn't disciplined, because Stanford didn't want to vic-
timize him or infringe on his right to free speech (112).

The Beethoven example shows that the preschool arguments over
whether or not black people can be "good guys," although childish, are not
just a preoccupation of children. Williams wonders if the lesson of the
Stanford incident is that the best that blacks can aspire to is being remembered as white like the mulattoes St. Augustine, Beethoven, Alexandre
Dumas, or Aleksandr Pushkin; that those who do remember the "good guys"
as black will be mocked; and that their tormentors will be absolved because it
is a reasonable mistake to assume that the "good guys" are white: they just
didn't know (113).

In *Report,* the white student was upset by "all this emphasis on race, on
blackness. Why can't we just all be human—I think it denies one's humanity
to be 'racial'" (111). Williams points out that this way of thinking implies
that blackness is a category inconsistent with humanity, that being raced is
not to be human. As I argued earlier, categories like *human, white,* and *American* masquerade as categories unmarked by race when in fact they are racially marked by whiteness. The Beethoven example goes to show once again
how whiteness operates as the norm, as racially unmarked, while people of
color are seen as the only ones racial or raced, and to be racially marked is
not to be "just human."

The notion that we have a color-blind society, or that we should act as
though we do even though we don't, reduces racism to an individual rather
than a social problem: according to the white student at Stanford, individuals who mention race are the problem because they refuse to let us all be "just

human." With decisions like *Croson* and *Hopwood,* social problems become irrelevant in a parade of individual rights and wrongs. Rather than see racism or sexism in their institutionalized forms, we see racism and sexism as personality traits or character flaws. Sometimes this character flaw is condemned, for example, when some Texas white men tie a black man to the back of their pickup and drag him to death. Or when a rapist stalks and kills college women in Florida. Sometimes this character flaw is admired as heroism, for example, when Bernhard Goetz emptied his gun into four black teenagers in a New York subway. Or when hundreds of thousands of men gather in sports arenas at Promise Keepers rallies and vow to regain authority in their homes by taking it away from their wives. Sometimes, paradoxically, this personality trait is excused as beyond one's control: "He can't help it—he was raised that way" (still ignoring the social institutions that raised him that way). Or sometimes this personality trait is funny, for example, in American icons of racism and sexism like Archie Bunker, Rush Limbaugh, or Howard Stern. When racism and sexism are turned into an individual problem, they can be dismissed as the result of a few bad or misguided individuals. That way, society—laws, government, businesses, educational institutions—don't have to face the problem. Indeed, with the renewed emphasis on individualism in our culture and courts, racism has become a matter of personal impropriety or an exercise of First Amendment rights rather than a social problem. And insofar as it is a social problem, according to our courts, it is not a legal problem.

The flip side of this individualistic attitude toward racism and sexism is that the victims' experiences of discrimination are explained away as imaginary, the product of paranoia or hysteria, or the result of some physical problem or illness. Their experiences are pathologized and they are made to feel as if there is something wrong with them rather than the social institutions, traditions, and stereotypes that are racist or sexist. Recall the example of Williams's son. His problematic relationship to colors was diagnosed as a physical limitation, as something wrong with him rather than the result of racism at school and his teachers' attempts to teach tolerance by denying that his difference was meaningful. This way of thinking is the product of the individualism that feeds empty notions of equality and counterfactual ideas about a color-blind society. It is the same individualism that supports the reasoning behind *Hopwood*: everyone who really wants to go to the university can because in America everyone can do anything they choose if they work hard enough; and if they don't succeed, then either they didn't deserve it or they didn't work hard enough.

This tendency to blame the victim is also apparent in the debates around

Washington State's Initiative 200. People of color and women are blamed for stealing jobs and opportunities that don't rightfully belong to them. The victims of discrimination are blamed for their own misfortunes—they deserve it because they are unqualified or don't work hard enough or aren't smart enough—and they are blamed for the misfortunes of the beneficiaries of discrimination. If white men are unemployed, it is because of affirmative action policies that have given their jobs to minorities and women—as if black women have all the best jobs. Turning racism and sexism into mental illness, paranoia, or hysteria, or reducing social problems to individual health issues, is another way of blaming the victim.

Blame-the-victim attitudes are fostered by an individualism that denies that any problems are social, governmental, or institutional in nature. Social problems, including racism and sexism, become family matters or individual character traits. The rhetoric of family values is a case in point. The corruption of family values is blamed as the cause of everything from teenage pregnancy and gang violence to urban decay. Instead of being seen as social problems in need of social programs, they are turned into personal or family problems as a way of justifying cuts in government programs. At the same time that politicians employing the rhetoric of family values deny abortion rights and prohibit condoms or other contraceptives from being distributed in schools, they hold young women responsible for teenage pregnancy. Even while they cut welfare, food stamps, medical benefits, day care facilities, and work programs, politicians using the rhetoric of family values hold households headed by women, primarily women of color, responsible for crime and drugs. At the same time that politicians employing the rhetoric of family values maintain that good mothers should be home caring for their children and keeping them off the streets, they complain that poor mothers are taking advantage of welfare benefits to stay home. The rhetoric of family values, with its underlying individualism, covers over the social realities of racism and sexism that work to keep black women in poverty and black men in danger of going to jail or losing their lives.

As we internalize individualistic ideals, we blame ourselves for our own victimization. Women believe that they are imagining things, that they are paranoid, or that they are inept and can't instill proper morals in their children. Blacks believe that they are responsible for racism: if only they were better mothers or fathers, there would be no gang violence or teenage pregnancy. This was the thinking behind the Million Man March when hundreds of thousands of black men gathered in Washington D.C., to "atone for their sins" and promise to be better husbands and fathers. Reducing social problems to personal sins implies that if their sons are in gangs, it is their fault. If their sons are in jail or killed on the streets, it is their fault. If those sons are more likely to be arrested, tried, and sentenced to prison terms than a white man, it is their fault. The consequences and realities of racism become personal sins rather than social problems. The recent Promise Keepers movement actually calls racism a personal sin; rather than address racism as a social problem, movement leaders ask white men to hug men of color and make friends with them at Promise Keepers rallies. The individualism behind notions of formal equality and a color- and gender-blind society reduces social problems to personal sins on the part of whites and men and mental instability or physical defects on the part of people of color and women.

While I was following stories about I-200 in the *Seattle Times,* I noticed an article titled "Biology Keeping Women Awake, Study Concludes" (October 23, 1998, A18). It said that "a study released . . . by the National Sleep Foundation shows that three specific biological events—menstruation, pregnancy and menopause—disrupt the sleep of a majority of women and interfere with how well they function during the day." The implication of this study is that women's inferior performance during the day is the result of a biologic fact. This kind of study harkens back to the idea that women are naturally inferior to men, that they just can't cut it in the professional and public world of men. Culturally and socially charged issues like menstruation, pregnancy, and menopause are reduced to mere biological facts that make women function poorly. The article tells us that the study was based on interviews with women, that is, women's own perceptions of themselves, their sleep patterns and how well they perform during the day. In a culture in which women internalize sexist ideas about their own inadequacy it should be no surprise that women perceive themselves as unable to function. The irony is that the women also report that their husbands' snoring keeps them awake, which suggests that biology may not be the cause of their sleeplessness and poor performance after all.

In *The Alchemy of Race and Rights* Patricia Williams uses a story about size to illustrate the way in which children are taught to discount their own experiences as false on the basis of what they are taught to believe about the world. She describes walking down Fifth Avenue in New York behind a couple and their four-year-old son. The boy was afraid of a big dog, and his parents were trying to convince him that all dogs are alike, that he shouldn't be any more afraid of the giant wolfhound in front of them than the little Pekinese nearby. When asked why he was afraid of big dogs, the little boy said, "They're big!" When asked what the difference between a big dog and a little dog was, the little boy said, "They're big!" The little boy's mother told him that there is no difference between big dogs and little dogs. And his father insisted that if he looked closely enough, he would see that there is really no difference, so he shouldn't be afraid of big dogs (1991, 12–13). In this situation, the parents discounted the fact that the dog was bigger than the child, that while they were looking down on the dog with his wagging tail, the little boy was looking up into a giant mouth full of big, sharp teeth. By universalizing their own relative bigness, they completely obliterated their child's relative smallness (13). To Williams the story illustrates "a paradigm of thought by which children are taught not to see what they see; by which blacks are reassured that there is no real inequality in the world, just their own bad dreams; and by which women are taught not to experience what they experience, in deference to men's ways of knowing" (13).

Rather than pathologize the experiences of women and people of color, it is time to examine the pathology of a culture in which gender blindness and color blindness operate as *hysterical symptoms* and in which race has become subject to *fetishism*, both seen and unseen, what we don't dare mention for fear of being rude, racist, or sued. Freud describes hysterical symptoms as those that "are substitutes—transcriptions as it were—for a number of emotionally cathected mental processes, wishes and desires, which by the operation of a special psychical procedure (repression), have been prevented from obtaining discharge in psychical activity that is admissible to consciousness" (1962, 30). Hysterical symptoms are what we would call psychosomatic symptoms, symptoms that have no physiological cause. Insisting that we are or should be color-blind manufactures a hysterical symptom, one that prevents us from "seeing" racial differences. The symptom, color blindness, takes the place of—or transcribes—emotionally charged issues of race and racism. Racial difference is repressed, and color blindness operates as a psychic substitute for racism. Although color blindness as hysterical symptom has cathected racist attitudes into what appears to be a socially acceptable affliction, racism continues to express itself in other, more violent ways. As Freud describes hysteria, it is prompted by tension between the repressed desire and a strong sense of social propriety. An exaggerated sense of social propriety that develops as a counterbalance to the repressed desire causes the hysteric to manifest the repressed desire as physical symptoms. In the case of hysterical color blindness, the tension between racism and social sanctions against racism redirects racism into the symptom.

In his essay "Psychogenic Visual Disturbance according to Psychoanalytic

Concepts," Freud identifies hysterical blindness with a dissociation between the unconscious and conscious caused by tension or opposition between drive forces. This dissociation becomes so extreme that Freud can say that the hysteric's consciousness is blind while his unconscious can see (1910, 212). Freud attributes this dissociation to a battle between sex drives and ego-preservation drives. He argues that certain organs that perform more than one function—genitals, mouth, eyes—are susceptible to conflict between their functions and the drives that motivate them. The tension or conflict between drives can cause symptoms to appear in these particular organs (216). He explains that hysterical blindness can result from the ego instincts refusing to see in order to curb the sex instincts, or from the sex instincts refusing to see in order to get revenge on the restrictive ego instincts (216). As a sort of cutting off the nose to spite the face, the drives cut off sight to spite each other.

As Freud describes it, hysterical blindness is a kind of punishment that the subject inflicts on himself for some evil or impropriety. A punishing voice within the subject chastises him for the misuse of an organ for evil purposes and ensures that the subject will never misuse the organ again by making that organ cease functioning altogether (217). Hysterical blindness, then, is a symptom of guilt. Freud insists that hysterical blindness is the expression and not the cause of a psychical state (212). Applying Freud's analysis to contemporary uses of color blindness in relation to race, we could interpret it as a symptom of racism. It does seem that color blindness, at least on the most generous reading, is motivated by a sense of guilt over racism.

Ruth Frankenberg's study of white women's relations to race makes this clear. Interviewing white women, she found that "for many white people in the United States, including a good number of the women I interviewed, 'color-blindness'—a mode of thinking about race organized around an effort not to 'see,' or at any rate not to acknowledge, race differences—continues to be the 'polite' language of race" (1993, 142). On the other hand, for many of the women she interviewed, "to be caught in the act of seeing race was to be caught being 'prejudiced'" (145). Frankenberg concludes that what she calls the color- and power-evasive relation to race—color blindness—is a response against earlier biological racism that operated by asserting a biological hierarchy of races:

> White women who grew up before the 1960s came to adulthood well before the emergence and public visibility of the movements that emphasized cultural pride and renewal among people of color. During their formative years,

there were only two ways of looking at race difference: either it connoted hierarchy or it did not (or should not) mean anything at all. Theirs was, then, a
historically situated rejection of the salience of race difference. (145)

This kind of color blindness as a reaction against racism supports Freud's
thesis that hysterical blindness is the result of feelings of guilt over some evil
or impropriety. Feeling guilty for racism of the past, the women whom
Frankenberg interviewed refused to "see" race at all.

The persistence of the metaphor of color blindness, even long after various prideful moments of the 1960s, suggests that color blindness is not just a
compensation for feelings of guilt over past racism. Color blindness is a
symptom of racism. Rather than see and acknowledge racial difference, we
would rather not see at all. Reversing Freud's description of the dissociation
between the unconscious and conscious, a person with racial color blindness
consciously sees race but remains willfully blind to the unconscious effects of
the sight of racial difference. Thus remaining blind to the effects of the sight
of race in a racist culture is a symptom of racism. In a culture that refuses to
see race, we develop a neurotic relation to race. As a culture we suffer from
hysterical color blindness, and so race becomes a type of fetish, both seen
and not seen.

Hysteria and fetishism are both neuroses in that they demand substitu-
tions that attempt to reconcile a tension between reality and unconscious desire. Whereas with hysteria the unconscious desire is manifest in the symptom, with fetishism the unconscious desire is manifest in the fetish. The
fetishist uses the fetish in order to deny some unacceptable reality. The classic fetishist both believes and denies the fact that women, particularly his
mother, do not have a penis; he substitutes some object or some other body
part for the missing maternal penis so that he can continue to believe that
she has one (see Freud 1927). Classic fetishism, then, among other things, is
a denial of sexual difference. The ideal of gender blindness is just such an attempt to deny sexual difference even while acknowledging it. The ideal of
gender blindness maintains that women are just like men; women are equal
to men. This is a particular type of denial of sexual difference that maintains
the masculine sex as the norm and turns everything else into it. Freud diagnoses the fetishist's tendency to deny sexual difference (or, as he says, the tendency to believe that woman is not castrated) as his attempt to protect his
own sex. Sexual difference poses a threat against which he protects himself
by denying that sexual difference and semihallucinating sexual sameness—
that all people have penises.

We could argue that the current attempts to deny racial difference operate in a similar way. The ideal of color blindness operates according to the logic of fetishism: seeing and not seeing at the same time. As the classic fetishist denies sexual difference, the ideal of color blindness denies racial difference. Moreover, as the classic fetishist turns all sex into masculine sex and makes it the norm, the ideal of color blindness makes whiteness the norm. So it is not just a matter of denying difference in color or race but the semihallucinatory insistence that all are white, or all are equal to white. Just as the classic fetishist denies sexual difference in order to protect his own sex from the threat of castration and the powerlessness that comes with it, the ideal of color blindness denies racial difference in order to protect whites from a type of symbolic castration that would undermine their power and normalcy. In addition, the attempt to deny racial difference can be read as an attempt to deny that white is itself a race or that as a category, like other racial categories, it has a history intimately tied to racial differences. The attempt to deny racial difference in order to protect the presumption of whiteness as the norm and a stable category is also an attempt to deny the reality of human history that has been a history of racial mixing, which has taken particular forms and transformations in the United States.

Even while as a nation we are subject to the fetishistic and hysterical ideal of color blindness, the reality of racial difference, whose threat is confirmed by that fetishism and hysteria, came out from under its symptoms and presented itself on November 3, 1998, when 38 percent of South Carolina voters voted to keep a 103-year-old passage in their state constitution that reads, "The marriage of a white person with a Negro or mulatto, or person who shall have ⅛ or more of Negro blood, shall be unlawful and void" (section 33, article 3 of the constitution of South Carolina). When more than a third of the voters in South Carolina think that blacks and whites shouldn't marry, the idea that we live in a color-blind society is at best a delusion that promotes turning a blind eye to the injustice of racism and sexism. We would rather wear blinders in the name of a color- and gender-blind society than work to end racism and sexism by facing the ways in which ours is still a racist and sexist society. We would rather cling righteously to principles of equality than face the ways in which those principles are being used to perpetuate real inequalities.

Facing the ways in which ours is still a racist and sexist society requires that we examine, elaborate, and interpret the process through which we come to see, or not to see, ourselves and others. This examination requires "looking" for what cannot be seen in seeing, the process of coming to see itself. To avoid injustice, we need to continually and vigilantly reinterpret how and why we see what we see and how and why we look for what we do. Working-through the hysterical symptoms and fetishes of racism and sexism requires elaborating our performances in relation to race and sex. The process of interpretation cannot rest. Recognizing that subjectivity and agency depend on the process of witnessing brings with it the responsibility to response-ability. Pathologizing otherness and difference does not enable a self-affirming response on the part of those whom it victimizes. Working-through the pathology of racism requires "seeing" and embracing the responsibility for the ability to respond—the responsibility to witnessing and witnessing subjectivity—even and especially in our blind spots.

8. Vision and Recognition

The ways in which the rhetoric of a color-blind society pathologizes seeing or not seeing race carry a particular set of symptoms that result from the concrete details of historical circumstance. Earlier, following Fanon, I argued that the pathology of racism or oppression cannot be reduced to the normal process of becoming a subject; oppression and domination are not normal products of this process. I have also argued against the normalization of abjection in the process of becoming a subject and developing subjectivity and agency. Throughout *Witnessing: Beyond Recognition*, I have tried to present an alternative account of subject formation, subjectivity, and agency. I have argued that recognition and the struggle or demand for recognition are symptoms of the pathology of oppression. Other manifestations of this pathology are the associations of recognition with criminality and guilt and with alienation and evil. Examining these connections may shed light on the guilt associated with seeing racial or sexual difference.

Rather than challenge the *priority of vision* in philosophy or history, which has already been done by many others, I want to explore the *notion of vision* presupposed by historians and philosophers of recognition.[1] My argument is not that the centrality of vision gives rise to problematic conceptions of subjectivity. Rather, I am arguing that a particular conception of vision is problematic when it is presupposed by theories of subjectivity. Much of the pathology of recognition that I have been diagnosing throughout this project is the result of the presupposition of an especially alienating conception of vision. By thinking through the presuppositions about vision underlying the notion of recognition, I hope to begin to suggest an alternative conception of vision that might change the way that we conceive of recognition, identity, subjectivity, and ethical relations.

Recognition's Visual Foundation

Etymologically, *recognition, witnessing,* even *vigilance* have visual connotations. This is why, in addition to resignifying *recognition, witnessing,* and *vigilance* by doubling their meanings, as I have been attempting to do, it is imperative to rethink the notion of vision that underlies the philosophical and historical uses of these terms. *Recognition* is defined in the *OED* in terms of reviewing, acknowledging, admitting, or confessing, perceiving that something is the same thing as one previously known, the mental process of identifying what has been known before, and color recognition. The connection between recognition and vision is even more explicit in the meaning of the verb *recognize,* from which *recognition* is derived; to recognize means to look over again, to acknowledge by admission or confession or avowal, to treat as valid or as having existence or as entitled to consideration, to take notice in some way, to know again. In addition to its connection to vision, some of the other problematic aspects of using recognition as the basis of identity and ethical relations are signaled in its definition: the idea that recognition is always of something already known, and the idea that to confer recognition is to confer validity, existence, and entitlement.[2]

If recognition connotes vision, what notion of vision does it presuppose? And how is this notion of vision constitutive of theories of subjectivity based on recognition? Martin Jay, in his comprehensive study of vision, *Downcast Eyes,* chronicles the role of vision in philosophy from the veneration of vision in Plato through what he calls the "denigration of vision" in contemporary French philosophy (1994). What Jay does not consider, however, is that this denigration of vision accepts a particular notion of vision. Jay describes various ways in which contemporary French theorists either criticize the priority of vision in Western philosophy or demonize it as a necessary evil. In his reading, philosophers like Jean-Paul Sartre and Jacques Lacan demonize vision as a necessary evil that in various ways alienates us from ourselves, while philosophers like Emmanuel Lévinas and Luce Irigaray criticize the priority given to vision and suggest replacing it with touch. Jay's interpretations of most of the French philosophers he engages share a particular view of vision as an alienating sense that separates us from the world; in his reading, the philosophers adopt different—denigrating—attitudes toward this view of vision.

I want to take a different tack. I want to investigate the notion of vision presupposed by philosophers who both venerate and denigrate vision. There are many different possible notions of vision. And while Jay often touches on different notions throughout the history of philosophy and science, he does not consider that the denigration of vision can be read as a denigration of a *particular notion* of vision. More than this, I will argue that some of the philosophers who supposedly denigrate vision effectively perpetuate this particular alienating notion of vision by presupposing it in their criticisms. Within the confines of my project, this analysis cannot be comprehensive or complete. Rather, I hope to sketch a trajectory that makes my thesis plausible: that much contemporary theory presupposes an especially alienating conception of vision.

This particular conception of vision imagines space as essentially empty and objects (or subjects) in space as points separated by the distance between them. Vision grasps objects at a distance and therefore is seen as either the privileged sense for knowledge or the sense that creates an illusion of mastery over the world. While this view of vision does create this illusion of mastery, there are alternative conceptions of vision that allow for more ethical relations to the world. The illusion of mastery or the privilege of vision in knowing (depending on whether you denigrate or venerate vision) is fortified by the notion that the physical eye is merely the medium for an immaterial mind's eye through which vision (perception) becomes Vision (thought). The separation and mastery over the world are sustained by the privileged perspective of the mind's eye.

For Plato as well as for René Descartes, vision is "the noblest of senses" only insofar as it informs or assists inner vision or the mind's eye.[3] For example, Plato privileges vision in the *Phaedrus* because it begins the process of recollecting beauty seen with the mind's eye; the process of recollecting the Form of Beauty begins with the sight of the beautiful boy. Plato maintains that "sight is the keenest mode of perception vouchsafed us through the body" because beauty can enter through the eyes to the soul and enable the soul to recollect its own sight of the Form of Beauty (1987b, 497: 250d). Descartes privileges inner vision in the *Meditations* when he concludes that clear and distinct ideas are illuminated by "the light of nature."[4] Although, significantly, Descartes does not conceive of space as empty because light "passes toward our eyes through the medium of air and other transparent bodies," he does use vision to separate the body from the mind and the mind from the world (1965, 66).

The separation of mind from world, which allows the mind to know or master the world, also alienates us from the world. This split between the mind and the world for the sake of controlling the world is what Teresa Brennan calls the "foundational fantasy" (1993; Brennan and Jay 1996). She describes the foundational fantasy as the first hallucination of autonomy and control through which the infant imagines itself in control of the maternal breast. Brennan argues that this control necessitates a passive dumb world or other and an active intelligent self or subject (Brennan and Jay 1996, 225). It also sets up the hierarchical split between material and immaterial, body and mind, reality and fantasy. The foundational fantasy of control becomes

> dominant psychically when human beings begin to deny their indebtedness in various forms: one was born free and equal in the marketplace; one owes nothing to nature, to the other, occasionally there is some debt to one's father but more certainly not one's mother. With these denials is born the illusion of autonomy. In this context, perhaps the most significant thing about the dematerialization of the active eye is that it makes us really separate from one another. If the way we see one another is no longer a way of touching, it makes us truly independent and alone. (225)

The imagined substitution of the mind's eye for the physical eye in vision replaces the interrelational dependent subject with an autonomous isolated subject. Vision becomes an alienating sense. Control and mastery are bought at the price of relationships. To give up the separation of the immaterial eye is to give up autonomy and mastery, even knowledge. Brennan argues that "the trend is always to insist that whatever cannot be seen and controlled is not real. The idea that the instrument for seeing, the eye itself, has invisible properties is beyond bearing. The idea that the eye *touches* others threatens autonomy and atomism alike" (227).

It is this radical separation between the mind and the world that some of the French philosophers mentioned by Jay either embrace as a necessary demon or reject along with vision altogether. In the next section, "The Eyes of the Law," I will explore connections between recognition, subjectivity, and criminality in the work of Maurice Merleau-Ponty, Louis Althusser, and Lévinas. I will analyze these connections in order to try to get beyond them. In the following section, "The Evil Eye," I will argue that Sartre and Lacan may "demonize" vision, but they also accept its alienating force. Lévinas, on the other hand, accepts the notion of vision as alienating but for that reason rejects it in favor of touch. Merleau-Ponty and Irigaray, I argue, go further to not only reject vision insofar as it is interpreted as a separating sense of mastery over the world but also suggest an alternative notion of vision based on touch. Rather than pass judgment on vision as either noble or demonic, using the work of psychologist J. J. Gibson, I hope to extend Merleau-Ponty and Irigaray's suggestions toward an alternative notion of vision that might found an alternative notion of subjectivity in relation to the world and others. I want to embrace the invisible, uncontrollable, foundation of vision and our relations with the world and other people in it. This relation, I argue, is based on witnessing, not recognition.

The Eyes of the Law

Strangely, contemporary philosophers have frequently associated recognition with criminality and guilt, specifically insofar as recognition is connected to vision. Seeing and being seen become guilty acts that, for philosophers like Sartre and Althusser, constitute our sense of ourselves as subjects. Metaphors of criminality become the models for subjectivity. Althusser gives us his famous example of ideological interpellation constituting the subject: being hailed by the police (1971, 174–75). Sartre gives us his famous example of the look constituting the subject: being caught peeking through a keyhole (1956, 347–49). Even Lévinas, who grounds his philosophy in the ethics of the face-to-face relationship embodied in the caress, maintains that the subject is constituted as a hostage to the other and that obedience to the other "slips into me 'like a thief'" (e.g., 1991, 11, 112–17, 148). And Merleau-Ponty, for all his attempts to describe fleshy connections across difference, resorts to the metaphor of a criminal recognized by a customs officer (1968, 142). From Sartre's keyhole to Althusser's hail from behind, recognition always makes one guilty.

Merleau-Ponty's metaphor of the criminal seems particularly strange returned to its original context. Simply put, at this point in *The Visible and the Invisible* Merleau-Ponty is trying to solve the problem of solipsism by postulating that I know the other's body (and consciousness) in the same way that I know my own body: "If my left hand can touch my right hand while it palpates the tangibles, can touch it touching, can turn its palpation back upon it, why, when touching the hand of another, would I not touch in it the same power to espouse the things that I have touched in my own?" (1968, 141). He argues that the relation between two people is like the relation between the two eyes in one body. First, he argues that the relation between the different sensations of the body—and therefore between the two eyes—is not a subject-object relation; rather, all sensations are part of one body and work together:

> This means that while each monocular vision, each touching with one sole hand has its own visible, its tactile, each is bound to every other vision, to every other touch; it is bound in such a way as to make up with them the experience of one sole body before one sole world, through a possibility for reversion, reconversion of its language into theirs, transfer, and reversal, according to

which the little private world of each is not juxtaposed to the world of all the others, but surrounded by it, levied off from it, and all together are a Sentient in general before a Sensible in general. Now why would this generality, which constitutes the unity of my body, not open it to other bodies? (142)

So just as there is reversion and reconversion of the language of one into the other such that the senses communicate, there is an analogous transfer and reversal between one person and another. Merleau-Ponty speculates that the synergy between our two eyes, between all of our senses, also exists between different organisms. He says that "their landscapes interweave, their actions and passions fit together exactly: this is possible as soon as we no longer make belongingness to one same 'consciousness' the primordial definition of sensibility, and as soon as we rather understand it as the return of the visible upon itself, a carnal adherence of the sentient to the sensed and of the sensed to the sentient" (1968, 142). The fit between actions and passions is related to the flesh of the world, which is responsible for the reversibility of sensed and sentient. The sensed and sentient fit together exactly. And for Merleau-Ponty, because we are all part of the same fleshy world, the same reversible system of sensibility and sensation, we have access to each other's sensations.

The idea that my body does not belong to me, and that sensation does not belong to consciousness, but that both belong to the world, begins to liberate us from a phenomenology premised on ownership. Still, as Irigaray and others point out, even as he opens up the borders of the body and autonomous self to the world and others, Merleau-Ponty's notion of reversibility that gives access to others inhabiting the same world homogenizes difference. Moreover, this notion ignores differences between sociohistorical subject positions in the world, and all differences between perspectives on the world. The anonymity of vision both liberates us from a subject-centered phenomenology and confines us to see everything in the same light: "For, as overlapping and fission, identity and difference, it brings to birth a ray of natural light that illuminates all flesh and not only my own" (1968, 142).

Merleau-Ponty uses color, and what appears to be an innocent metaphor of the criminal, to substantiate his claims about the accessibility of another's sensations. Since I would like to spend some time thinking through this metaphor, I will quote the passage at length:

It is said that the colors, the tactile reliefs given to the other, are for me an absolute mystery, forever inaccessible. This is not completely true; for me to have not an idea, an image, nor a representation, but as it were the imminent experience of them, it suffices that I look at a landscape, that I speak of it with someone. Then, through the concordant operation of his body and my own, what I see passes into him, this individual green of the meadow under my eyes invades his vision without quitting my own, I recognize in my green his green, as the customs officer recognizes suddenly in a traveler the man whose description he had been given. There is here no problem of the *alter ego* because it is not *I* who sees, not *he* who sees, because an anonymous visibility inhabits both of us, a vision in general, in virtue of that primordial property that belongs to the flesh, being here and now, of radiating everywhere and forever, being an individual, of being also a dimension and a universal. (1968, 142)

What does it mean to recognize "his green" as the customs officer recognizes a wanted man? Why does Merleau-Ponty, seemingly unthinkingly, connect recognition with the law recognizing the outlaw? How does the anonymity of vision guarantee this recognition? In what sense does the operation of recognizing the criminal give me access to the other's perception?

Merleau-Ponty uses the customs officer's recognition to describe how I recognize the green that you see as the same green that I see. He describes looking at a meadow together and talking about it. Through the bodily operations of looking and talking together, my vision "invades" yours as what I see "passes into" you. At this point, after the invasion of vision and the passing of sight, I recognize your green in my green as the customs officer recognizes the wanted man. In this scenario, we both look together and then we talk about what we see, presumably describing it to each other. Next, because we are embodied, and because visibility is anonymous and does not belong to either of us but, rather, to flesh itself, what I see passes through you, and the green of the meadow invades you. The green flesh of the meadow makes its impression on both of us. But how do I know that? I know that the green you see is the same green that I see because I recognize your green—once again, presumably the green that you have been describing—in my green, the green that I see. What does it mean that this recognition is like the customs officer recognizing the wanted man?

The customs officer has been given a description of the wanted man. He is on the lookout for a man who fits the description. He is looking for the characteristics described in what he sees. As a result, he is suspicious and takes note of anyone bearing those characteristics and possibly matching the description. When he sees a man who matches the description, suddenly that man is transformed from a traveler to the wanted man. When you describe the green of the meadow to me, it seems that I am on the lookout for the green that fits your description. I take note of any color bearing those characteristics. When I see a color that matches your description, it becomes your green, which I also recognize as my green. Suddenly, my green becomes your green, just as the traveler becomes the wanted man. The recognition that brings us together is analogous to the customs officer's "Aha, that's him!" But the officer's recognition is the result of suspicion. It is a recognition that is at the same time an accusation. The man on the side of the law recognizes the man outside the law.

Is it because the customs officer and the wanted man are both subject to the law that defines their relationship that we are both subject to the anonymity of vision that defines our relationship? Or, rather, in the analogy does visibility occupy the place of the outlaw? The wanted man occupies the place of the green of the meadow. The green of the meadow forces a recognition in the same way that the criminal does, through our descriptions of it/him. Or is it, rather, that your green occupies the place of the criminal? I am looking at my green and after your description I see in it your green just as the customs officer looks at the traveler and in the description of the wanted man sees him as the criminal. Your green is the wanted man that I recognize through your description. Your green is the outlaw that I see from my position on the side of the law. Does Merleau-Ponty mean to suggest that the perception and experience of the other are recognized as outlawed? This unfortunate metaphor seems to act as an indictment of recognition itself. It accuses recognition of involving criminal activity outside the law. Recognition is of the wanted man, the criminal, the outlaw, from the position of the law, through some sort of all-points bulletin. Recognition, which is supposed to bring us together in a shared vision, is born out of suspicion and fulfilled in accusation.

Like the customs officer always on the lookout, it may seem that I have made too much of this marginal character in Merleau-Ponty's phenomenology of recognition; but the criminal is impossible to avoid in Althusser's account of ideological recognition. While Merleau-Ponty describes the officer's recognition of the wanted man, Althusser describes the recognition of the wanted man through the officer's hail. At stake in Merleau-Ponty's account is how we recognize the other's experience or perception, which he claims is prior to recognizing either ourselves or the other as subjects. Merleau-Ponty suggests that the bodily recognition he describes circumvents the subject-object/other distinction (even if it doesn't avoid guilt and suspicion).

Althusser, on the other hand, is concerned precisely with how we are constituted as subjects. He claims that ideology "acts" or "functions" in such a way that it "recruits" subjects among the individuals (it recruits them all), or "transforms" the individuals into subjects (it transforms them all) by that very precise operation which I have called interpellation or hailing, and which can be imagined along the lines of the most commonplace everyday police (or other) hailing "Hey, you there!" (1971, 174)

In Althusser's scenario, an individual becomes a subject by turning around in response to the police officer's hail. Althusser uses this example to try to break away from the mere "'consciousness' of our incessant (eternal) practice of ideological recognition" and begin to develop what he calls a "scientific (i.e., subjectless) discourse on ideology" (173). He suggests that what he identifies as everyday rituals of recognition—handshakes, calling people by their names, responding "It's me" to the question "Who's there?"—do not give us scientific knowledge of the mechanism of this recognition (173). His example is intended to give us scientific insight into the mechanism of recognition.

In a footnote, Althusser says that "hailing as an everyday practice subject to a precise ritual takes on a quite 'special' form in the policeman's practice of 'hailing' which concerns the hailing of 'suspects'" (174). In addition, he claims that the fact that "the one hailed always recognizes that it is really him who is being hailed . . . cannot be explained solely by 'guilt feelings,' despite the large numbers who 'have something on their consciences'" (174). What, then, does the police hail example show us about the mechanism of recognition that other more "friendly" examples don't if it is not that recognition operates through suspicion and guilt?

Judith Butler extends Althusser's analysis and example in order to substantiate her argument that the subject is constituted in its subjection to the law (1997b). Her reading confirms that suspicion and guilt are necessary parts of the mechanism of recognition. Rather than reject this view of recognition, or reject recognition altogether in favor of another model, Butler accepts this pessimistic view of subject formation and argues that interpellation always fails even as it succeeds. While I prefer to go beyond recognition and think of subject formation as outside of an economy of guilt and suspicion, Butler's reading is helpful in understanding the mechanisms at work in Althusser's conception of recognition. Understanding his conception will be instructive in diagnosing the pathology of recognition models of subject formation, especially insofar as recognition is complicit with a particularly pathological notion of vision.

Butler makes the visual aspect of Althusser's scenario explicit:

> Why would the person on the street respond to "Hey, you there!" by turning
> around? What is the significance of turning to face a voice that calls from be-
> hind? This turning toward the voice of the law is a sign of a certain desire to be
> beheld by and perhaps also to behold the face of authority, a visual rendering
> of an auditory scene—a mirror stage or, perhaps more appropriately, an
> "acoustic mirror"—that permits the misrecognition without which the so-
> ciality of the subject cannot be achieved. (1997b, 112)

The officer's hail is prompted by the recognition of the sort that Merleau-
Ponty describes, which is based on seeing someone suspicious. Then the suspect is caught in the gaze of the officer and turns around out of a desire to be
seen by and to see the law. Butler compares this mechanism of recognition to
the Lacanian mirror stage, or what Kaja Silverman calls the "acoustic mirror," which Butler suggests points to an "irreducible ambiguity between the
'voice' of conscience and the 'voice' of law" (Butler 1997b, 210; Silverman
1988).

Like the Lacanian mirror recognition, Althusser's ideological recognition
is always necessarily a misrecognition of agency and authority. The Althusserian subject recognizes itself as a subject only through its subjection
and subordination to the law as a guilty suspect. Butler describes the process:

> Social existence, existence as a subject, can be purchased only through a guilty
> embrace of the law, where guilt guarantees the intervention of the law and,
> hence, the continuation of the subject's existence. If the subject can only as-
> sure his/her existence in terms of the law, and the law requires subjection for
> subjectivation, then, perversely, one may (always already) yield to the law in
> order to continue to assure one's existence. (1997b, 112)

As a case study, and a defining moment in the ideology of recognition,
Althusser turns to religion to substantiate his theory. In his discussion of religion, the Althusserian mirror becomes explicit when he claims that man as
subject to God mirrors God as the Absolute Subject. The mirror is doubled
when God sends his Son, his duplicate, to earth (1971, 179). Through this
duplication of mirrors, Althusser identifies a double specularity at the heart
of recognition. All recognition, he argues, is based on this specular duplication: "This mirror duplication is constitutive of ideology and ensures its
functioning" (180). The double mirror connection *subjects* subjects to the
Subject/God and at the same time guarantees their uniqueness as the ones
recognized by God. By being subjected, they are recognized, and they are rec-

ognized by being subjected. Since they are the mirror image of God, after all, God is sure to recognize them. In her study of Althusser, Butler concludes that the attempt to critique religion necessarily engages its reinforcement. She argues that "the exemplary status of religious authority underscores the paradox of how the very possibility of subject formation depends upon a passionate pursuit of a recognition which, within the terms of the religious example, is inseparable from a condemnation" (1997b, 113).

At the center of his case study in ideology Althusser uses the example of God's call to Moses and Moses's answer, "It is (really) I! I am Moses thy servant, speak and I shall listen!" (179). Like the policeman, God hails Moses and Moses is compelled to answer. Althusser argues that like the wanted man Moses is interpellated as a subject at the moment that he recognizes himself as a subject in the hail from the Law/God. The moment of recognition is the moment that the addressee realizes that the call is really addressed to him, as a unique irreplaceable subject. Moses recognizes himself as a subject of God just as the police suspect recognizes himself as subject to the law. The proof, says Althusser, is that Moses obeys God, just as the suspect obeys the policeman (179).

Of course, Moses does not behave like Althusser's police suspect. Moses does not turn to see God; he hides his face. Moses does not immediately and without question obey God. It seems that Moses may not be predisposed to obey the command. In fact, he argues with God that he cannot speak to Pharaoh because of his "slow tongue" and "uncircumcised lips," and God subsequently threatens him with death, only after which he obeys without argument (see Exodus 3–6). Althusser's example of Moses works against his suppositions about the role of recognition in the constitution of the subject. Moses does not recognize himself as a subject through God's hail. While he does respond, "Here am I," he immediately turns away from God and tries to hide. More than that, he keeps insisting that he cannot speak and that the children of Israel do not listen to him (Exodus 4:10; 6:12). He does not recognize himself as the unique and singular addressee of the hail; instead, he denies that the hail could be addressed to him. It is not the rituals of recognition that constitute Moses as an obedient subject. Rather, it is the repetition of the rituals of the covenant—God's contracting—that is continually reinscribed in his relationship to Zipporah, his wife.[5] The covenant precedes and motivates God's revelation of the Law to Moses. Before Moses, there is no Law per se, but instead the repetitions of the contract or covenant that God makes with Israel.[6]

It will be instructive to compare Lévinas's use of the biblical "Here I am" with Althusser's. We could say that whereas Althusser imagines subject constitution within an economy of criminal law, Lévinas imagines subject constitution within an economy of contract law. For Althusser, the hail or command from God or the policeman constitutes the subject as unique through the subject's own subjection to the law in his turn to face the Law. Lévinas describes a similar scenario in which the subject is constituted as unique through the call of the other. Like Althusser's hail, Lévinas's call is a command that the subject is compelled to obey. Both Althusser and Lévinas describe the subject's predilection to turn, to obey the hail or call. Before the hail, the "subject" already has been subjected to the law; the "subject" already has what Butler calls the desire or passion for the law (1997b, 128–29). Reading Althusser, Butler diagnoses this readiness to turn as a sign that the subject is already in relation to the law, to the voice of the law; that the subject is already implicated in its own subjection to authority and its subsequent misrecognition of itself as a subject with its own authority. She suggests that "turning is merely a sign of an inevitable submission by which one is established as a subject positioned in language as a possible addressee. In this sense, the scene with the police is a belated and redoubled scene, one which renders explicit a founding submission for which no such scene would prove adequate" (1997b, 111).

Lévinas also maintains that "obedience precedes any hearing of the command" (1991, 148). He says that this predilection to obedience is "an anarchic being affected, which slips into me 'like a thief' through the outstretched nets of consciousness" (148). Lévinas uses metaphors of criminality—burglary, thieves, hostages—to describe the readiness to obey the law. In this regard, like Althusser's, his discourse evokes criminality. Yet Lévinas is not comparing the subject to a criminal or a suspect, but, rather, the law itself is the metaphorical criminal that slips in to constitute subjectivity. Subjectivity is constituted through this clandestine operation of the other in the same, the clandestine command of the other at the foundations of subjectivity. Criminality is the result not of my guilt—although Lévinas's subject is accused—but of the command binding me before I become an *I*. The criminal is evoked by the fact that I am contracted to obey. The agency of the contract itself is criminal. At the extreme, we might say that for Lévinas, God/the infinite is the criminal that sneaks in like a thief or burglar to hold me hostage. And it is this bondage that constitutes me as a subject.

If the Althusserian subject is criminal, the Lévinasian subject is a martyr. Lévinas says that "the subjectivity of the subject is persecution and martyrdom" (1991, 146). The subject is not self-conscious and does not choose to martyr itself for the other. Yet paradoxically, and at the same time, without choice the subject has a responsibility to the other, to be for the other. It seems that in order to make his point that the ethical obligation is not symmetrical—I have always one more responsibility for the other's responsibility—Lévinas uses extreme metaphors of bondage and persecution. He says that "the one is exposed to the other as a skin is exposed to what wounds it, as a cheek is offered to the smiter. . . . it is a denuding beyond the skin, to the wounds one dies from, denuding to death . . . being torn up from oneself . . . one-penetrated-by-the other" (49). While I appreciate the urgency of Lévinas's call to ethics, and the necessity of extreme formulations in order to remain vigilant in response to it, I am not convinced that we gain much by privileging martyrdom of the self over murder of the other. Is it better to be penetrated by some criminal Lévinasian force that slips in like a thief or to be caught in oneself like an Althusserian criminal turning to answer the hail of the policeman?

Lévinas's notion of response is promising, and yet like Althusser's interpellation its echoes of an authoritative God make it suspect. For all of their metaphors of criminality, neither Lévinas nor Althusser offers us any true outlaws. Rather, for both, in significantly different ways, subjectivity is always circumscribed by law. By exploring some of the differences in their notions of law and obedience, I hope to open up the possibility of getting beyond the associations between subjectivity, recognition, and criminality. For Lévinas, the hail or call from the other does not operate in the realm of ideology or even the realm of justice, but the realm of the ethical, which he associates with prophecy and revelation.

The biblical "Here I am" is a response to the call from God, but it is a response that anticipates the call in the realm of what Lévinas calls prophecy or revelation. Trying to describe the law of prophecy or inspiration, Lévinas quotes Isaiah: "Before they call, I will answer" (1991, 150). For Lévinas, this "obedience prior to the hearing of the order" is not a sign that the subject is always already implicated in ideology à la Althusser; rather, it is a sign of the infinite otherness at the center of subjectivity. Lévinas says that "this singular obedience to the order to go, without understanding the order, this obedience prior to all representation, this allegiance before any oath, this responsibility prior to commitment, is precisely the other in the same, inspiration and prophecy, the *passing itself* of the Infinite" (150). The movement of infinity through the subject compels response because response itself is infinite. As Lévinas says, there is always one more response to give: "Beyond any responsibility attributed to everyone and for everyone, there is always the additional fact that I am still responsible for that responsibility" (1989, 226).

Paradoxically, infinity manifests itself in this infinite responsibility through the subject's response to the other even while responsibility is the movement of the Infinite itself. The ethical obligation of infinite responsibility is the Covenant: "In the Covenant, when it is fully understood, in the society which fully develops all dimensions of the Law, society becomes a community" (1989, 226). The Covenant or the contract is the ethical contract that makes community and communion possible. This Covenant is the ethical contract that exists before any contract or oath as the infinite bond between human beings. As response, the obedience to the call is not the obedience to a repressive or authoritative law that subjects me even while it constitutes me as subject in my turn toward it (1989, 150). This covenant is the law of prophecy. Rather than choosing Moses, Lévinas picks Isaiah's "Here I am" to exemplify responsibility. The law of prophecy is not like criminal law or any other kind of restrictive law. Although this law compels obedience, it does so from the foundation of subjectivity itself, which is the otherness or infinite out of which it is born. In his introduction to Lévinas's *Basic Philosophical Writings,* Adrian Peperzak describes this Lévinasian law:

> This formulation does not refer to some private, secret, or mystical experience; instead it exhibits me as being-for-the-other (and not for my self in the interiority of an encompassing Cogito). Even against my wish or will, my Saying already testifies to the Infinite, which reveals itself in giving me breath for this very Saying. Inspiration is the condition for all Saying and human life as such. This, and not the inner adventure of a self-contained soul, is the "secret" of all prophecy: to speak in obedience to the "law" of inspiration. (Quoted in Lévinas 1996, 97)

As response, obedience to the "law" of inspiration or prophecy is an obedience to the saying in the said, to the performance of my subjectivity in relation to others. As response, obedience is bearing witness to the infinite responsibility that makes us human subjects:

> "Here I am" as a witness of the Infinite, but a witness that does not thematize what it bears witness of, and whose truth is not the truth of representation, is not evidence. There is witness, a unique structure, an exception to the rule of being, irreducible to representation, only of the Infinite. The Infinite does not appear to him that bears witness to it. On the contrary, the witness belongs to the glory of the Infinite. It is by the voice of the witness that the glory of the Infinite is glorified. (Lévinas 1989, 146)

For Lévinas, the turning toward the law is not a subjection that is necessary in order to be a subject but, rather, a response to the Infinite by virtue of which we are subjects.

Taking a step away from Lévinas and leaving behind some of his religious language, we could say that response—to a hail, or a call, or a question, or a cry, or a plea, or a gesture—is obligated by our very subjectivity. We are by virtue of our relations with others. Our sense of ourselves as subjects and agents is born out of witnessing relations. The fact that we speak, what Lévinas calls the Saying in the Said, is testimony to our connection with others. We can speak only because we are spoken to and only because someone listens. The possibility of an interlocutor is what makes subjectivity possible. This possibility is what Dori Laub calls the "inner witness." Subjectivity depends on, is constituted and nourished by, witnessing. As such, witnessing bears witness to itself in all human interaction. The Lévinasian Infinite could be reinterpreted as the transcendence that is born in human relationships. Like what Irigaray refers to as the sensible transcendental, what happens between people, what happens in human relationships, what makes human relationships human is what take us beyond ourselves and toward otherness. Through relationships humanity gives birth to divinity.

The Evil Eye

Lacan's influential account of ego formation in "The Mirror Stage" is another model of the essential link between vision and recognition. There, Lacan argues that unlike other animals, as infants human beings compensate for lack of real motor coordination with images that anticipate motor coordination. Human beings are especially reliant on visual images because of our "premature birth," "anatomical incompleteness," and "residual humors from the maternal organism" (Lacan 1977, 4). We are even more dependent on vision than pigeons and locusts, the animals that Lacan uses to make his argument that mimicry is essential to identity.

For Lacan, the mirror stage inaugurates the infant's entrance into the outside world in which things are visibly distinct from each other. As such, Lacan calls it the threshold of the visible world (1977, 3). But the mirror image is not just any other visible image available to the sense of sight. Rather, its most important function is the initiation of a psychic image or imago that is not sensible but mental. The mirror image is the threshold between the inner world and the outside world (4). It is the threshold of the visible world and the psychic world, the outside world and the inner world, the body's eye and the mind's eye. It is the threshold between *vision* and *visions.* And, therefore, it is in fact the threshold of the I. At the threshold of the visible world we slip from physical to psychic, from material to immaterial, from sensible to mental, from body to mind, from eye to I.

What makes this transition from vision to visions, from eye to I, possible? Why does this visible, physical image in the mirror give rise to an invisible psychic image? I want to argue that for Lacan it is the empty space or gap between the body of the infant and its mirror image that opens up the space of visions or the inner world. Lacan maintains that the infant's ego or sense of agency is developed in relation to its mirror image and sets up the ego-ideal. The discrepancy between the ideal and reality leaves the subject with an inevitable sense of alienation and frustration. This discrepancy is the result of the fact that the image is always elsewhere, cut off from the infant's body. This cut prefigures Lacan's insistence that the real is impossible or forever cut off from the realm of images or symbols. At a fundamental level, however, this split between the real and the imaginary or symbolic returns to the empty space between body and image that produces the first sense of alienation in the mirror stage. In a sense, by imagining the empty space between the infant and the mirror, it seems that Lacan's analysis creates the very split between the inner and outer worlds that his theory attempts to reconnect with the mirror stage as threshold.

If Lacan's analysis of the misrecognition in the mirror stage is dependent on the gap or empty space between the body and its image, this is because that gap is seen as a void or abyss that permanently separates "us" from our "object," even if this object is our own image or another self-consciousness. Lacan's analysis of misrecognition (which is always the flip side of recognition—doesn't misrecognition suppose that something could be recognized but isn't?) supposes that we are fundamentally separated from others and objects because of the empty physical space between us that can only be bridged by vision. Yet it is the presupposition that vision operates across distance and separation that creates this gap in the first place. So vision is imagined as a sense that inaugurates an abyss, which is in fact created by the faulty presupposition that vision traverses empty space. Space, after all, is not empty, and there is no physical gap between the infant and his mirror image. The infant, the mirror, and his image inhabit the same world of air, light, heat, and the continual movement of matter that keeps them in constant connection.

In his later work, Lacan seems to revise and complicate his mirror stage account when he explicitly theorizes vision in *The Four Fundamental Concepts of Psychoanalysis* (1981). One of the most obvious contrasts between "The

Mirror Stage" essay and this later work is his treatment of mimicry. In the earlier essay he suggests that subject formation is the result of mimicry and the two-sided relation of image to self; he says that just as the image of like beings sets off sexual development in insects and birds, so too the image of like beings sets off subjective development in human beings. In the later work, mimicry is not the one-directional miming of an image in a two-sided relationship. Rather, in a sense Lacan asks whether the "original" may not hold its fascination because of its resemblance to the "mime" and not the reverse (1981, 74). He gives the example of insects with parts that look like eyes, *ocelli*, but aren't. He asks "whether they impress by their resemblance to eyes, or whether, on the contrary, the eyes are fascinating only by virtue of their relation to the form of the *ocelli*" (74).

This discussion of mimicry appears in a section titled "The Split between the Eye and the Gaze" in which Lacan proposes that subject is always split between the eye—its own perspective—and the gaze, the fact that it can be seen from all other perspectives: "I see only from one point, but in my existence I am looked at from all sides" (1981, 72). Lacan posits that the gaze "preexists" the eye and therefore our vision is always "stained" by the gaze (72, 74). Vision, what he associates with the eye, can act as a way to avoid the gaze and deny its effects on one's own subjectivity (74). The illusion of the eye—that we are autonomous, self-controlled subjects who see from the perspective of a unified consciousness, and that we are conscious of what we see, indeed that we are self-conscious—is used to avoid the gaze. In other words, the illusion of autonomy avoids the fact that we are already situated by the gaze of the Other.

While Lacan's notion of the gaze is reminiscent of Sartre's, Lacan is quick to point out that his gaze is not Sartre's (1981, 84).[7] For Sartre, the look of the Other catches me in the act and turns my consciousness back on itself to confront the dialectic of being and nothingness at my core, which is thereby constitutive of a world that is always for me. For Lacan, however, the look or gaze does not originate with another subject who by virtue of his subjectivity makes me into an object, and at the same time gives me and robs me of my freedom, and throws me face to face with the nothingness at the core of my being. Rather, the Lacanian gaze preexists the subject's own seeing and positions the subject in relation to desire. This is to say that the Lacanian subject is not the center of the universe. This seems to be one of the lessons of Lacan's story of his fishing trip in which a fisherman points to a can and tells him, "You see that can. Do you see it? Well, it doesn't see you!" (95). Lacan uses this story to make the point that the subject is not the center of the universe or the other's gaze: he argues that in a sense the can does see you because you are looked at from all sides; and he claims that this experience made him feel like "nothing on earth" (96).

The Lacanian gaze, then, is not the look of another person or another subject: "The gaze in question is certainly the presence of others as such. But does this mean that originally it is in the relation of subject to subject, in the function of the existence of others as looking at me, that we apprehend what the gaze really is?" (1981, 84). Lacan answers that the gaze belongs neither to the subject nor to the other, but to the field of the Other. Thus the Lacanian gaze is not from any particular other but from the Other, the Symbolic, or the realm of Meaning itself.

While the Sartrean look moves from one subject to the next in a linear progression of guilt—the woman in the room is being looked at through the keyhole by the peeping Tom who is caught in the act by the footsteps he hears coming up the stairs—the Lacanian gaze moves through the triangular structure of desire. Lacan insists that "the subject in question is not that of the reflexive consciousness, but that of desire" (1981, 89). In the fisherman story it is not that Lacan is caught by the fisherman's look; if anything, he is caught by the look of the can. Rather, the fisherman, the can, and Lacan form the triangle through which the gaze operates.

The dilemma of Lacan's prisoner is another example of the triangulation of the gaze, desire, and recognition (1966, 206–8). In this story, prisoners are given white or black discs on their backs. By looking at the discs of the other prisoners, they try to determine the color of their own discs. If they determine that they have a white disc, then they are free to go. Lacan uses this story to describe the process of recognition through which one attains subjectivity. Subjectivity is dependent on recognizing the recognition of the other (Does he move to the door when he sees my disc?). The subject knows his own color only by looking at the colors of the others and by looking at the others' reactions when they look at him. Here again the connection between vision and recognition, between vision and Vision, is essential.

Lacan's other famous story of seeing and not seeing, from his analysis of Poe's "The Purloined Letter," also exhibits this triangular structure of desire in which everyone is seen seeing from another position but never from their own. In his reading of Poe's tale, Lacan identifies three positions of the glance that trap subjects in an endless repetition: "The first is a glance that sees nothing: the King and the police. The second, a glance which sees that the first sees nothing and deludes itself as to the secrecy of what it hides: the Queen, then the Minister. The third sees that the first two glances leave what should be hidden exposed to whomever would seize it: the Minister, and finally Dupin" (1988, 32). The King and the police have only the illusion of vision, which for Lacan is all there is to vision. They naively assume that they are self-possessed seers who see what is there. The Queen and the Minister who occupy the second position are also duped into believing that their secret is safe because the others do not see. From the third position, the Minister and Dupin see more than the other two because they see the others' glance, but they are still blind to their own vision, which is to say their own blind spot. One's own perspective is really always a blind spot.

Sartre's look, then, would be nothing more than Lacan's eye or vision, a blind spot parading as self-consciousness. So, too, the image in the mirror stage would be associated with the eye or vision caught up in the specular fantasy of wholeness and agency. Lacan's gaze, on the other hand, moves us from the linear line of sight to the triangular operation of desire that blinds us to our own perspective. It moves us from the Imaginary two-dimensional world of the mirror stage to the three-dimensional world of the Symbolic and desire. In this sense, Lacan's later formulation privileges the Symbolic over the Imaginary and renders a more social account of subjectivity, determined as it is by the gaze of the Other. In addition, with the later theory it becomes impossible to say, as Lacan does earlier, that the mirror stage is the threshold of the visual world; vision no longer gives birth to Vision. Martin Jay summarizes some of the differences between the mirror stage and later account of vision:

> Whereas in the mirror-stage argument, vision was involved in an imaginary identification with a gestalt of corporeal wholeness, an identification due to a specular projection of narcissistic sameness, now it was connected as well with desire for the other. . . . vision necessarily enters the realm of the Symbolic in which language is paramount. (1994, 368)

At least one thing remains constant from Lacan's earlier remarks to his later ones on vision: vision opens a contestatory space that initiates aggressivity and alienation. In *The Four Fundamental Concepts of Psychoanalysis* Lacan insists that alienation is not the result of the fact that the subject finds himself in the field of the Other—that he recognizes himself through the Other, or that his meaning is from the Other. Rather, he argues that there is a fundamental ontological split between being and meaning such that the subject cannot have both at once: the subject either is (being) or has meaning, but not both at once. This alienation is not the specular alienation of the mirror stage but the alienation essential to signification and the subject's relation to language. As language becomes paramount, the alienation inherent in language also becomes paramount.

Separation is a crucial operation of signification, which Lacan associates with alienation (1981, 214). He develops his theory of the alienation and separation inherent in language using the distinction between the eye and the gaze and a particular notion of vision. Even while he criticizes the notion that Vision or self-consciousness is separated from vision by virtue of turning back on itself (the separation between the mind's eye and the eye, the self-reflective act of seeing myself seeing enabled by that distance), he proposes a hypothesis about the dynamics of sight itself based on separation and distance: "The eye is a sort of bowl—it flows over, too, it necessitates around the ocular bowl, a whole series of organs, mechanisms, defenses. The iris reacts not only to distance, but also to light" (94). Sight is based on light and distance. And because of this, for Lacan it is also caught up with the gaze, which defies self-reflection or any real relation with another person. Lacan maintains that "that which is light looks at me.... the shimmering of a surface that is not, in advance, situated for me in its distance. This is something that introduces what is elided in the geometrical relation—the depth of field, with all its ambiguity and variability, which is in no way mastered by me" (96). Here Lacan claims that this is not optical space but something visual that is inherent in subjectivity itself. In his earlier essay on the mirror stage, Lacan presupposes the emptiness of optical space and the distance it creates between and within subjects and the world; in his later writing, he displaces that emptiness and distance onto the plane of the visual and the gaze. Alienation moves from the imaginary to the properly Symbolic.

Alienation and the paranoid nature of the gaze share something with Sartre's look. Recall that for Sartre, shame is the primary experience of one caught by the look of the other. We make doubtful improvement with Lacan, for whom alienation is the primary experience of one caught in the gaze. Presenting a psychoanalytic reading of Sartre's notion of the look, René Held argues that the look exhibits pathological fear, anxiety, and masochism, which he associates with the myth of the power of the evil eye (1952). With Lacan, the evil eye becomes the essence of the gaze.

Describing the relation between the gaze and the eye, Lacan wildly suggests that the eye of the gaze is "the eye filled with voracity, the evil eye" (1981, 115). This is not an individual evil eye controlled by its bearer. Rather, it is a universal evil eye that for Lacan comes to define the eye in relation to the gaze. In this paranoid universe the subject "operates by remote control" in response to the evil eye of the gaze. Fundamental to the power of the evil eye is the power to separate, which is what causes the subject's alienation, condemnation, and even damnation: "It is striking, when one thinks of the universality of the function of the evil eye, that there is no trace anywhere of a good eye, of an eye that blesses. What can this mean, except that the eye carries with it the fatal function of being in itself endowed—if you will allow me to play on several registers at once—with a power to separate?" (1981, 115). From beginning to end, the subject is separated from the object of his desire. And for Lacan this separation is connected to vision.

The presupposition that space is empty and vision both traverses and fails to traverse that empty space is what leads Lacan and some of his predecessors to conclude that all intersubjective relationships are aggressive and alienating encounters. The *sight* of the other incites aggression because sight only serves to remind us of the abyss separating us from others. For Hegel it is the sight of the other self-conscious body mimicking your actions that makes you want to kill it: "Each *sees* the *other* do the same as it does; each does itself what it demands of the other, and therefore also does what it does only insofar as the other does the same" (Hegel 1977, 112; my emphasis). For Freud the sight of the supposedly castrated sex of females initiates all of the rage, jealousy, and murderous impulses of the Oedipal situation: "Probably no male human being is spared the terrifying shock of threatened castration at the *sight* of the female genitals" (Freud 1972a, 216; my emphasis); "The *observation* that finally breaks down the [male] child's unbelief [in castration threats] is the *sight* of the female genitalia" (1972a, 178, my emphasis); "They [females] notice the penis of a brother or playmate, strikingly *visible* and of large proportions, at once recognize it as the superior counterpart of their own small and inconspicuous organ, and from that time forward fall a victim to envy for the penis" (1972b, 187; my emphasis). For Freud, the castration threat and penis envy that both initiate and resolve the Oedipal situation revolve around looking at the other. For Lacan the alienating function of the I as it is misrecognized in the mirror releases aggressivity in relation to any other (1977, 6). In the mirror stage, it is in fact the gap between the recognition of my own limitations and my misrecognition of the ideal other as myself that inaugurates the antagonism between self and others in the struggle for recognition.

In these theories, vision creates a sense of lack, castration, or alienation, the sense of being cut off from the world or being alone. It seems that what we see when we recognize ourselves or the other is the distance between us, and the rest of our lives are spent in the futile and alienating attempt to fill that gap. In this scenario we imagine that by getting rid of the other we can close the space between us and overcome alienation. But what we cannot see are the elements that make vision possible—light, air, matter—and that fill the space between us. What we do not recognize makes recognition possible. What we cannot see in this notion of vision are the elements that connect us. What is it, then, about the sense of sight that makes us feel cut off and thereby opens psychic space?

9. Toward a New Vision

Ironically enough, vision traditionally has been separated from the other senses because it gives us privileged access to the invisible world. This access, as I have been arguing, is dependent on the distance presumed to be maintained through vision, a distance seemingly not inherent in our other (less reliable) senses. Yet perhaps unlike taste and touch, hearing and smelling are senses that also work across distance just like vision. Like vision, they depend on the movement of particles, waves, or vibrations under the influence of forces of heat, pressure, density, and so forth. So what is special about vision? Perhaps it is the idea that our other senses operate through orifices that not only open onto the world but also allow the world access to our bodies that the other senses don't maintain the gap or abyss that sends us into a self-reflective swoon. Our eyes *appear* to be solid, mirrors reflecting images on their pupils, windows onto the soul. But, as we know, they are porous and fluid. We see only because light travels into our eyes and meets our optic nerves. Like the other senses, vision is the result of pressures, vibrations, particles, and waves affecting the nerves. And visual images are surrounded and informed by tastes, smells, sounds, and palpitations. Indeed, the senses necessarily work together and cannot be neatly separated.

Ecological Optics and Affective Energy

Psychologist J. J. Gibson has developed what he calls "ecological optics" in order to explain how vision works as a perceptual system (1950, 1961, 1966).[1] Gibson argues that there are not just five senses but various perceptual systems. He points out that even textbooks list anywhere from six to a dozen or more senses (1966, 48). He rejects the notion of a sense or sense organ in favor of perceptual systems, which are the result of cooperative efforts between parts of the body and the body as a whole. Every perceptual system operates through the whole body along with a set of organs, not just one sense organ such as the eyes or ears. The basic perceptual system on which all others depend is our orientation to gravity. Gibson explains that the hairs in the inner ear operate as a sense organ receptive to gravitational pull. All living beings respond to gravity. When awake and upright, animals are constantly negotiating the force of gravity in order to maintain their posture and position. The other perceptual systems depend on this basic orienting system because "the postures of the sensitive organs in the head depend on the posture of the head, and the postures of the extremities depend on the posture of the body. Hence the exploratory searching of the eyes, ears, nose, mouth, and hands depends on an upright body, and the orienting of these organs rests on orientation to gravity" (1966, 51).

As I mentioned in the introduction, more recent work from psychologists Andrew Meltzoff and Keith Moore confirms that every perceptual system operates in conjunction with others. For instance, Meltzoff and Moore have shown that newborn infants can imitate facial and manual gestures of adults around them (1977, 1983). They conclude that infants imitate because of an inherent coordination between visual and motor systems that develops before recognition. From the beginning of human development, we have the ability to "represent actions intermodally" (1983, 708). Their work suggests that this ability to imitate is not the result of recognition or social conditioning. Rather, it comes out of the infant's inherent responsiveness to its environment and to others. In related research, Shaun Gallagher and Meltzoff have found that from birth "an experiential connection between self and others exists" (1996, 212). Thus echoing Gibson, these studies suggest that primary social interactions result from complex sensory systems that are inherently responsive.

Gibson argues that perceptual systems are attentive to the information in the environment. Information is available in various forms of energy—electrical, chemical, thermal, mechanical, photic, magnetic, and so on. The body is receptive to these various types of energy. Evolution has made different plants and animals more or less sensitive or receptive to different kinds and frequencies of energy. Different species have different types of eyes and therefore have different types of sight. When thinking about the nature of vision, it might be provocative to remember that only animals with two eyes on the front of their heads focus on objects in front of them. Moreover, what is seen is determined not only by the type and placement of eyes but also by the movement of the eyes and the body as a whole. Movements of the body attend to the information available in energy. According to Gibson, it is argued that "these adjustments constitute modes of attention, and they are senses only as the man in the street uses the term, not as the psychologist does. They serve to explore the information available in sound, mechanical contact, chemical contact, and light" (1966, 58). Energy, then, is the medium through which we perceive the world.

The density and temperature of the medium determine what kind and how much information we can gather from our environment. Most basically, the density and temperature of the medium determine how we move through our environment. We move more quickly and easily through air than through water. We don't move through solids. Other animals move through water or fly through the air. "The bodies of animals, their behavior, and their organs for receiving stimulation depend profoundly on elements in the Greek sense—on whether they live *in* the water or *on* the land, or fly in the air" (1966, 8). Gibson maintains that the air or atmosphere is a medium through which we perceive the world: "The atmosphere, then, is a medium. A medium permits more or less unhindered movements of animals and displacements of objects. Fundamentally, I suggest, this is what is meant by 'space'" (14). Space is a medium. It is not empty but full of various forms of energy, vibrations, particles, and waves. In Gibson's analysis space is the medium through which information is available to perceptual systems; space enables and facilitates the movement of information that connects us to our environment.

Taking a step away from Gibson's discussion of information, we could say that space enables and facilitates communication and communion. Rather than functioning as an obstacle, an empty abyss between us, space is full of the energy of life that connects us to the environment sustaining us. Moreover, space and the energies that move through it connect us to each other. The space between us facilitates rather than prevents relationships.

In Gibson's analysis light is another medium, which enables seeing. Gibson says that "terrestrial airspaces are 'filled' with light; they contain a flux of interlocking reflected rays in all directions at all points. This dense reverberating network of rays is an important but neglected fact of optics, to which we will refer in elaborating what may be called *ecological* optics" (1966, 12). His notion of ecological optics is "neither mentalistic nor physicalistic, but treats light as a means by which things are seen" (222). He maintains that

the environment consists of *opportunities* for perception, for *available* information, of *potential* stimuli. Not all opportunities are grasped, not all information is registered, not all stimuli excite receptors. But what the environment affords an individual in the way of discrimination is enormous. . . . The animate environment affords even more than the physical environment does since animals have more characteristics than things and are more changeable. (23)

By *information* Gibson does not mean something registered by the intellect; rather, information is registered by the body (2–3). Gibson develops his ecology of perception to counteract theories of perception that attribute it to either the physical world itself or the mind of man. Perception originates neither in the world nor in the subject; instead, perception is a relationship between the two. Gibson considers the environment in which we see as ecological optics. Sight is the result of a relationship with, and responsiveness to, our environment.

He uses this theory to solve the problem of virtual images or the status of images that appear as objects but aren't, for example, reflections in a mirror. He argues that images, whether virtual or real, are the result of a complex of relations that he calls information (1966, 226–27). Sight is the result of a response to differences between light and energies. It is in essence relational. More than this, Gibson suggests, the connection between the subject and the world is not a linear subject-object relationship or a simple stimulus-response relationship, but a circular responsive relationship, especially when it concerns relating to other animals:

> Sensitivity to action or behavior is clearly of a special kind, unlike the more familiar sensitivity to the prods and pushes of the external world or the pangs and pressures of the internal environment. The stimuli are self-produced, and the causal link is from response to stimulus as much as from stimulus to response. The classical stimulus-response formula, therefore, is no longer adequate; for there is a loop from response to stimulus to response again, and the result may be a continuous flow of activity rather than a chain of distinct reflexes. (31)

If Gibson is right and our relation to other animals is a response loop, then it is misleading for him to say that the stimuli are self-produced. At least the notion of self-production must be reformulated to refer to activity that is always already part of a response loop. By extrapolation, I suggest that the subject itself becomes part of a response loop that we call subjectivity.

So we are constantly responding to different types of energy in our environment—mechanical, chemical, heat, photic—which is registered by the human body in different ways. We are more or less aware of the processes of our response to this energy. We feel hot or cold in response to heat or thermal energy and radiation. We see daylight or darkness in response to light or photic energy. We smell and taste in response to chemical energy. We hear in response to mechanical energies. But we are less aware of other energies that affect us constantly. For example, we aren't conscious of our body's response to the forces of gravity, even though it takes constant effort to remain upright and stable in relation to the earth. Only recently, with more attention being paid in the mainstream press to seasonal depression, have we become aware of the effects of sunlight and light energy on our moods. When we consider the energy that surrounds, sustains, and connects us to the world and other people, the phrase "the forces of nature" takes on a new meaning.

A crucial, yet often ignored, part of the forces of nature are the social forces that enable communication and communion. Just as heat, chemical, mechanical, and photic energy sustain life, psychic energy or the energy of affects also surrounds us, connects us, and moves through us to sustain us. All relationships and all of human experience are the result of the flow and circulation of affective energy. Affective energy circulates between and among us. It is never contained. It migrates from person to person. We are constantly negotiating affective energy transfers. Our affective energy radiates out of us like light from the sun. Like other forms of energy, affective energy is invisible but has a powerful effect.

For example, has it ever happened that you are upset and by talking to your lover you start feeling better, getting it off your chest, but afterward your lover feels worse? You started out upset but now feel fine, while your lover started out fine but now feels upset. Or have you ever felt fine until your lover tells you about his or her depression, and then you start feeling depressed, too? Emotions migrate between people. Our moods and feelings are not just a response to what is said or what happens. They are also a response to the currents of emotional energy that flow between people. Emotional energy is transferred between people. This psychic or affective energy has profound effects on our moods and behavior. Just as we respond, most times unaware, to forces in our environment, so too we respond, unaware, to affective energy. In order to begin to understand human relationship and responsibilities, we need to begin to understand how affective or psychic energy works.

Gibson describes illusions and misperceptions as sensory misinterpretations of the information in energy. Just as an optical or auditory illusion can be the result of the body's inability to register and respond to photic or mechanical energy, miscommunication can be the result of the inability to register and respond to psychic or affective energy. He maintains that we can refine our perception by attending to particular energies and their effects. For example, the wine connoisseur can train her palate to taste and differentiate between subtle chemical differences. The art critic can train her eye to distinguish between subtle differences in light. The musician can train her ear to distinguish between differences in sound wavelengths. So, too, we can train ourselves to be attuned to subtle differences in affective energies in relationships. In fact, it seems that just as some people are better able to distinguish between differences in chemical, photic, or mechanical energies, some are better at distinguishing between psychic energies. In order to cope in the social world, we learn to respond to psychic energy, even if we aren't consciously aware of it, as with other forms of energy.

My argument is that we need to become consciously aware of affective energy not only to continue to try to understand ourselves and enable a process of interpretation that opens up rather than closes off the possibility of relationship, but also to fulfill our ethical obligation to do so. The possibility of subjectivity is founded on responsiveness to psychic and affective energy. Psychic and affective energies are social energies. These energies, along with other forms of energy, connect us to the world and other people. Whereas our dependence on other forms of energy may bring their own ethical obligations to the earth and atmosphere, the social energies—psychic and affective—bring with them special obligations to humanity, which may include other animal species.

Throughout her work, Teresa Brennan discusses social energy (1992, 1993, 1997). She emphasizes Freud's physical model of the psyche based on the notion of conflicting forces complemented by bound and free energy. Brennan explains that for Freud the binding of psychical energy gives neuronal pathways their stability (1997, 261; 1992). This bound energy can lead to psychic rigidity while freely mobile energy leads to psychic flexibility. The question for Brennan becomes how to keep psychic energy mobile and free. Frustration, she explains, is the result of a buildup of expectations or psychic energy that is not satisfied and has no outlet (1997, 262). In this way, bound energy can lead to disappointments, repression, and symptoms, while freed-up energy can lead to working-through those problems.

In addition, Brennan argues that mobile energy is supplied by living attention from others. In *The Interpretation of the Flesh* she introduces her notion of living attention as the source of ego support and development. She argues that psychic development depends on living attention from others. She suggests that since women are more likely to be caregivers than care receivers, they do not get the living attention that enables them to function as effectively and confidently as men. Her notion of living attention substantiates the notion that energy migrates from one person to another. If directed energy nurtures psyches, then it is conceivable that directed psychic and affective energy moves from one person to another. Moreover, social energy is essential to human life, as well as many forms of animal life.[2]

In a recent article titled "Social Pressure," Brennan argues that social pressure operates as physical energy. She suggests that social pressures are pressures to conform but also those exerted on the psyche in the same way that physical pressures are exerted on the body. She insists that social forces are material forces. She finds corroboration in Durkheim's discussions of social energy, forces, and pressure. In his discussion of religious life, Durkheim identifies social energy as a sort of "electricity" generated when people are gathered together (Durkheim 1995, 217). The experience of social electricity should be familiar to anyone who has attended a powerful religious service, a rock concert, a political rally, or even an aerobics class. The sum of collective energy is greater than its individual parts. This is why group experiences can be so powerful. This is also why we can feel energized by being part of a group. So we can feel energized, or drained of energy, by interpersonal relations.

Durkheim's analysis of religious experience suggests that social energy operates as or like physical energy: "The heat or electricity that any object has received from outside can be transmitted to the surrounding milieu, and the mind readily accepts the possibility of that transmission. If religious forces are generally conceived of as external to the beings in which they reside, then there is no surprise in the extreme case with which religious forces radiate and diffuse" (1995, 326–27). Durkheim also proposes "the radiation of mental energy" (210). Just as our bodies radiate heat and electromagnetic energies, our psyches radiate affective energy. Just as thermal energy from our bodies can warm the bodies of others, affective energy from our psyches can affect the psyches of others. In important ways, the psyche is a material biological phenomenon, a biosocial phenomenon.[3]

Brennan calls for a physics of social pressure to accompany the physics of other sorts of physical pressures. She maintains that physics should attend to the questions of social pressures so that we can better understand our social environment:

> The failure to discover the effects of CFCs [chlorofluorocarbons] for so long is an excellent illustration of how hard it is to couch physical experimentation in ways in which low-grade effects can be isolated. Something far more complex, such as the cumulative effects on persons of manifold energetic additions to their environment, would be very difficult to gauge. Of even greater difficulty

is the notion of a sum total of affects operations as "social pressure" in a given environment. But the difficulties should not be confused with the notion that the effects are nonexistent. Were more physicists to address the systematic questions concerning the nature of the changes wrought in the environment by social pressure, we might be better placed to know if these thoughts about social pressure, the social as a physical force in itself, are more than mere speculations, and whether the social is in fact something that weighs one down more in some environments than others. (1997, 282–83)

The idea that our environment is filled with dynamic energy opens up an alternative to the idea that we exist as self-contained units separated from our environment. If the dynamic energy that surrounds us touches, permeates, affects, and nourishes us, then we are neither self-contained nor separated. Rather, we are profoundly dependent on our environment and other people for the energy that sustains us. Far from being alienated from the world or others, we are intimately and continually connected, and responding, to them. We are by virtue of our response to the biosocial energy that surrounds us. Biosocial energy operates, is sustained, and expands through responsive energy loops. We are energized in our relationships with others. Vision is another form of the circulation of energy that involves not only photic energy or light but also psychic energy or affect. We see in and through this circulation of biosocial energy. Moreover, the circulation of dynamic energy guarantees that we are connected to our environment and other people.

Touching Eyes

Merleau-Ponty's later phenomenology of perception will be helpful to continue to imagine an alternative notion of vision that makes possible connection rather than alienation in relation to others. Against Sartre, Merleau-Ponty rejects the view that "the other can enter into the universe of the seer only by assault, as a pain and a catastrophe" (1968, 78). The other is not my negation or destruction, because "there is an intersection of my universe with that of another" (80). Merleau-Ponty insists that radical alterity requires neither that we are in conflict with others nor that we are forever cut off from others. Also in contrast to Sartre, Merleau-Ponty argues that I am not fixed by the accusing gaze of the other:

> One knows the other not only in what he suffers from him, but more generally as a witness, who can be challenged because he is also himself accused, because he is not a pure gaze upon pure being any more than I am, because his

views and my own are in advance inserted into a system of partial perspectives, referred to one same world in which we coexist and where our views intersect. For the other to be truly other, it does not suffice and it is not necessary that he be a scourge, the continued threat of an absolute reversal of pro and con, a judge himself elevated above all contestation, without place, without relativities, faceless like an obsession, and capable of crushing me with a glance into the dust of my world. (82)

For Merleau-Ponty, the body itself mediates the relationship between subject and object, self and other. The body is both subject and object "because a sort of dehiscence opens my body in two, and because between my body looked at and my body looking, my body touched and my body touching, there is overlapping encroachment, so that we must say that the things pass into us as well as we into the things" (1968, 123). Rather than reject any philosophy of subjectivity, Merleau-Ponty rethinks subjectivity through the body. The thickness of flesh and permeability of skin make "intercorporiety" possible (141); they make communication with the world and other possible (135). The thickness of the flesh guarantees relations, while the skin ensures that we can distinguish our experience from the other's. Yet since the flesh and skin are not objects but synergetic, we are never cut off from the other. The skin is a boundary, but a permeable boundary.

Flesh makes communication possible because, as Merleau-Ponty says, it is the "reversible." By *reversible*, he means that we are both sensing and sensible, both subject and object. By virtue of our flesh, we can sense and be sensed by others and by ourselves. The reversibility of the tangible opens up an "intercorporeal being," which extends farther than any one individual and founds the "transitivity from one body to another" (1968, 143). Merleau-Ponty goes so far as to suggest that I can almost experience something of the other's embodiment. He gives the example of the difference between hearing one's own voice and hearing the voice of another. I have a different relation to my own voice because it emanates from my body, and I am affected by the vibrations of my body as I speak: "But if I am close enough to the other who speaks to hear his breath and feel his effervescence and his fatigue, I almost witness, in him as in myself, the awesome birth of vociferation" (144). At this point, Merleau-Ponty suggests the radical notion that I can feel the other's pain. There can be an exchange of synergy between bodies, and if I am close enough to another person, I can experience the movements of their body in the same way that I experience the movements of my own. More than this, I can feel their effervescence and fatigue. This opening of the boundary between self and other resonates with the theory of biosocial energy that I sketched earlier.

It is precisely in this opening, which is our difference and the distance between us, that relationships and communication take place. For Merleau-Ponty, "This distance is not the contrary of this proximity, it is deeply consonant with it, it is synonymous with it. It is that the thickness of the flesh between the seer and the thing is constitutive for the thing of its visibility as for the seer of his corporiety; it is not an obstacle between them, it is their means of communication" (1968, 135). Distance is not alienating or threatening. It does not forever separate me from the world and from others. Rather, for Merleau-Ponty distance is enabling and vision is precisely how: "Vision alone makes us learn that beings that are different, 'exterior,' foreign to one another, are yet absolutely together, are 'simultaneity'" (1964, 187). Unlike Lacan's gaze that either cuts us off from the world and others à la the mirror stage or fixes us in a triangle of unfulfillable desire à la *The Four Fundamental Concepts,* Merleau-Ponty imagines vision as a means of connection and communion. Rather than the alienation and conflict at the heart of either Sartre's or Lacan's notions of the gaze, with Merleau-Ponty we find wonder at the gap between us, the distance that enables us to relate to each other.

Merleau-Ponty does not accept the Cartesian conception of space that privileges the perspective of some God's-eye view on my seeing, what becomes represented in Lacan's *The Four Fundamental Concepts* as the floating can that sees me looking. He insists that "space is no longer what it was in the *Dioptric,* a network of relations between objects such as would be seen by a witness to my vision or by a geometer looking over it and reconstructing it from the outside" (1964, 178). Thus Merleau-Ponty's conception of space and vision stands opposed not only to Descartes' *Dioptric* but also to Lacan's triangle of desire that defines the gaze in terms of a third party by whom we are seen in our relationship. Merleau-Ponty, it seems, should accept neither Lacan's characterization of vision as a deluded self-centered enterprise of the autonomous subject nor his notion of the anonymous gaze as more accurate to our relationships, or their ultimate impossibility.

While for Lacan the anonymity of vision makes it alienating, for Merleau-Ponty the anonymity of vision makes relationships possible without subjects dominating their objects: "There is here no problem of the alter ego because it is not *I* who sees, not *he* who sees, because an anonymous visibility inhabits both of us, a vision in general, in virtue of that primordial property that belongs to the flesh, being here and now, of radiating everywhere and forever, being an individual, of being also a dimension and a universal" (1968, 142). For Merleau-Ponty vision is not the product of an autonomous self-centered subject; and although it may be anonymous, vision is not inhuman. He argues against the "inhuman gaze" (1962, 361). Humanity is the reversibility of flesh, an openness to the world, the eye's welcome to the world. Humanity is the intertwining of being and meaning, and the intertwining of visible and invisible is the relation between being and meaning. While Lacan insists that meaning and being are caught in an exclusive either-or relationship, Merleau-Ponty suggests that we live in both: "Meaning is invisible, but the invisible is not the contradictory of the visible: the visible itself has an invisible inner framework, and the in-visible is the secret counterpart of the visible" (1968, 215).

One fundamental reason why Merleau-Ponty can imagine vision as bringing us together is that he has a different conception of vision and space. For him, vision is part of a system of sensation, and space is filled with the flesh of the world. He describes palpitations of the eyes as analogous to tactile palpitations in what he calls a "vision-touch system." "Vision is a palpitation with the look" (1968, 134), and the world is visible because it is tactile. Vision is dependent on tactility and the necessary connection, even reversibility, between the body and the visible world. For Merleau-Ponty the corporeality of the visible world is the connective tissues that nourish and sustain the possibility of seeing. He describes vision in terms of thickness, corpuscles, tissues, grains, waves, channels, circuits, currents, embryos, and pregnancy, the very corporeality out of which sensation, thought, and language are born.

In addition to describing vision as part of a vision-touch system, he argues that all of the senses are interconnected. He insists that the notion of the separation of the senses is misguided because all of the senses are interconnected in one body: each sense is really a complex of sensations that fundamentally implicates the others, and sensation operates in the reversible world of sensible and sentient, which folds the senses back onto themselves in a way that produces new levels of sensation and consciousness. The senses translate each other and work together to form perception. In this way, vision never works merely through the eyes. It is always the result of a coordinated effort between all senses. More than this, the so-called mind's eye or mental image supposedly connected to visual images is also the result of a coordination of the senses. The mirror, then, is not the threshold of the visual world, as Lacan maintains. Rather, the mirror image is perceived through a complex network of sensations working together, developed primarily from the most proximal sense, touch.[4]

Merleau-Ponty's vision-touch system clearly resonates with Gibson's theory of perceptual systems. Both Merleau-Ponty and Gibson resist cataloging the senses according to separate sense organs. Both insist that perception involves the whole body. Whereas Merleau-Ponty tries to revise traditional notions of vision by associating it with touch, Gibson develops his ecology of optics in which vision is part of a system of perception. Influenced by Gestalt psychology, both Merleau-Ponty and Gibson attend to the environment in which perception takes place. While Merleau-Ponty associates vision with touch in order to make it a more proximal sense, Gibson points out that touch is not as proximal as it seems, since more often than not only hairs protruding from the skin touch other objects: "The tactual system is not, then, strictly a 'proximity sense' as traditionally assumed, for the appendages of the skin protrude into the environment" (Gibson 1966, 100). If vision can be proximal and touch is not as proximal as it seems, then distinctions between the senses begin to break down.

As part of the vision-touch system for Merleau-Ponty, vision is proximal in that it is possible because our flesh touches the flesh of the world. It is possible because the world also has flesh. Vision touches the world and people in it not in order to fix it or them in the gaze. Rather, vision is movement, more like a caress than a grip, more like a motion picture than a photograph (1964, 162). And space is thick with the flesh of the world. Merleau-Ponty criticizes Descartes' conception of space as "having no true thickness" (1964, 174). Space is not made up of Cartesian points separated by infinite gaps between them in some geometrical arrangement. Rather, space is full of light and motion that cannot be located in any one point. There are no gaps between us and the world, since we touch it with our eyes, working as they do in coordination with all of sensation. As Merleau-Ponty says, "It is more accurate to say that I see according to it, or with it, than that I *see it*"; "The world is all around me, not in front of me. . . . I live in it from the inside; I am immersed in it" (1964, 164, 178). I do not see the world; I see according to it, with it. So, too, I do not see other people in the world; I see with them. In this regard, Merleau-Ponty's phenomenology of vision again resonates with Gibson's theory of ecological optics.

For Merleau-Ponty the distance necessary for vision is not alienating but enabling because of the interconnection between the senses and the elements that make vision possible. We are not separated from ourselves, others, and the world by an abyss. If vision is part of a sensory system that includes what we take to be more proximal senses like touch, taste, or smell, vision becomes a sort of touching, a palpitation with the eyes. Vision itself becomes a proximal sense. If the eyes are flesh—porous membranes—and not solid mirrors or windows or Lacanian bowls, then vision like the other senses necessitates a type of interpolation of elements that cannot be imagined as an impassable abyss or alienating gap (cf. Lacan 1981, 94). If various interconnected, inter-acting elements—air, light, waves, particles, nerves, tissues—make vision possible, then distance is never empty space, an unbridgeable gap, or an abyssal void. Rather, the distance between us is the connective tissues of earthly elements. Stephen Melville nicely describes the trajectory of Merleau-Ponty's philosophy of vision:

> Vision is the place where our continuity with the world conceals itself, the place where we mistake our contact for distance, imagining that seeing is a substitute for, rather than a mode of, touching—and it is this anesthesia, this senselessness, at the heart of transparency that demands our acknowledgment and pushes our dealings with the visual beyond recognition. (1996, 109)

Luce Irigaray challenges Merleau-Ponty's attempt to think the visual be-yond recognition when she accuses him of solipsism. She argues that the no-tion of reversibility reduces the other and the world to another part of myself (1993b, 153, 157, 160, 169, 172, 184). The reversibility between the seer and the visible defines everything in terms of the seer. In a sense, she reads the Husserlian transcendental ego back into Merleau-Ponty's phenomenology. She argues that Merleau-Ponty's emphasis on the reversibility between the visible and the invisible suggests a desire to master the invisible (163). She claims that he reduces touch to vision and privileges vision over all other senses (162, 175). And she maintains that he forgets or ignores the invisible maternal womb that gives birth to the possibility of vision.

Rather than stage a dialogue between Irigaray and Merleau-Ponty, let alone negotiate between them, I use what I see as some of the more radical aspects of Merleau-Ponty's philosophy.[5] Merleau-Ponty's philosophy is sug-gestive in its attempts to renegotiate the subject-object relationship by reconceiving of vision. His notion of the flesh of the world is provocative in its implications for reconceiving of space as full rather than empty. And his theory of a vision-touch system in which all the senses work together opens up the possibility of conceiving vision as touch, in order to circumvent the philosophical battle over which sense is primary or privileged. Hopefully, reading Merleau-Ponty together with Irigaray and Lévinas can provide a corrective to the more solipsistic moments in Merleau-Ponty's phenome-nology, especially the problematic notion of reversibility. While Irigaray, fol-lowing Lévinas, makes an essentially orthopedic gesture when she insists that relations of difference are irreversible and always carry a remainder, it is important to note that Merleau-Ponty does not endorse reducing difference to sameness or defining the other in terms of the subject. Rather, he explicitly insists on difference. What he wants to avoid is the alienating hostile difference of the neo-Hegelian theories of Sartre and, I would add, Lacan. Like Lévinas and Irigaray after him, he attempts to theorize communication between differences, communication beyond recognition.

Caressing Eyes Closed

Like Merleau-Ponty, Lévinas rejects Cartesian space and optics in favor of a touch-based sensation. Taking a different tack from that of Merleau-Ponty, Lévinas seems to dismiss vision as a distancing sense that mistakenly puts the subject at the center of the universe. Rejecting a Sartrean notion of the objectifying gaze or look, Lévinas rejects vision-centered philosophy in general. "Social relations," he says, "are the original deployment of the relationship that is no longer open to the gaze that would encompass its terms, but is accomplished from me to the other in the face to face" (1969, 290). The face-to-face relationship takes us further than vision. While I see parts of the face, according to Lévinas, I do not see the face itself. Moreover, that which cannot be seen—infinity—shines through the face. The face is never an intentional object—or an object of any sort—for a subject. For Lévinas, the face-to-face relationship breaks the hostile gaze and transforms empty space and distance into the marvel of an ethical encounter:

> The true essence of man is presented in his face, in which he is infinitely other than a violence like unto mine, opposed to mine and hostile, already at grips with mine in a historical world where we participate in the same system. He arrests and paralyzes my violence by his call, which does not do violence, and comes from on high. The truth of being is not the image of being, the idea of its nature; it is the being situated in a subjective field which deforms vision, but precisely thus allows exteriority to state itself, entirely command and authority: entirely superiority. This curvature of the intersubjective space inflects distance into elevation; it does not falsify being, but makes its truth first possible. (290–91)

Lévinas calls the face-to-face encounter a "curvature of intersubjective space" that transforms distance into elevation or transcendence. This transformation of space breaks with Cartesian space in which subjects and objects are located at specific points certain distances from each other. In Lévinasian ethical space, there is proximity rather than distance. And the distance between us becomes what he calls "exteriority," which guarantees radical alterity and the possibility of welcoming peaceful relationships: "Exteriority is not a negation, but a marvel" (292).

The sense of negation, distance, or alienation is created by the notion of vision as grasping objects in empty space. Criticizing what he calls the objectifying Platonic "schema of vision from Aristotle to Heidegger," Lévinas says that empty space is the condition for the relationship between the hand and its objects or the objectifying relationship in general (1969, 191). He maintains that light and vision condition relations between objects but do not enable a face-to-face approach (191). In order to go beyond the egoistic subject-object relation and approach what he calls the face-to-face relation, Lévinas privileges touch over vision. For him, touch enables proximity whereas vision enables only distance. He explains that "proximity, which should be the signification of the sensible, does not belong to the movement of cognition. . . . Sight, by reason of its distance and its totalizing embrace, imitates or prefigures the 'impartiality' of the intellect and its refusal to hold to what the immediacy of the sensible would dispose, or what it would constitute" (1991, 63). This is why he insists that all "sensibility must be interpreted as touch first of all" (1993, 118).

Again taking and turning from Merleau-Ponty, Lévinas makes a distinction between touch as palpation and touch as caress. To get beyond the subject-object hierarchy, Lévinas suggests that we also have to get beyond the notion of touch as palpation. Touch is not intentional, and rather than return me to myself, it takes me out of myself toward the other (1993, 119). As a caress, touch has no object. A caress *is* relationship and not its aim or medium: "What is caressed is not touched"; rather, the caress is an anticipation of a "future without content" (1987, 89). The caress is a promise, but not a promise of some thing. The promise and future of the caress are simply the erotic loving relationship itself. The caress seeks the continuation of relationship, the future of relationship, even while it constitutes it. But the caress cannot possess the other or the relationship; this is why it is a future without content, a promise yet to come.

Basing sensibility, and therefore intelligibility, on touch as caress, Lévinas tries to go beyond objectifying notions of vision and recognition:

> In starting with *touching*, interpreted not as palpation but as caress, and *language*, interpreted not as the traffic of information but as contact, we have tried to describe proximity as irreducible to consciousness and thematization. . . . Incapable of remaining in a theme and of appearing, this invisibility

that becomes contact does not result from the nonsignifyingness of what is approached but rather from a way of signifying wholly other than that of exhibition from a *beyond* the visible. (1996, 80; cf. 1991, 100)

Starting with touch, Lévinas imagines a way of relating and signifying other than objectifying operations like thematizing or exhibiting. Even Merleau-Ponty's palpation is too subject-centered for Lévinas. The caress, on the other hand, does not take place between subjects and objects. And all sensibility, even vision, begins with caress: "Sensibility must be interpreted as touch first of all. . . . The visible caresses the eye. One sees and one hears like one touches" (1993, 118).

Lévinas's touch-based ethics takes us beyond knowing or grasping the other through vision—the mind's eye or the body's—toward a relationship beyond recognition. He insists that our relation with others cannot be one of recognition and be ethical at the same time. Recognition seeks only itself and not the other. Recognition is not open to otherness, but only to confirmations of itself. This is why Lévinas maintains that communication can take place only beyond recognition:

> But communication would be impossible if it should have to begin in the ego, a free subject, to whom every other would be only a limitation that invited war, domination, precaution and information. To communicate is indeed to open oneself, but the openness is not complete if it is on the watch for recognition. It is complete not in the opening to the spectacle of or the recognition of the other, but in becoming a responsibility for him. (1991, 119)

Beyond recognition there is responsibility. And for Lévinas responsibility is for the other's response; it is response-ability.

I am responsible for the other, for the other's response, and the other's ability to respond. Subjectivity is an openness to the other. Even the ego, or the idea of the subject in its solidarity as something identical to itself, as a monad, necessarily "begins by bearing witness of itself to the other" (1991, 119). The illusion of the ego as monad makes communication impossible, "save by a miracle" (119). The ego *is* insofar as it bears witness of itself to the other. Bearing witness, in this context, means not only listening to the other but also telling oneself to the other. It is not the content of its testimony that solidifies the ego; rather, it is the bearing witness itself, the relationship of telling oneself to the other, that solidifies the ego. On a phenomenological level, my experience of myself comes through the narratives that I construct in order to tell myself and my life to another, especially on a mundane everyday basis. I construct and reconstruct my experiences for another, even if I don't ever actually tell them the narrative that I have prepared for them. It is the bearing witness to the other itself, spoken or not, that gives birth to the *I.*

Lévinas's insistence on the "bond between expression and responsibility, the ethical condition or essence of language," resonates with Dori Laub's insistence on the inner witness that earlier I suggested is necessary for subjectivity (Lévinas 1969, 200). What Laub describes as the inner witness is the result of relationships with loving or supportive others who listen. The "inner" witness is formed in relation to "outer" witnesses who respond to testimony. Subjectivity and a sense of one's self as an agent depend on this inner witness, which is born out of, and sustained by, one's relations to others. Lévinas privileges the face as that which gives birth to and sustains discourse and thereby subjectivity. He says that "the face opens the primordial discourse whose first word is obligation. . . . It is that discourse that obliges the entering into discourse" (1969, 201).

Roughly, we could say that for Lévinas the face-to-face encounter brings us into contact with the otherness that constitutes humanity—the infinite within the finite, the transcendent within the embodied, the meaning of being. This contact is not a knowing or grasping, because this otherness cannot be controlled by a subject. Yet it is this otherness through which the subject comes to be and is sustained. The face-to-face encounter is grounded in discourse: it both grounds and presupposes discourse. As the very foundation of human life and language, the face-to-face encounter brings with it an ethical obligation and responsibility. In a sense, this ethical responsibility is to become that which we are, to be bound to that which constitutes us. Once again reformulating Eva Kittay's analysis of relations of dependency, a subject who "refuses to support this bond absolves itself from its most fundamental obligation—its obligation to its founding possibility" (1998, 131).

For Lévinas, insofar as we are constituted as subjects in our relations with others and otherness, we have an obligation to and for the other. I am responsible, before all others. The ethical imperative or command inherent in this obligation comes from the fact that, according to Lévinas, one's responsibility is not reciprocal or symmetrical:

> Responsibility is what is incumbent on me exclusively, and what, *humanly,* I cannot refuse. I am I in the sole measure that I am responsible, a noninterchangeable I. I can substitute myself for everyone, but no one can substitute himself for me. Such is my inalienable identity of subject. It is in this precise sense that Dostoyevsky said: "We are all responsible for all for all men before all, and I more than all the others." (1985, 101)

To refuse this responsibility is to refuse our own humanity. This responsibility is an obligation to acknowledge my dependence on others and otherness for my sense of myself as *I*, as a subject or agent. The ethical obligation to acknowledge dependence commands me to open myself to otherness rather than try to possess it as mine; for there is no *mine* without the other. And while justice may require reciprocity, according to Lévinas, the force of the ethical obligation to the other begins with my unique asymmetrical responsibility beyond all recognition (1985, 99–101). Although Lévinas admits that infinite responsibility is an ideal, it is "one which is inseparable from the humanity of human beings" (1989, 226).

Loving Eyes

Rather than trying to think outside of a Hegelian notion of recognition by abandoning recognition altogether, Irigaray reconceives of recognition as a connection between two different sexes. In *i love to you,* she describes an alternative nonhierarchical recognition that does not and cannot dominate the other. She argues that to recognize another person requires that neither party is the One against the Other nor the Whole against its part (1996, 103). We cannot recognize that of which we are a part, whether it is the Whole or the One. Therefore, recognition requires two who are not greater or lesser than each other. Yet these two are also not equivalent; their differences cannot be sublimated in a Hegelian dialectic. They cannot be substituted for each other or reduced one to the other: "I recognize you goes hand in hand with: you are irreducible to me, just as I am to you. We may not be substituted for one another" (103). Recognition requires that we are two different beings, inaccessible to each other, and yet able to communicate because of what is between us.

Communication does not demand subordination or assimilation. It does not require a master-slave relationship. But "in order to avoid master(s)/slave(s) relations," says Irigaray, "we have to practice a different sort of recognition from the one marked by hierarchy, and thus also by genealogy" (105). Difference that is irreducible cannot be categorized or prioritized according to hierarchy or genealogy, because it cannot be reduced to one system. Irigaray argues that when difference is recognized as irreducible, "the power of the one over the other will be no more. Difference that is irreducible never ceases to curb the capitalization of any such power, of mere authority over" (105). For difference to be recognized as irreducible, it must be recognized as beyond recognition. Ultimately, for Irigaray, "only the recognition of the other as sexed offers this possibility" (105): only the recognition of sexual difference opens up difference that is irreducible. I agree with her that sexual difference is irreducible, but it is just a strategic opening onto other irreducible differences. In *Womanizing Nietzsche: Philosophy's Relation to "the Feminine,"* I interpret Irigaray's insistence on sexual difference as the primary difference and her emphasis on *two* sexes as a strategic move to open up multiplicity (1995). I argue that she is working within the paradigm of the One and the Many such that in order to get multiplicity we first must have two.

Irigaray suggests that we are different and that we can communicate because of what she calls the "labor of the negative" between us. Most simply, the labor of the negative is the labor of limitation. Each individual has its limits that define it in relation to others. While these limits cannot be penetrated, they enable rather than disable communication:

> I recognize you is the one condition for the existence of I, you and we. . . . This *we* is the work of the negative, that which cannot be substituted between us, the transcendence between us. It is constituted by subjects irreducible one to the other, each one to the others, and thus capable of communicating out of freedom and necessity. Spiritual progress can be understood, then, as the development of communication between us, in the form of individual and collective dialogue. Speech *between* replaces instinctual attraction or the attraction of similitude. (1996, 104)

We is the result of a recognition of our limitations that brings us together. Gender is one of our primary limitations in the sense that we cannot know the other gender. Irigaray explains that "I is never simply mine in that it belongs to a gender. Therefore, I am not the whole: I am man or woman. And I am not simply a subject, I belong to a gender. I am objectively limited by this belonging" (106). Irigaray goes so far as to say that the limitation of gender might serve as a third term in the psychoanalytic sense, which implies that the paternal function or law of the father is not necessarily the only third term that brings with it the possibility of social relations. It is through our limitations, or the labor of the negative between us, that we come together. It is through a recognition of our limits that we become social beings capable of relationships. For Irigaray limit and limitations do not have *negative* connotations, because the negative itself is reworked as a positive labor, a giving birth.

Irigaray says that it is the "negative that enables me to go towards you" (1996, 104). It is the negative in the sense of the phrases "I cannot know you," "I cannot be you," "I will never master you" that allows for relationships beyond domination, beyond recognition. As soon as I am sure that I know you, that I know what you will do next, I have stopped having a relationship with you and instead have a relationship with myself, with my own projection onto you. When I think that I know you, our relationship is over.

The notion of recognition that Irigaray proposes is not connected to vision or seeing someone. In fact, she believes that recognition is acknowledgment of that which cannot be seen in vision, the invisible or beyond recognition. It is precisely what we do not see, what we cannot witness with our eyes, that attracts us to each other: "I recognize you supposes that I cannot see right through you. You will never be entirely visible to me, but thanks to that, I respect you as different from me. What I do not see of you draws me toward you. . . . I go towards you as towards that which I shall not see but which attracts me" (1996, 104). Recognition is a form of love that requires bearing witness to that which is beyond recognition, bearing witness to what cannot be seen. For Irigaray, love is bearing witness to that which is between us, the invisible bond created through the labor of the negative, which is not nothing. In order to emphasize the between in love, Irigaray insists on saying "I love to you" rather than "I love you." The *to* adds the dimension of movement and the in-between *I* and *you* missing from the formulation that sounds as if my love can assimilate you (1996, 109–13).

With Irigaray, I will argue that the *between* is missing from dominant conceptions of vision. Irigaray's work on Heidegger, *Forgetting of Air in Martin Heidegger* (1999), is especially suited to developing an alternative account of vision that does not presuppose that space is empty and that that emptiness leads to some fundamental alienation. Extending Irigaray's analysis of air beyond the confines of her engagement with Heidegger is an important step toward conceiving of the fullness of space and the elements that connect us to the world and each other. Irigaray's insistence on a recognition of the role of material elements in vision, perception, thought, and philosophy in general suggests a new direction for theories of recognition and intersubjective relations. Throughout her work she is concerned to recall and remember the material elements—water, earth, fire, and air—out of which we are born and through which we live, together. In *Marine Lover of Friedrich Nietzsche* (1991) she reminds us of the importance of water and fluids, especially those out of which we were born. In *Forgetting of Air* she suggests that air has a special place among the elements: "Is not air the whole of our habitation as mortals? Is there a dwelling more vast, more spacious, or even more generally peaceful than that of air? Can man live elsewhere than in air? Neither in earth, nor in fire, nor in water is any habitation possible for him"

(1999, 8). My concern here is how to expand Irigaray's theories of air and light in order to develop a new conception of vision that can give birth to a new conception of relationships beyond subject-object/other hierarchies.

Unlike Lévinas, rather than just discounting vision in favor of touch because traditional theories of vision presuppose subjects dominating their objects, Irigaray also tries to reconceive of vision. Unlike Merleau-Ponty, Irigaray refuses to fuse vision and touch and instead insists that they cannot be reduced one to the other.[6] In her book *Textures of Light*, Cathryn Vasseleu argues that Irigaray goes further than either Merleau-Ponty or Lévinas toward developing an alternative theory of vision by developing an alternative theory of light (1998). Primarily working with Irigaray's engagement in *An Ethics of Sexual Difference* (1993a) with Merleau-Ponty and Lévinas, Vasseleu shows how Irigaray develops a theory of what she calls the "texture" of light. Rather than reduce vision to touch, which is one of her (debatable) criticisms of Merleau-Ponty, Irigaray emphasizes the touch of light on the eye. It is not, then, that vision and touch are not separate senses but, rather, that vision is dependent on the sense of touch. Vasseleu describes a texture as

> a disposition or characteristic of anything which is woven into a fabric, and comprises a combination of parts or qualities which is neither simply unveiled or made up. Texture is at once the cloth, threads, knots, weave, detailed surface, material, matrix and frame. Regarded in this way, light is not a transparent medium linking sight and visibility. It is not appropriate to think of light as a texture either perspectively as a thing, or as a medium which is separable from things. In its texture, light is fabrication, a surface of depth that also spills over and passes through the interstices of the fabric. The dichotomy between visible and invisible is itself a framing of photology that gives light its texture. As a texture, the naturalness of light cannot be divorced from its historical and embodied circumstances. It is neither visible nor invisible, neither metaphoric nor metaphysical. It is both the language and material of visual practices, or the invisible interweaving of differences which form the fabric of the visible. (1998, 12)

Vasseleu argues that conceiving of light's texture challenges the traditional separation of the senses that serves the separation of sensible and intelligible. She explains that the separation between sensible and intelligible, between body and mind or soul, has been constructed around the notion of the mind's eye and an immaterial seeing cut off from the body and sensation, a more accurate seeing. The split between the mind's eye and the body's eye is interlaced with the split between objective theoretical knowledge and

subjective personal feeling. Objective theoretical knowledge requires a notion of vision as a distancing sense that separates the mind's eye from the
body and gives it a privileged perspective devoid of contaminating sentiment. Information gathered through touch and more proximal senses is
thought to provide only subjective feeling and cannot be the grounds for
knowledge. Martin Jay's analysis of the nobility and then denigration of vision in philosophy substantiates this analysis (1994).

If vision is founded on touch, says Vasseleu, then the split between mind
and body, between objective and subjective, can no longer be sustained: "The
distance and space for reflection and insight that comes with vision through
the mediation of light are lost as the sense of sight passes to the sense of
touch" (1998, 12). She finds in Irigaray a theory of vision in which

> tactility is an essential aspect of light's texture, where texture refers not only to
> the feeling of a fabric to the touch, or the grasping of its qualities, but also to
> the hinges or points of contact which constitute the interweaving of the mate-
> rial and ideal strands of the field of vision. An elaboration of light in terms of
> texture stands as a challenge to the representation of sight as a sense which
> guarantees the subject of vision an independence, or sense in which the seer is
> distanced from an object. (13)

If vision involves touching light, then we are touched by and touching everything around us even as we see the distance between ourselves and the world
or other people in the world. The texture or fabric of vision is even more
tightly woven than Merleau-Ponty's reversible flesh. It is not just that the fabric of vision is reversible between subject and object, invisible and visible,
ideal and material; rather, the texture of vision is the result of an interweav-
ing of elements both distinct and intimately connected in their sensuous
contact.

The texture of light is what is between us and other people in the world.
We are both connected and made distinct by the texture of light that wraps
us in the luxury and excesses of the world. In addition to Vasseleu's mar-
velous rendering of Irigaray's texture of light, Irigaray's insistence on material elements, especially air, provokes us to rethink vision. Irigaray concludes
her *Elemental Passions* with an ode to the density of air:

> I opened my eyes and saw the cloud. And saw that nothing was perceptible
> unless I was held at a distance from it by an almost palpable density. And that
> I saw it and did not see it. *Seeing it all the better for remembering the density of
> air remaining in between.* But this resistance of air being revealed, I felt some-

thing akin to the possibility of a different discovery of myself. (1992, 105; my emphasis)

Space is not empty, because it is filled with the density of air. And the density of air connects and separates everything on earth. Remembering air and the density of air reminds me that I am both connected to and different from those around me. Remembering what cannot be seen, the density of air, allows me to better see what cannot be seen, the difference and communion between myself and others. Seeing what is different from me and what is between me and difference opens the possibility of a different discovery of myself.

Irigaray's most sustained reflections on air and the density of air are in *Forgetting of Air*. There she takes Heidegger to task for forgetting the air that makes possible any clearing, being, or Being of being. Leaving behind her criticisms of Heidegger, which are interesting in themselves, I am interested in her descriptions of air and how they can help reconceive of vision. Throughout this work Irigaray suggests that the philosopher has forgotten air and thereby forgotten that he is nourished and supported by air. By forgetting air, the philosopher imagines that he is thrown into an empty abyss, where he confronts only nothingness. The abyss, she reminds us, is not empty; it is full of air. And air is not nothing. Applying her analysis to Lacan and my earlier comments, we could say that the alienating gap or separation inherent in vision or the gaze (or language) is the product of what Irigaray calls the oblivion of air. She says that "the elementality of *physis*—air, water, earth, fire—is always already reduced to nothingness in and by his own element: his language" (1999, 74). Irigaray asks what happens when the philosopher focuses on the things within air and forgets air itself: "And what becomes of air when the being appears within it? It is reduced to nothingness" (162). By forgetting the elements, the philosopher forgets that space is not empty. By forgetting that space is not empty, the space between us and others or our own image seems unbridgeable, empty, alienating. But what if space is full and not empty?

Even light is dependent on air. The texture of light cannot touch without the air that opens onto that touch. Vision, speech, and life itself require air. In response to Heidegger, Irigaray says:

It is not light that creates the clearing, but light comes about only in virtue of the transparent levity of air. Light presupposes air. No sun without air to welcome and transmit its rays. No speech without air to convey it. Day and night, voice and silence, appear and disappear in air. The extent of space, the horizons of time, and all that becomes present and absent within them are to be found gathered together in air as in some fundamental thing. The originary intuition of which recedes indefinitely. Free beyond all vision. Dwelling out of sight. . . . And thought attains the heart of this assembly only by assimilating itself to this serene spatiality—air. (1999, 166–67)

The serene spatiality that is air cannot be seen and yet there is no seeing without it. It fills space with the plenitude of life.

For Irigaray, air occupies a unique place among the elements in that it is place:

> No other element can for him take the place of place. No other element carries with it—or lets itself be passed through by—light and shadow, voice or silence. . . . No other element is in this way space prior to all localization, and a substratum both immobile and mobile, permanent and flowing, where multiple temporal divisions remain forever possible. Doubtless, no other element is as originarily constitutive of the whole of the world, without this generativity ever coming to completion in a primordial time, in a singular primacy, in an autarchy, in an autonomy, in a unique or exclusive property. (1999, 8)

The air generates life but without hierarchy, genealogy, domination, or ownership. More than this, Irigaray marvels at the way that air gives without demanding anything in return: "But this element, irreducibly constitutive of the whole, compels neither the faculty of perception nor that of knowledge to recognize it. Always there, it allows itself to be forgotten" (1999, 8). The acknowledgment of this giving without demand for recognition is what opens the possibility of a different discovery of myself in relation to what gives me life and nourishes me.

Irigaray's discussion of gifts and indebtedness to the elements and mediums of perception adds an ethical dimension to Gibson's notion of ecological optics. Gibson emphasizes that space is filled with air; in fact, he uses the term "airspace." He also insists that air and light are mediums through which we see. Irigaray suggests that because we see and live in and by air and light, we have an ethical obligation to the earth and sky. Our indebtedness is not the debt of some economic exchange that must be paid off in full or in kind; rather, our indebtedness can only be acknowledged through wonder, marvel, love, and care.

Irigaray proposes that remembering air and the gift of life that it gives provides us with another way of looking. The look is no longer the philosopher's gaze that rips open and penetrates the other or fixes us in its piercing intensity. Reminiscent of Merleau-Ponty, she says that the look is the look of the flesh living in and off the air. The flesh does not respond to the demanding gaze of the philosopher but to the loving look of another body. Her poetic philosophy suggests this alternative:

> The flesh sources indefinitely, never moving away from the setting that gives rise to it. The flesh opens, petal after petal, in an efflorescence that does not come about for the look, without for all that avoiding the look. These blooms are not seen. Unless by another sort of look? A look that allows itself to be touched by the birth of forms that are not exposed in the bright light of day? Yet, nonetheless, are there. Invisible substrate for the constitution of the visible. These gifts give themselves in the direction of an outside that does not cross the threshold of appearance. They suffuse the look without being noticed by sight. Irrigation by a sense-intuition that flows back and forth from the flesh to the look, from the look to the flesh, with neither the ek-stasis that attends a contemplation that has been resolved, nor a confinement in lack of light. Irradiances that imperceptibly illuminate. (1999, 116)

The unseen source of sight is a sensuous caress that touches and is touched by another sort of look, a tactile look that does not pry or gaze but caresses in the flow of irrigation and irradiances. This look that sees without seeing, this look that touches the unseen substrate of the visible, seems to be an immersion in the ebb and flow of the moving elements that give birth to and nourish sensation and therefore thought, vision, and visions. Thus we have moved from Sartre's or Lacan's hostile and alienating gaze to a loving look that caresses. A loving look becomes the inauguration of "subjectivity" without subjects or objects. In *Être deux*, Irigaray suggests that the loving look involves all of the senses and refuses the separation between visible and invisible (1997, 79). A body in love cannot be fixed as an object (78). The look of love sees the invisible in the visible; both spiritual and carnal, the look of love is of "neither subject nor object" (78). Irigaray describes the look of love as that which brings us together through our difference by virtue of both embodiment and transcendence: "Perhaps loving one another asks us to gaze together at the invisible, to abandon our sight to the breathing of the heart and the soul, to maintain this breathing as carnal without fixing it on a target"(78).[7]

The look of love is an example of what Teresa Brennan calls living attention. When we look at someone with love, when we caress with our eyes, we are giving living attention necessary for psychic life. Irigaray's suggestions about the possibility of loving looks turn Sartre's or Lacan's antisocial gaze into a look as the circulation of social energy. The gaze does not have to be a harsh or accusing stare. Rather, affective psychic energy circulates through loving looks. Loving looks, then, nourish and sustain the psyche, the soul.

Irigaray's formulation of the loving look as an alternative to the objectifying look, and her reformulation of recognition beyond domination through love, resonates with Fanon's call for the ethical and political power of love to overcome oppression. If objectification is essential to domination and oppression, and love can bring us together outside of the hierarchy of subject/object/other, then relations beyond domination are possible: "The caress does not seek to dominate a hostile freedom" (Irigaray 1993a, 188). In the caresses of love, there is no subject or object/other. The caress is the between, both carnal and divine, both sensible and transcendental. As such, the caress, and the look as caress, does not fix an object for a subject but opens a realm in which the two remain two but cannot be separated. Irigaray insists that "the other of sexual difference is each time contiguous and transcendent to me, and subjective and objective; he is matter and spirit, body and intention, inclinations and liberty" (1997, 165). Love and difference take place in between. Love does not exist without difference. And difference is not recognized beyond recognition without love.

The love imagined by Irigaray, however, is itself beyond recognition. Irigaray's discourse of love would challenge many, if not most, of our contemporary cultural representations of love. The notion of love itself—the experience of love and its representations, which cannot be separated—must be open to social and political transformation. Love too must be reinterpreted and elaborated, especially in terms of its performative dimension. What is love beyond domination?

Conclusion: Witnessing the Power of Love

Trying to imagine love beyond domination brings us full circle back to Fanon's suggestion that through love we can overcome domination. For Fanon, love is a means to overcome the objectification of the oppressed and restore a sense of subjective agency. Love operates on both the psychic and social levels by restoring the agency necessary to imagine oneself as an ethical and political actor. Fanon, however, actually says very little about love. I am imagining what he means by love by extrapolating from what I find most compelling in his analysis. Still, there is much more to be said about the possibility and necessity of love beyond domination.

As we have seen, Axel Honneth insists on the necessity of love in order to form the self-confidence needed to operate as an agent. He identifies love as the first and primary form of recognition necessary for subject formation, which becomes the foundation for later social and political forms of recognition. Honneth's notion of love, however, is a traditional patriarchal notion chained to the nuclear family. His notion of love is ahistorical and nonpolitical. Even Maria Lugones, who imagines love outside of the context of the nuclear family, still proposes a notion of love that privileges the subject over the other. Love is at the center of Maria Lugones's notion of playful world traveling. She claims that we love each other by traveling to each other's worlds and seeing through each other's eyes. Earlier, I argued that this notion of love presupposes a form of domination. Even while she refuses to "kneel and pray" at the altar of love, Judith Butler insists on the totalizing power of love to dominate (1997b, 128). She argues that love is a form of dependency that traumatizes the fledgling subject. She also maintains that the melancholic subject is the result of a lost love. For Butler, it seems that love is always and necessarily another form of domination. So how can we conceive of love outside of domination?

Irigaray proposes love outside of domination as a nonhierarchical love between two. She emphasizes the between, which both connects and separates the lovers. This negative limit, which is not a negation, sets up the boundaries necessary to imagine a nontotalizing love across difference. She imagines a love that does not fix a beloved as an object, a love that does not reduce one to the other, love as a dynamic movement toward another: I love to you. She suggests that by reconceiving love we can transform ethical, social, and political relations. Indeed, in order to transform ethical, social, and political relations, we must reconceive of love.

In some of her latest work, bell hooks points out that "there is no powerful discourse on love emerging either from politically progressive radicals or from the Left" (1994a, 243).[1] Hooks insists that an ethic of love must be part of any political movement: "Without an ethic of love shaping the direction of our political vision and our radical aspiration, we are often seduced, in one way or the other, into continued allegiance to systems of domination—imperialism, sexism, racism, classism" (243). Love is the ethical agency that motivates a move toward others, across differences. Love motivates a move beyond self-interested political action, which is necessary to move beyond domination. Hooks argues that in order to see beyond our blind spots, the blind spots that perpetuate domination, we need to consciously and decisively adopt an ethic of love. We negotiate blind spots only by acknowledging them, which is possible only through a vigilant concern for others, what hooks calls an ethic of love: "The ability to acknowledge blind spots can emerge only as we expand our concern about politics of domination and our capacity to care about the oppression and exploitation of others. A love ethic makes this expansion possible" (244).

Hooks's call to acknowledge blind spots resonates with my analysis on bearing witness to what is beyond recognition, what is beyond the eyewitness. In order to "see" what we cannot see, in order to move beyond our blind spots, we need to be vigilant in interpretation, elaboration, and analysis. We need to interpret the ways that our performances both perpetuate and challenge institutions and structures of dominance. Only through this process of continual reinterpretation and reassessment can we be vigilant in an attempt to think through our blind spots and transform ourselves and our culture. This process of loving, but with critical interpretation, opens up the possibility of working-through rather than merely repeating the blind spots of domination.

Hooks comments on the importance of awareness in her own experience of love:

When I look at my life, searching it for a blueprint that aided me in the process of decolonization, of personal and political self-recovery, I know that it was learning the truth about how systems of domination operate that helped, learning to look both inward and outward with a critical eye. Awareness is central to the process of love as the practice of freedom. (1994a, 248)

The loving eye is also a critical eye. And, I would add, learning "the truth" is an ongoing process that must be undertaken continually and vigilantly in order to love. Moreover, self-awareness as self-recovery of this sort demands a new conception of self. Just as the truth of the self is not transparent or fixed, the structure, contents, and consciousness of the self are not unified or self-contained. The process of self-interpretation necessary for love requires a new concept not only of love but also of self and self-reflection.

Self-awareness resulting from self-reflection cannot mean the reflection of a self-contained, unified self. Instead, self-reflection must be the reflection of otherness that constitutes the self as a subject. The interpretation or elaboration necessary for the process of what hooks calls self-recovery, and what Kristeva identifies with the process of working-through in psychoanalysis, depends on constantly renegotiating self and other to expose the connections between them. Identity and difference need not be opposed. Identity need not be the result of expelling or excluding difference. Rather, identity constantly renegotiated through interpretation and elaboration of the performative aspect of signification will yield new forms of relationships, both with one's self and with others.

Reflection and self-reflection can no longer be conceived as mirroring operations that lead to either recognition or misrecognition. Self-reflection is not a turn inward but a turn toward otherness. It is not a return but a detour. If the self is by virtue of a witnessing relation to another, then self-reflection is the reflection of that relationship. If witnessing is "seeing" what cannot be seen, the unseen in vision, the process of witnessing itself, then self-reflection is the reflection of what makes reflection possible, the process of reflecting that makes mirrors send back images. The loving eye is a critical eye in that it demands to see what cannot be seen; it vigilantly looks for signs of the invisible process that gives rise to vision, reflection, and recognition. The loving eye is a critical eye in that it insists on going beyond recognition toward otherness. The loving eye is a critical eye in the sense that it is necessary, crucial for establishing and nourishing relationships across difference.

Whether we are talking about intimate love relations or loving one's "enemies," the loving eyes of "self-reflection" are critical. Love must be alive and kicking in order to move us beyond our selves and beyond recognition. Only by continually reinterpreting and elaborating our relations, including self-relations, can we hope to maintain them as loving relations. Love is an openness to otherness. But this openness requires reflection as a turn toward others. It requires the insomnia of a vigilance that recognizes the urgency of opening toward what is beyond recognition. When love or the beloved becomes fixed, stable, recognizable, part of an economy of exchange, then love cannot be maintained; love becomes a two-dimensional mirror image of itself that flattens the psychic depth necessary for it to be meaningful. The operations of the imaginary in the process of interpretation and elaboration are the movements of love.

As Kristeva says in *Tales of Love,* we are extraterrestrially wandering and lost without love: "Today Narcissus is an exile, deprived of his psychic space, an extraterrestrial with a prehistory bearing, wanting for love. An uneasy child, all scratched up, somewhat disgusting, an alien in a world of desire and power, he longs only to reinvent love" (1987, 382–83). For Kristeva, love provides the support for fragmented meanings and fragmented subjectivities. Love provides the support to reconnect words and affects. She says that "love is something spoken, and it is only that" (277).

Our lives have meaning for us—we have a sense of ourselves—through the narratives that we prepare to tell others about our experience. Even if we do not tell our stories, we live our experience through the stories that we construct in order to "tell ourselves" to another, a loved one. As we wander through our days, an event takes on its significance in the narrative that we construct for an imaginary conversation with a loved one as we are living it. The living body is a loving body, and the loving body is a speaking body. Without love we are nothing but walking corpses. Love is essential to the living body, and it is essential in bringing the living body to life in language through witnessing.

Bell hooks associates the testimony of love, a testimony that I identify with witnessing, with the practice of freedom: "The moment we choose to love we begin to move against domination, against oppression. The moment we choose to love we begin to move towards freedom, to act in ways that liberate ourselves and others. That action is the testimony of love as the practice of freedom" (1994a, 250). Hooks emphasizes that love is a choice; it is a willful decision. We can choose to love or we can choose not to love. In this regard, love is an attitude that we willingly cultivate toward others. We can choose to close ourselves off to others or we can choose to try to open ourselves toward others. But only through vigilant reinterpretation and elaboration of our own performance of that opening can we maintain this loving attitude. Love is not something we choose once and for all. Rather, it is a decision that must be constantly reaffirmed through the vigilance of "self-reflection."

Hooks cites Martin Luther King Jr.'s proclamation "I have decided to love" (1994a, 247). She argues that the civil rights movement had the power to move the masses because it was rooted in this love ethic. Martin Luther King Jr. was a charismatic leader because he called for love. Hooks suggests that any progressive movement that compels the masses must do so by compelling the hearts and souls through the promise and proclamation of love. Opening a public space of love and generosity is crucial to opening a space beyond domination. Yet only by maintaining the critical capacity of the loving eye do we resist the temptation to "kneel and pray" at the altar of love.

If love is divine, it is not because it is alien or separated from us. Love, born from critical reinterpretation, is the affirmation of our relationship to the world and other people. The critical self-reflection of the loving eye is a reflection through full and not empty space, a reflection that is communicated not on the smooth hard resistance surface of a mirror but in the tissues of the flesh of the world. If we reconceive of recognition from a notion of vision that emphasizes the fullness of space and the connections—interdependence even—between the visible world and vision, between the seer and the seen, then we begin to move away from the Hegelian struggle for recognition and toward an acknowledgment of otherness. Starting from this alternative notion of vision, otherness or others are not forever cut off from subjects or seers, threatening alienation and annihilation. Rather, the gaps or spaces between us open up the very possibility of communication and communion. Vision itself becomes a process, a becoming, rather than the sovereign of recognition. Vision becomes a circulation of energy between and among rather than an artificial and inadequate bridge between a subject and an alien world.

As Merleau-Ponty, and Irigaray following him, so powerfully suggests, there is no unbridgeable gap between the visible and the invisible. The invisible, what Lacan calls the inner world, is one side of a reversible corporeality through which the thickness of the flesh makes relationships possible. For Irigaray, the invisible is nourished by material elements to which it is indebted to the point of calling into question any dualistic or alienating distinction between visible and invisible. J. J. Gibson's ecological optics goes even further to suggest that we are connected through photic or light energy as well as other types of energy. Vision is the result of responsiveness to differences and relationships of "invisible" energy. The implications of this deconstruction of visible and invisible for notions of subjectivity are vast.

If the visible and invisible are both elements circulating in a system of communication, then we have crossed the moat surrounding the fortress of consciousness traditionally protecting its privacy or ownness, an ownership always tied to recognition. We have broken the mirror that reflects only our alienation from others, which in Lacan's mirror-stage scenario is based on the alienation between my body and my ego-ideal or the outer and inner worlds. Subjectivity is no longer tied to a notion of vision that revolves around seers recognizing (or misrecognizing) their objects. Subjectivity is no longer the origin or source of recognition but part of a process, which rather than eliminate the *relata* makes relationships possible. Subjectivity is a response to energy that connects us to our environment.

I have attempted to reconstruct notions of recognition, witnessing, and vigilance not to challenge the privilege of the visible but to reconstruct a positive notion of vision. Vision is a type of circulation between and through the tissues of bodies, elements, and language. Like blood circulating in the body to nourish all of its members, light circulates through air, elements, and our eyes to engender vision. As we have seen, however, seeing is not just a matter of matter, but also a matter of the circulation of ideas, language, and images. Vision is the result of a process of relationships between bodies in the world, between images, traditions, institutions, laws, myths. What we see is the product of the process of coming to vision that is invisible yet can be interpreted and elaborated in its performance and effects. Vision is the result of the circulation of biosocial energy.

From a new conception of vision as connection, notions of recognition and subjectivity are transformed. If space is not empty, then vision does not have the impossible task of crossing an abyss between the subject and the world or others. Subjects do not have to be motivated to control the world in order to compensate for their separation from it. If the abyss is an illusion, so is the need to dominate objects that lay always on the other side. The notion that space is empty and that vision is alienating sets up a dominating resentful subject attempting to control the alien hostile world around him. But if the world is not alien and the subject is not separated but essentially connected to the world and others, then domination is not a compensation for alienation. We don't have to be extraterrestrially longing for an impossible love. If the subject is using vision not to grasp or fix alien objects that it seeks to control but to connect and touch others on whom it depends for its agency, then connection rather than alienation becomes primary.

Once we reconstruct a positive vision we can reconstruct a positive recognition that is not based in domination or assimilation. Recognition does not have to compensate for some primary alienation or abyss. It does not have to be the result of an illusory need to control as compensation for separation. If we are connected through vision, then we can be connected through a recognition that does not dominate otherness but moves toward it. If vision does not fix objects, then recognition need not fix objects. Vision and recognition become dynamic processes that demand reevaluation and reinterpretation in order to open into the tissues of space in which to imagine ourselves together.

A new conception of vision leads to a new conception of recognition beyond recognition. Imagining vision as circulation of energy through connections and touch, even caress, allows us to imagine our fundamental dependence on each other. Subjectivity is not the result of a war against all others. Rather, it is the result of a process of witnessing that connects us through the tissues of language and gestures. The notion of vision as circulation through the tissues of bodies, the tissues of elements, and the tissues of language resonates with the notion of subjectivity as witnessing that I have been developing throughout *Witnessing: Beyond Recognition*.[2] Subjectivity is a circulation of bodies, images, and language; it is a responsive biosocial loop. Subjectivity is the result of a continual process of witnessing. Only by witnessing the process of witnessing itself, the unseen in vision, the unsaid in language, can we begin to reconstruct our relationships by imagining ourselves together.

This conception of subjectivity as the process of witnessing transforms our images of subjects and others. The other is not an object or determined by the subject's gaze. The other is no longer *the* other. There is no the other, but a multitude of differences and other people on whom my sense of myself as a subject and an agent depends. This first step opens up the possibility of thinking of othered subjectivity by insisting on acknowledging the process on which any discussion of subject and objects or self and other depends. There is no other except as the result of a process of domination through which subjects are turned into objects, othered subjectivities. Subjectivity is not located in a subject who takes it away from his object or other. Rather, subjectivity is the process of witnessing, of addressing oneself to others, of responding to the address from others. Subjectivity as fundamentally response-ability does not require domination or subordination, although they may be facts of life. Instead, domination and subordination work to erode the very conditions of possibility of subjectivity, the possibility of responding and response-ability. The conditions of possibility of subjectivity are developed in a process of witnessing, continually becoming, beyond recognition.

Relations with others do not have to be hostile alien encounters. Instead, they can be loving adventures, the advent of something new. Difference does not have to be threatening; it can be exciting, the source of the meaning of life. In the thrilling adventure of love, the unknown and incomprehensible excite rather than threaten. Falling in love, the otherness of the other, is the greatest joy; and vulnerability in the face of the other is a sweet surrender, a gift rather than a sacrifice. The other's potential to make me better than I am is the power of love. In this case, I fall in love with love, with the precarious process of subjectivity that connects the tissues of my sensations, affects, thoughts, and words—the tissues of my being—to the tissues of others. To love is to bear witness to the process of witnessing that gives us the power to be, together. And being together is the chaotic adventure of subjectivity.

Notes

Introduction

1. Judith Butler will serve as one of the main representatives of this position in this book. In *Womanizing Nietzsche* (1995) and *Family Values* (1997) I consider Derrida as one of the main representatives of this position.

2. I am especially grateful for the comments of Cynthia Willett. Her insights gave me a new perspective on the impact of my project on multicultural ethics.

3. Later in the text I will argue that Charles Taylor and Maria Lugones present such models.

4. Some examples of theorists of misrecognition with whom I engage are Judith Butler, Julia Kristeva, and Jacques Lacan.

5. The two main theorists of visibility with whom I engage in the body of the text are Judith Butler and Patricia Williams.

6. Ironically, since Foucault focused on discursive analysis and subjugated discourses, this obsession with visibility in social theory seems to be in some sense a Foucauldian legacy.

7. Susan Hurley concludes that "not only are creatures with perspective, who perceive and act, essentially situated in environments. Perception and action are also co-constituted" (1998, 400).

8. Thanks to Shaun Gallagher for helpful comments and citations on the connection between motor systems and sensation.

9. Teresa Brennan (1997) talks about social energy in terms of social pressures.

1. Domination, Multiculturalism, and the Pathology of Recognition

1. See, for example, Lewis Gordon (1995a, 1995b, 1997) and Pellegrini (1997).

2. Ann Pellegrini (1997, especially chap. 6) suggests that Fanon's analysis could be productively applied to the relation between race and gender. T. Denean Sharpley-Whiting (1997) tries to rescue Fanon's analysis for feminism. Since many others have taken up the question of the relation between Fanon and feminism, and since his texts seem so problematic on the issue of gender, I will try to extrapolate from his theories—as he does himself—a general theory of the psychology of oppression.

3. Throughout this section on Fanon, I will use the masculine pronouns because it is clear in Fanon's text that he is usually talking about a male.

4. In a graduate seminar at SUNY, Stony Brook, that I taught in the spring of 1999, Johanna Burton suggested comparing Fanon's mirroring operations to Luce Irigaray's mimetic strategies. The comparison between Irigaray's taking up the place as mirror and Fanon's mirroring the mirror back again is useful.

5. The move from vision to Vision will be explained in later sections on vision.

6. Ann Pellegrini cites this passage in her deference to the tradition of interpreting Fanon as a theorist of recognition (1997, 91). Lewis Gordon also interprets Fanon as a theorist of recognition and authenticity (1995a, 1995b, 1997). In a documentary on Fanon made by Isaac Julien, Stuart Hall describes Fanon as embracing Hegel's master-slave dialectic of recognition (in Julien 1995).

7. For example, see Pellegrini (1997), Doane (1991), and hooks (1994b, 49).

8. For an insightful criticism of Taylor on this point, see Dominick LaCapra's *Representing the Holocaust* (1994, 183–87).

2. Identity Politics, Deconstruction, and Recognition

1. Senem Saner made this point very persuasively in my fall 1998 graduate seminar at SUNY, Stony Brook.

2. See chapter 4 of *Family Values* (1997, 214–26) where I argue that Derrida overlooks the gift of life in his *Gift of Death*.

3. For an insightful analysis of the pessimism of Young's starting point, see Lorenzo Simpson's "Communication and the Politics of Difference: Reading Iris Young," forthcoming in *Constellations* (2000).

4. Fraser's relation to the redistribution-recognition dilemma as she sets it out is suspect. She begins her argument by describing the dilemma in stark terms that make it appear to be an unresolvable contradiction between those who advocate redistribution and those who advocate recognition (1997). She goes on to argue that transformative remedies (deconstructive notions of recognition and socialist notions of distribution) resolve the dilemma. Yet her account of transformative remedies changes the terms of her original dilemma entirely. In other words, she defines a dilemma to motivate her analysis and then she resolves the dilemma by abandoning the very definition with which she constructed her dilemma in the first place. And she does so without acknowledging what in this circumstance looks suspiciously like a sleight of hand with her definitions. Even more peculiar is Fraser's insistence at the end of the chapter, after resolving her seemingly artificial dilemma, that the dilemma is "real." Her investment in the reality of the dilemma seems to undermine her attempts to resolve it. This is to say, the status of the dilemma and Fraser's relation to it are problematic. Iris Young criticizes the arbitrary nature of this dilemma in her response to Fraser (see Young 1998).

3. Identity as Subordination, Abjection, and Exclusion

1. It is interesting to note that in *The Psychic Life of Power* Butler attributes the distinction between repression and foreclosure to Freud: "Freud distinguishes between re-

pression and foreclosure, suggesting that a repressed desire might once have lived apart from its prohibition, but that foreclosed desire is rigorously barred, constituting the subject through a certain kind of preemptive loss" (1997b, 23). Only in a footnote in *Excitable Speech* does she suggest that Freud does *not* in fact make this distinction. Freud discusses disavowal and repudiation as forms of psychotic repression. Laplanche and Pontalis maintain that the distinction between foreclosure and repression originates with Lacan, whom Butler does not cite in this connection in *Bodies That Matter* or *The Psychic Life of Power*. See Laplanche and Pontalis (1973, 166–67).

2. See also my *Womanizing Nietzsche* (1995), *Family Values* (1997), and *Subjectivity without Subjects* (1998).

3. Elsewhere (1995, 1997, 1998), I attempt to formulate a theory of subjectivity that does not limit us to these extremes. Precisely because subjectivity is necessarily relational, because we are dependent, excess and transformation are possible. It is through our relationships and not as self-made subjects that we can "escape" violence.

4. It is interesting that Kristeva emphasizes the melancholic's sadness while Butler emphasizes the melancholic's rage.

5. Butler's use of the capital O to designate the Other of the social norm (not other people) also suggests that she sees melancholic rage as directed against other people.

6. The translation from the French is by Lisa Walsh.

7. Although Butler once mentions "working-through" in passing, she never develops it. Working-through is not a central concept in her theory. In fact, as I argue elsewhere, it is difficult to see how her theory allows for a concept like working-through (1997, 191).

4. The Necessity and Impossibility of Witnessing

1. Eva Kittay made this point in a seminar we team-taught in the fall of 1998. I am indebted to her for many insightful comments and lively discussions about Jacobs's narrative and issues of recognition in general.

2. Even objectification of the victim during trauma may not be purely oppressive in that the victim may, through splitting or objectifying herself, protect herself through numbing or disassociating from the experience as it is happening. On the other hand, objectification on the part of the psychoanalyst does not necessarily deny the subjective agency of the analysand but protects the analyst from a projective identification with the trauma of the victim.

5. False Witnesses

1. This rhetoric also presumes an economy of scarcity. Of course, the presumption of scarcity and antagonistic struggles over resources is an illusion in a country that owns well over a majority of the entire world's wealth and resources. In reality, there is plenty to go around.

2. In her book *Alchemy of Race and Rights*, Patricia Williams analyzes some of the rhetorical devices the Supreme Court used in order to justify its decision. She points out that the Court sets up discrimination and its harms as a "'slippery slope' at the bottom of

which lie hordes-in-waiting" ready to bring their "competing claims" from "every disadvantaged group" (1991, 105).

3. Although issues of race, class, and gender, and racism, classism, and sexism relate in complicated ways that I am not addressing now—ways that need to be addressed—crucial insights into the failure of abstract principles of equality and color or gender blindness can be gained by juxtaposing, even mixing, these issues.

4. The absurd, complex logic of formal equality and gender blindness was recently brought home to me. At the age of twenty-nine my sister contracted a rare liver disease from taking birth control pills for only a few months. At the age of thirty-five she was waiting for a liver transplant. Her liver failure caused kidney failure and as a result she is on kidney dialysis and a low sodium diet. Various family members, including my parents, take turns caring for my sister. My sister asked that those living with her follow a low sodium diet so that she wouldn't be tempted to eat what she shouldn't. In response, my father said that he didn't have to follow a special diet because he didn't ruin his liver with birth control pills. His remark left me speechless. But now I see that this kind of perverse denial of difference is exactly what gender or color blindness leads us to.

5. Since *Hopwood,* the numbers of black and Hispanic students at the University of Texas has dropped dramatically. At the end of October 1998, twenty students held a sit-in at the administration building. They refused to leave and another two hundred students rallied outside demanding that the university reinstate affirmative action and that the president hold town hall–style meetings to discuss the issue. President Larry Faulkner's immediate response was to cut off all electricity, water, and food supplies to the students. Is the color-blind university also deaf to demands on behalf of those excluded from equal educational opportunities for all Americans?

6. I wonder what the court would say about racism at the law school after UT law professor Lino Graglia's remarks after the *Hopwood* decision that blacks and Mexican Americans aren't ambitious enough for law school.

6. History, Transformation, and Vigilance

1. See the work of Julia Kristeva, Luce Irigaray, Cynthia Willett, and Lisa Walsh. Walsh engages specifically with *Archive Fever* in "You Are Not Your Self: Toward an Alternative Ethics of Maternity" (1998). There she argues that the origin in *Archive Fever* is clearly connected to Freud's mystification of the maternal body (125) and that Derrida does not suggest the possibility of memory without violence, because he too closely follows Freud's theories of the mother as the first other to be incorporated or fended off (164).

2. Thanks to Krzysztof Ziarek for suggesting this connection to me.

3. For associations between Heidegger, Lévinas, and Kierkegaard on the blink and the wink, see Llewelyn 1995.

7. Seeing Race

1. In *Family Values* I indicate how the notion of ownership operates in traditional philosophies of the subject (1997, part II).

2. This example reminds me of the extreme situation in Latvia where language police check to make sure employees have the proper language certificates. See Steven Johnson's article in *Transitions* (1998).

3. It is notable that literal color blindness affects almost only men. This is because color blindness is determined by a sex-linked X chromosome. Since women have two X chromosomes, they are less likely to be affected by color blindness because it is less likely that both their X chromosomes will carry the color-deficient gene. It is also interesting to note that color blindness is not the inability to see colors, but the inability to distinguish some colors from others.

4. Compare Ruth Frankenberg's analysis in *White Women, Race Matters,* chap. 6, "Thinking through Race" (1993).

8. Vision and Recognition

1. Martin Jay's *Downcast Eyes* (1994) provides a thorough exposition of various (particularly French) philosophers who have challenged the primacy of vision.

2. In *Subjectivity without Subjects* (1998) I raise criticisms of the notion of recognition on the basis of its insistence on the already known or sameness.

3. For an account of the priority of vision in Western philosophy and the relationship between vision and the mind's eye, see Hans Jonas, "The Nobility of Sight" (1982). See also Jay 1994.

4. See, for example, Dalia Judovitz, "Vision, Representation and Technology in Descartes" (1993).

5. Zipporah's role in Exodus is to renew not only the alliance of the covenant but also the marriage alliance, which was also an alliance between the Levites and the Midianites. Zipporah's father, Reuel or Jethro, was the priest of Midian (Exodus 2:18, 3:1). Until Exodus 4:25–26 there is no mention of Moses's circumcision (he was raised as an Egyptian), which would symbolize his proper entrance into the people of Israel, renewing their alliance with God; nor is there mention of Moses's marriage, which would symbolize his alliance with Zipporah and the alliance between the Levites and the Midianites. In Exodus 4:25–26 the alliances between man and woman, between one tribe and another, and between man and God are reaffirmed through Zipporah's circumcision of her son and her symbolic circumcision of Moses: "Then Zipporah took a flint, and cut off the foreskin of her son, and cast it at his feet; and she said: 'Surely a bridegroom of blood art thou to me.' So he let him alone. Then she said: 'A bridegroom of blood in regard of the circumcision.'" With the circumcision, Zipporah proclaims Moses a bridegroom of blood or a husband of blood to indicate that they are blood relatives. They are by blood Israelites. This bond of blood is stronger than that of all others. It is frequently invoked to symbolize the strength of the covenant and, eventually, the binding strength of God's law over Israel. After Moses receives the Ten Commandments and subsequent laws, he kills an ox and sprinkles the people of Israel with its blood to remind them that they are bound to God and His laws by blood. Israel is the Son of God. The ritual circumcision, insisted on in preparation for the night of Passover (Exodus 12:44–48), binds the sons of Israel to God

through blood that signs a pact of regeneration. For a more detailed argument, see my *Family Values* (1997, 71–74).

6. The Hebrew word *berith,* translated as covenant, means an ordinary contract. *Covenant* is used in connection with God's promise to Noah and his posterity, His promise to Abraham and his posterity, marked by circumcision, His dispensation of the Mosiac Law and its applications, and the prophesies (see the *OED* definition of *covenant*).

7. For a brilliant account of the differences between Sartre and Lacan on vision see Stephen Melville's "Division of the Gaze" (1996).

9. Toward a New Vision

1. I would like to thank Edward Casey for recommending Gibson's work to me.

2. Think of H. F. Harlow's famous studies of monkeys clinging to soft-cloth mother surrogates for "contact comfort" (1958).

3. For a more developed analysis of the psyche as a biosocial phenomenon, see my *Family Values* (1997). See also my discussion of the psyche as biosocial in the work of Julia Kristeva in the introduction to *The Portable Kristeva* (Kristeva 1997a). And see Brennan's "Social Pressure" (1997).

4. Cynthia Willett makes a very persuasive case that the mirror-stage recognition is the result of a touch, along with the mother-infant song and dance (1995).

5. For discussions of Irigaray and Merleau-Ponty, see Grosz 1993; Vasseleu 1998; Jay 1994.

6. In her essay on Merleau-Ponty in *An Ethics of Sexual Difference,* Irigaray argues that he reduces touch to vision. She objects that while vision needs touch, touch does not need vision, and therefore these senses are not reciprocal or reversible (1993a, 162). Her criticism of Merleau-Ponty may not be fair, in that he does not claim that touch can be as-similated into vision or that one sense can be reduced to another; rather, he argues that the senses are interrelated and always work together to produce sensation and perception. For Merleau-Ponty vision is tactile in that it is analogous to touch, and dependent on it. In my reading, Irigaray's thesis that vision is founded on touch seems to echo rather than contra-dict Merleau-Ponty. For another interesting comparison between senses, see Irigaray's dis-cussion of the connection between sight and sound in "Flesh Colors" in *Sexes and Gene-alogies* (1993b). There, Irigaray argues that sight and sound operate in different registers, and yet she endorses bringing them together to talk about the color of sound and the sounds of colors.

7. Translation from the French by Lisa Walsh.

Conclusion

1. Marilyn Edelstein's (1998) recent work on hooks and Kristeva on love is a step to-ward returning love to progressive political discourse.

2. In *Subjectivity without Subjects* (1998) I develop the notion of vision as circulation based on the model of the circulation of blood between the maternal body and the fetus.

Works Cited

Althusser, Louis. 1971. *Lenin and Philosophy and Other Essays.* Trans. Ben Brewster. New York: Monthly Review Press.

Benjamin, Jessica. 1988. *The Bonds of Love.* New York: Pantheon.

Bibring, Edward. 1943. "The Conception of the Repetition Compulsion." *Psychoanalytic Quarterly* 12:486–519.

Brennan, Teresa. 1992. *The Interpretation of the Flesh.* London: Routledge.

———. 1993. *History after Lacan.* New York: Routledge.

———. 1997. "Social Pressure." *American Imago* 54, no. 3: 257–88.

Brennan, Teresa, and Martin Jay, eds. 1996. *Vision in Context.* New York: Routledge.

Butler, Judith. 1991. *Gender Trouble.* New York: Routledge.

———. 1993. *Bodies That Matter.* New York: Routledge.

———. 1997a. *Excitable Speech.* New York: Routledge.

———. 1997b. *The Psychic Life of Power.* Stanford, Calif.: Stanford University Press.

———. 1997c. "Sovereign Performatives in the Contemporary Scene of Utterance." *Critical Inquiry* 23, no. 2: 350–77.

Casey, Edward. 1992. "Forgetting Remembered." *Man and World* 25:281–311.

Chanter, Tina. 1995. *Ethics of Eros: Irigaray's Rewriting of the Philosophers.* New York: Routledge.

Derrida, Jacques. 1992. "Psyche: Inventions of the Other." In *Acts of Literature,* ed. D. Attridge. New York: Routledge.

———. 1996. *Archive Fever.* Trans. Eric Prenowitz. Chicago: University of Chicago Press.

Descartes, René. 1965. *Discourse on Method, Optics, Geometry, and Meteorology.* Trans. P. J. Olscamp. Indianapolis: University of Indiana Press.

———. 1989. *The Meditations Concerning First Philosophy.* In *Philosophical Essays.* Trans. Laurence LaFleur. New York: Macmillan.

Doane, Mary Ann. 1991. "Dark Continents: Epistemologies of Racial and Sexual Difference in Psychoanalysis and Cinema." In *Femmes Fatales,* 209–248. New York: Routledge.

Durkheim, Émile. 1995. *The Elementary Forms of Religious Life.* Trans. Karen Fields. New York: Free Press.

Edelstein, Marilyn. 1998. "What's Love Got to Do with It?" Presented at the Modern Language Association annual meeting, San Francisco.

Fanon, Frantz. 1967. *Black Skin, White Masks.* Trans. Charles Lam Markmann. New York: Grove Press.

———. 1968. *The Wretched of the Earth.* Trans. Constance Farrington. Harmondsworth: Penguin.

Felman, Shoshana, and Dori Laub. 1992. *Testimony: Crises of Witnessing in Literature, Psychoanalysis, and History.* New York: Routledge.

Frankenberg, Ruth. 1993. *White Women, Race Matters: The Social Construction of Whiteness.* Minneapolis: University of Minnesota.

Fraser, Nancy. 1997. *Justice Interruptus.* New York: Routledge.

Freud, Sigmund. 1910. "Psychogenic Visual Disturbance According to Psychoanalytic Concepts." In *The Complete Works of Sigmund Freud: Standard Edition,* ed. James Strachey, 11:211–18. London: Hogarth.

———. 1914. "Remembering, Repeating, and Working-Through." In *Standard Edition,* 12:147.

———. 1923. "The Ego and the Id." In *Collected Papers.* In *Standard Edition,* 19:12–66.

———. 1927. "Fetishism." In *Collected Papers.* In *Standard Edition,* 20:77.

———. 1962. "Three Essays on the Theory of Sexuality (1905)." Trans. James Strachey. Basic Books: New York.

———. 1972a. "The Passing of the Oedipus-Complex (1924)." In *Sexuality and the Psychology of Love.* Trans. Joan Riviere. New York: Collier Books.

———. 1972b. "Some Psychological Consequences of the Anatomical Distinction between the Sexes (1925)." In *Sexuality and the Psychology of Love.* Trans. Joan Riviere. New York: Collier Books.

———. 1989. "Mourning and Melancholia." In *The Freud Reader,* ed. Peter Gay. New York: Norton.

Gallagher, Shaun, and Andrew Meltzoff. 1996. "The Earliest Sense of Self and Others: Merleau-Ponty and Recent Developmental Studies." *Philosophical Psychology* 9:211–36.

Gates, Henry Louis Jr., ed. 1991. *Bearing Witness: Selections from African-American Autobiography in the Twentieth Century.* New York: Pantheon.

Gibson, J. J. 1950. *The Perception of the Visual World.* Boston: Houghton Mifflin.

———. 1961. "Ecological Optics." *Vision Research* 1:253–62.

———. 1966. *The Senses Considered as Perceptual Systems.* Boston: Houghton Mifflin.

Gordon, Lewis. 1995a. *Bad Faith and Antiblack Racism.* Atlantic Highlands, N.J.: Humanities Press.

———. 1995b. *Her Majesty's Other Children.* Lanham, Md.: Rowman & Littlefield.

———. 1997. *Fanon and the Crisis of European Man.* New York: Routledge, 1997.

Grosz, Elizabeth. 1993. "Merleau-Ponty and Irigaray in the Flesh." *Thesis Eleven* 36:37–59.

Harlow, H. F. 1958. "The Nature of Love." *American Psychologist* 13:673–85.

Hegel, G. W. F. 1977. *Phenomenology of Spirit.* Trans. A. V. Miller. Oxford: Clarendon Press.

Heidegger, Martin. 1962. *Being and Time.* Trans. J. Macquarrie & E. Robinson. New York: Harper.

Held, René. 1952. "Psychopathologie du regard." In *L'Evolution psychiatrique* (April–June).

Henderson, Mae Gwendolyn. 1992. "Speaking in Tongues: Dialogics Dialectics, and the Black Woman Writer's Literary Tradition." In *Feminists Theorize the Political,* ed. Judith Butler and Joan Scott, 144–66. New York: Routledge.

Honneth, Axel. 1996. *The Struggle for Recognition.* Trans. Joel Anderson. Boston: MIT Press.

hooks, bell. 1990. *Yearning: Race, Gender, and Cultural Politics.* Boston: South End Press.

———. 1993. *Sisters of the Yam, Black Women and Self-Recovery.* Boston: South End Press.

———. 1994a. *Outlaw Culture, Resisting Representations.* New York: Routledge.

———. 1994b. *Teaching to Transgress: Education as the Practice of Freedom.* New York: Routledge.

Hurley, Susan. 1998. *Consciousness in Action.* Cambridge: Harvard University Press.

Irigaray, Luce. 1983. *L'Oubli de l'air.* Paris: Les Éditions de Minuit.

———. 1991. *Marine Lover of Friedrich Nietzsche.* Trans. G. Gill. New York: Columbia University Press.

———. 1992. *Elemental Passions.* Trans. J. Collie and J. Still. New York: Routledge.

———. 1993a. *An Ethics of Sexual Difference.* Trans. C. Burke and G. Gill. Ithaca, N.Y.: Cornell University Press.

———. 1993b. *Sexes and Genealogies.* Trans. G. Gill. New York: Columbia University Press.

———. 1996. *i love to you.* Trans. A. Martin. New York: Routledge.

———. 1997. *Être deux.* Paris: Grasset.

———. 1999. *Forgetting of Air in Martin Heidegger.* Trans. Mary Beth Mader. Austin: University of Texas Press.

Jacobs, Harriet. 1987 (1861). *Incidents in the Life of a Slave Girl.* In *The Classic Slave Narratives,* ed. Henry Louis Gates Jr., 333–515. New York: Penguin.

Jameson, Fredric. 1992. *Signatures of the Visible.* New York: Routledge.

Jay, Martin. 1994. *Downcast Eyes: The Denigration of Vision in Twentieth-Century French Thought.* Berkeley and Los Angeles: University of California Press.

Johnson, Steven. 1998. "Watch Your Tongue: On the Streets with Latvia's Language Patrol." *Transitions* 5, no. 11: 46–47.

Jonas, Hans. 1982. "The Nobility of Sight: A Study in the Phenomenology of the Senses." In *The Phenomenon of Life: Toward a Philosophical Biology.* Chicago: University of Chicago Press.

Judovitz, Dalia. 1993. "Vision, Representation and Technology in Descartes." In *Modernity and the Hegemony of Vision,* ed. D. M. Levin. Berkeley and Los Angeles: University of California Press.

Julien, Isaac. 1995. *Frantz Fanon: Black Skin, White Mask.* Documentary, California Newsreel, Los Angeles.

Kittay, Eva. "Welfare, Dependency, and a Public Ethic of Care." *Social Justice* 25, no. 71 (spring).

Kristeva, Julia. 1981. *The Kristeva Reader,* ed. Toril Moi. New York: Columbia University Press.

———. 1982. *Powers of Horror.* Trans. Leon Roudiez. New York: Columbia University Press.

———. 1984. *Revolution in Poetic Language.* Trans. Margaret Waller. New York: Columbia University Press.

———. 1987. *Tales of Love.* Trans. Leon Roudiez. New York: Columbia University Press.

———. 1989. *Black Sun.* Trans. Leon Roudiez. New York: Columbia University Press.

———. 1995. *New Maladies of the Soul.* Trans. Ross Guberman. New York: Columbia University Press.

———. 1996. *Sens et non-sens de la révolte.* Paris: Fayard.

———. 1997a. *The Portable Kristeva.* Ed. Kelly Oliver. New York: Columbia University Press.

———. 1997b. *La Révolte intime.* Paris: Fayard.

———. 1998a. *L'Avenir d'une révolte.* Paris: Calmann-Lévy.

———. 1998b. *Contre la dépression nationale.* Paris: Les éditions textuel.

———. 2000. *The Sense and Nonsense of Revolt.* Trans. Jeanine Herman. New York: Columbia University Press.

Lacan, Jacques. 1966. *Écrits.* Paris: Éditions du Seuil.

———. 1977. *Ecrits.* Trans. Alan Sheridan. New York: Norton, 1977.

———. 1981. *The Four Fundamental Concepts of Psychoanalysis.* Trans. Alan Sheridan. New York: Norton.

———. 1988. "Seminar on 'The Purloined Letter.'" Trans. J. Mehlman. In *The Purloined Poe,* ed. J. Muller and W. Richardson. Baltimore: Johns Hopkins University Press.

LaCapra, Dominick. 1985. *History and Criticism.* Ithaca, N.Y.: Cornell University Press.

———. 1989. *Soundings in Critical Theory.* Ithaca, N.Y.: Cornell University Press.

———. 1994. *Representing the Holocaust, History, Theory, Trauma.* Ithaca, N.Y.: Cornell University Press.

Laplanche, L., and J.-B. Pontalis, 1973. *The Language of Psycho-Analysis.* Trans. Donald Nicholson-Smith. New York: Norton.

Lévinas, Emmanuel. 1969. *Totality and Infinity.* Trans. Alphonso Lingis. Pittsburgh: Duquesne University Press.

———. 1985. *Ethics and Infinity: Conversations with Philippe Nemo.* Trans. Richard Cohen. Pittsburgh: Duquesne University Press.

———. 1987. *Time and the Other.* Trans. Richard Cohen. Pittsburgh: Duquesne University Press.

———. 1989. *The Levinas Reader,* ed. Seán Hand. Cambridge, Mass.: Blackwell.

———. 1991. *Otherwise Than Being.* Trans. Alphonso Lingis. Boston: Nijoff.

————. 1993. *Collected Philosophical Papers.* Trans. Alphonso Lingis. Boston: Kluwer Academic Publishers.

————. 1996. *Emmanuel Levinas: Basic Philosophical Writings,* ed. A. Peperzak, S. Critchley, and R. Bernasconi. Bloomington: Indiana University Press.

Llewelyn, John. 1995. *Emmanuel Levinas: The Genealogy of Ethics.* New York: Routledge.

Lugones, Maria. 1987. "Playfulness, 'World' Travelling, and Loving Perception." *Hypatia* 2, no. 2 (summer): 3–19.

Meltzoff, Andrew, and Keith Moore. 1977. "Imitation of Facial and Manual Gestures by Human Neonates." *Science* 198:75–78.

————. 1983. "Newborn Infants Imitate Adult Facial Gestures." *Child Development* 54:702–9.

Melville, Stephen. 1996. "Division of the Gaze; or, Remarks on the Color and Tenor of Contemporary 'Theory.'" In *Vision in Context,* ed. Teresa Brennan and Martin Jay, 101–16. New York: Routledge.

Merleau-Ponty, Maurice. 1962. *Phenomenology of Perception.* Trans. Colin Smith. London.

————. 1964. *The Primacy of Perception.* Ed. James Edie. Evanston, Ill.: Northwestern University Press.

————. 1968. *The Visible and the Invisible.* Trans. Alphonso Lingis. Evanston, Ill.: Northwestern University Press.

Mohanty, Chandra Talpade. 1987. "Feminist Encounters: Locating the Politics of Experience." *Copyright* 1 (fall): 30–44.

Morrison, Toni. 1987. *Beloved.* New York: Plume Publishing Group.

Nietzsche, Friedrich. 1967. *On the Genealogy of Morals.* Trans. Walter Kaufman. New York: Random House.

Oliver, Kelly. 1995. *Womanizing Nietzsche: Philosophy's Relation to "the Feminine."* New York: Routledge.

————. 1997. *Family Values: Subjects between Nature and Culture.* New York: Routledge.

————. 1998. *Subjectivity without Subjects: From Abject Fathers to Desiring Mothers.* Lanham, Md.: Rowman & Littlefield.

Pellegrini, Ann. 1997. *Performance Anxieties: Staging Psychoanalysis, Staging Race.* New York: Routledge.

Plato. 1987a. *Meno.* In *The Collected Dialogues of Plato,* ed. Edith Hamilton and Huntington Cairns. Princeton, N.J.: Princeton University Press.

————. 1987b. *Phaedrus.* In *The Collected Dialogues of Plato,* ed. Edith Hamilton and Huntington Cairns. Princeton, N.J.: Princeton University Press.

Santner, Eric. 1990. *Stranded Objects: Mourning, Memory, and Film in Postwar Germany.* Ithaca, N.Y.: Cornell University Press.

Sartre, Jean-Paul. 1956. *Being and Nothingness.* Trans. Hazel Barnes. New York: Washington Square Books.

————. 1976. *No Exit.* Trans. Stuart Gilbert. New York: Alfred Knopf.

Scott, Joan. 1992. "Experience." In *Feminists Theorize the Political,* ed. Judith Butler and Joan Scott, 22–40. New York: Routledge.

Sharpley-Whiting, T. Denean. 1997. *Frantz Fanon: Conflicts and Feminisms.* Lanham, Md.: Rowman & Littlefield.

Silverman, Kaja. 1988. *The Acoustic Mirror: The Female Voice in Psychoanalysis and Cinema.* Bloomington: Indiana University Press.

Simpson, Lorenzo. 2000. "Communication and the Politics of Difference: Reading Iris Young," *Constellations* (forthcoming).

State of Washington Voters Pamphlet. 1998. General Election, November 3. Edition 15. Published by the Office of the Secretary of State and King County Records and Elections.

Taylor, Charles. 1994. "The Politics of Recognition." In *Multiculturalism,* ed. Amy Gutman. Princeton, N.J.: Princeton University Press.

———. 1989. *Sources of the Self.* Cambridge: Harvard University Press.

Vasseleu, Cathryn. 1998. *Textures of Light: Vision and Touch in Irigaray, Levinas and Merleau-Ponty.* London: Routledge.

Walsh, Lisa. 1998. "You Are Not Your Self: Toward an Alternative Ethics of Maternity." Ph.D. diss., French Department, University of Texas at Austin.

West, Cornel. 1994. *Race Matters.* New York: Random House.

Willett, Cynthia. 1995. *Maternal Ethics and Other Slave Moralities.* New York: Routledge.

———, ed. 1998. *Theorizing Multiculturalism.* New York: Blackwell.

———. 2001. *The Soul of Justice.* Forthcoming.

Williams, Patricia. 1991. *The Alchemy of Race and Rights.* Cambridge: Harvard University Press.

———. 1995. *The Rooster's Egg: On the Persistence of Prejudice.* Cambridge: Harvard University Press.

———. 1998. *Seeing a Color-Blind Future: The Paradox of Race.* New York: Farrar Straus.

Young, Iris. 1997. *Intersecting Voices.* Princeton, N.J.: Princeton University Press.

———. 1998. "Unruly Categories." In Willett 1998.

Index

Kelly Oliver is professor of philosophy and women's studies at SUNY, Stony Brook. She is the author of *Subjectivity without Subjects: From Abject Fathers to Desiring Mothers, Family Values: Subjects between Nature and Culture, Womanizing Nietzsche: Philosophy's Relation to "the Feminine,"* and *Reading Kristeva: Unraveling the Double-Bind.* She has also edited several books, including *Ethics, Politics, and Difference in Kristeva's Writings, Feminist Interpretations of Nietzsche,* and *The Portable Kristeva.*